Affection and Trust

Harry Truman with Dean Acheson in the Oval Office on December 21, 1950, discussing Acheson's meetings with foreign and defense ministers of North Atlantic Treaty Organization (NATO) countries in Brussels, Belgium.

Affection and Trust

THE PERSONAL CORRESPONDENCE OF HARRY S. TRUMAN AND DEAN ACHESON, 1953–1971

With an Introduction by
David McCullough

Alfred A. Knopf · New York · 2010

THIS IS A BORZOI BOOK
PUBLISHED BY ALFRED A. KNOPF

www.aaknopf.com

Knopf, Borzoi Books, and the colophon are registered trademarks
of Random House, Inc.

Library of Congress Cataloging-in-Publication Data

Truman, Harry S., 1884–1972.
Affection and trust : the personal correspondence of
Harry S. Truman and Dean Acheson, 1953–1971 / by
Harry S. Truman and Dean Acheson ;
edited by Ray Geselbracht and David C. Acheson.—1st ed.
p. cm.
ISBN 978-0-307-59354-2
1. Truman, Harry S., 1884–1972—Correspondence.
2. Acheson, Dean, 1893–1971—Correspondence.
3. United States—Politics and government—
1945–1953—Sources. 4. United States—Foreign relations—
1945–1953—Sources. I. Acheson, Dean, 1893–1971.
II. Geselbracht, Raymond H.
III. Acheson, David C. IV. Title.
E814.A4 2010
973.918—dc22
2010016904

Manufactured in the United States of America

First Edition

Contents

Editorial Note

Minor style changes in punctuation and capitalization have been made to these letters without notice. Titles of books and periodicals have been italicized. Dates to the letters and other items have been regularized by being placed in the top right position in a month-day-year format.

*Harry Truman, Dean Acheson, and Chief Justice Fred Vinson
in the Oval Office on January 21, 1949, at Acheson's swearing-in
as Secretary of State.*

Introduction

The younger and taller of the two eminent Americans, the former Secretary of State, stood six foot one and, to judge by his exquisitely tailored suits and neatly trimmed, ever so slightly upturned mustache, he might have stepped from the pages of an English fashion magazine of the day. The other, older man, the former President of the United States, was a good three inches shorter and about as unmistakably midwestern American as anybody could be.

Where one, the patrician Dean Gooderham Acheson, had attended Groton, Yale, and the Harvard Law School, the other, Harry S. Truman, was the only President of the twentieth century who had no more than a high-school education. Truman was the son of a farmer; Acheson, the son of an Episcopal bishop. Acheson had begun his rise in the profession of the law under the tutelage of the learned Supreme Court Justice Louis Brandeis. Truman owed much of his success in the rough-and-tumble of Missouri politics to the notorious boss Tom Pendergast. Acheson was known to suffer fools hardly at all, Truman had long since become a master of the art. Truman, as he said, liked a little H_2O flavored with bourbon, Acheson preferred his martinis extremely dry.

At the time the correspondence in these pages began, early in 1953, both men had come to regard themselves as oldsters, to use Truman's word. He was sixty-nine, Acheson, sixty, and they seemed still, as they had at the summit of their careers, as incongruous a pair as might be imagined, separated now not only by the thousand miles between Independence, Missouri, and Washington, D.C., but by so much else that was obvious—that is, if one chose to judge only by the obvious.

For as conspicuously different as they were in background, appearance, and manner, they were two principled men who lived by the same code, and, importantly, each had the capacity to see beyond what met the eye. Truman had understood at once how much more there was than the fashion plate to Acheson. Acheson had seen from the beginning the rare common sense and underlying greatness of the plainspoken supposed nobody who had taken the place of the fallen Franklin Roosevelt.

Some similarities between the two were as marked as the differences. Both had a small-town background. (Acheson came from Middletown, Connecticut.) Both loved books—and history and biography in particular. (The breadth of Harry Truman's reading—the fact that he read Latin for pleasure, for example—came as a surprise to those who did not know him.) Both liked a morning walk at a good clip and neither had the least ability to speak any language other than his own. If Acheson paid inordinate attention to how he looked, Truman was not far behind with his bow ties, his invariably well-pressed suits, crisp shirts, and insistence that five points of a fresh handkerchief be showing just so from his breast pocket. The failed haberdasher, as his critics liked to label him, loved clothes and from boyhood had cared very much about how he looked.

In explanation of Acheson's attention to wardrobe, his son, David, has written that it was not vanity so much as part of "a perfectionist drive that touched everything he did." To a degree that could be said of Truman as well.

Both men were devoted to their wives and families. Each had an active sense of humor and was capable of laughing at himself. And they were both profound patriots. An unfailing loyalty to their country was bedrock to their code and one of their strongest bonds.

They were the same in their dislike of cheap political preening and hypocrisy, not to say the use of public office primarily as a means of self-aggrandizement. But at the same time, both relished politics, and Acheson quite as much as Truman. Many of his happiest hours, Acheson once confided to a reporter, were spent in the back rooms of the Capitol working with the leaders of both parties. "Some of my worst enemies on the Hill were my best friends," he said.

They were alike in their exceptional vitality and their belief in straightforward leadership. They deplored the tendency in politicians to avoid hard choices. They had tried always to make decisions in the best interest of the country in the long run, and to adhere to decisions once made. Though they made mistakes, both showed again and again uncommon courage in the face of adversity, each drawing strength from the other's resolve.

As mentioned in the pages that follow, an English writer once observed that a great play could be written about Truman and Acheson. How right he was!

In an interview with the writer Merle Miller, shortly after returning to stay in Independence, Truman said, "I tried never to forget who I was, where I came from, and where I would go back to." And on the morning of his first full day at home, in February 1953, when asked by the NBC correspondent Ray Scherer what was the first thing he planned to do, Truman said he was going to "carry the grips up to the attic," a remark the country took to heart, because it seemed so perfectly in character, so like a man glad to be back where he came from.

In truth, being off the world stage and taking up the part of a plain citizen again was no easy thing for Truman, or for Acheson either, as they were to confide in their remarkable exchange of letters.

The correspondence began on February 7, 1953, with Truman telling Acheson, "I hope that we will never lose contact," and continued for fully eighteen years, until Acheson's death in 1971. There has been nothing like it in our history, except for the post-presidential exchange, known as the Retirement Series, between John Adams and Thomas Jefferson, as Acheson was quick to point out, telling Truman that the Adams-Jefferson letters were among "the most glorious" he had ever read. What Truman and he wrote had more to do with the bonds of friendship, less with political philosophy than what the two Founders had taken up with each other. Acheson wrote at greater length than Truman, but then Acheson loved to write and had an exceptional gift for expressing himself.

Above all, it seems, each wanted the other to know how much their friendship mattered. To a large degree this remarkable collection of letters is a testament to friendship.

Most of the letters were handwritten, and on two sides of the paper. The handwriting of both of the correspondents is clear and straightforward. Truman writes a bit larger and the lines are more forward moving in spirit. Acheson's writing is tighter, perfectly neat and trim. They had both learned well in school to maintain a legible hand, to dot *i*s and cross *t*s.

Much is said about the particular activities each had taken up in his new life. Acheson was devoting large amounts of his time to Yale, as a member of the Yale Corporation, the ruling board of the university. Though he continued to live in Washington on P Street in Georgetown, his repeated trips to Connecticut and the time spent there seem to have been his way of going back where he came from. In the spring of 1958, he arranged for Truman to come to New Haven for several days as a visiting lecturer. Truman was an enormous hit with the students. "I hope you can understand how very much I enjoyed my visit to Yale," he writes Acheson afterward. "I have never had a better time any-where. It is what I have always wanted to do. . . ."

Truman writes of his part in the creation of the Truman Library in Independence. And then there were his memoirs, about which he and Acheson both have much to say. "The cursed manuscript" proved an awful ordeal, the work far greater and more demanding than Truman had ever reckoned. He had come home from the White House without a salary or pension, and would refuse to serve on any corporate boards or to take fees for lobbying or commercial endorsements. But the offer of a publisher's advance for an autobiography he thought an acceptable source of income.

He desperately needed Acheson's editorial help, and the help Ache-son provided, as his critical comments on the subject so abundantly document, was no easy matter for either of them. Once, in 1951, at the start of his seventh year serving under President Truman, Acheson had written, "We have always spoken the truth to one another and we always will." And there could be no waiving of that rule now, however awkward or outright painful that truth might be.

At one point, responding to the manuscript of the memoir in a letter dated June 27, 1955, Acheson warns Truman about the excessive use of the first person singular and refers to a page where the pronoun *I* appears eleven times. In a following letter, Acheson says bluntly that two entire chapters of the memoir are "pretty heavy going": "Somehow I don't think that a general exposition of budgetary principles adds a great deal to your autobiography."

Truman was being assisted by a cluster of "helpers," and the manu-script kept growing ever larger. Acheson read every page, carefully, thoughtfully, questioning facts and doing his part to weed out redun-dancies and such excess lumber as budgetary principles. The book was too much the work of others, Acheson saw, and far too long-winded. One of Acheson's letters, written on July 18, 1955, could serve as a model of expert editorial questioning and guidance. "Was the final meeting with Marshall re China on December 14 or 15?" he asks at one point. "My recollection is the latter." "The CIA is not the Presiden-tial advisor on the effects of policies. This is the State Department," he reminds Truman, adding, "The illustration does not illustrate; it con-fuses." The hours of thought and effort that went into this one letter can be imagined, not to say the discomfort Acheson must have had over hurting Truman's feelings. Most unfortunate and infuriating, he writes, were those pages that seemed more like what Horatio Alger might have said than Harry Truman. Your ghost writers are doing you in, Acheson is telling him. And then follows a superb, two-paragraph Acheson synopsis of Truman's first term which is one of the golden moments in the collection.

At times Acheson's criticism verges on the caustic. But Truman took it all in stride. "Damn it, Dean," he later writes, "you are one man who can say to me what you please any time, anywhere on any subject."

When reading these letters between old friends it is well to pause now and then and remember that these are the two who established the Truman Doctrine of assistance to Greece and Turkey, who worked together in the creation of the Marshall Plan, who faced the decision of whether to go into Korea. They had worked together continuously, their respect and admiration for each other growing steadily, over the seven years of Truman's presidency, during which Acheson served first as Undersecretary of State, then for four years as Secretary of State. Acheson saw himself as "the faithful first lieutenant" to Truman, whom he called "the captain with the mighty heart," echoing a line from Edwin Markham's poem about Lincoln. In 1946 he was the sole member of the President's official "family" who came to the railroad station to greet Truman on his return to Washington after the humiliating defeat for the Democrats in the off-year elections. It was something Truman would never forget, and he had stood by Acheson when Acheson was under continuous attack from Senator Joe McCarthy. Truman considered George Marshall the greatest American of the time, but regarded Acheson, as he says in the letters, as his greatest Secretary of State.

I first encountered the post-presidential letters between Truman and Acheson more than twenty years ago, while reading in the Research Room at the Truman Library. I was in the last stages of work on a biography of Truman and these particular letters provided some of the most pleasurable hours of all. I remember being especially struck by Acheson's enthusiasm for the Adams-Jefferson correspondence. It was the first I had heard of that classic exchange and it started me on the path that led to my biography of Adams. (In writing history, as in history, one thing does very often lead to another.)

That the "oldster" letters of Truman and Acheson are now at last in print and in such handsome fashion is a grand step forward. They pro-

vide interest and amusement aplenty, as well as further human delin-
eation of two Americans who are so immensely important for us to
understand and appreciate.

One of my favorite samples of vintage Truman is the good-humored
observation, in his letter of January 28, 1954, that while "the past
had always interested me for use in the present . . . I'm bored to
death [when writing his memoirs] with what I did and didn't do nine
years ago."

> But Andrew Johnson, James Madison, even old Rutherford B.
> Hayes I'm extremely interested in as I am King Henry IV of France,
> Margaret of Navarre, Charles V, Philip II of Spain, and Charlie's
> Aunt Margaret.
>
> Wish to goodness I'd decided to spend my so called retirement
> putting Louis XIII, Gustavus Adolphus, Richelieu and five tubs of
> gold together instead of writing about me and my mistakes. Any-
> way I made no mistake in my Great Secretary of State.

I love, too, what Acheson wrote in 1955 to Bess Truman after he and
his wife, Alice, visited Independence, staying as guests in the Truman
home at 219 North Delaware Street, in that it expresses so much that
countless others have felt after spending time in Independence, and I
am one of them: "It made us feel all over again the strength and
grandeur of the fabric of this America of ours."

For two who had such a sense of history and who had played such
outsized parts in history, they rarely seem to be writing for the benefit
of history, but to each other only. As old friends do, they report on birthdays, anniversaries, and their travels, they exchange photographs. Still
the arena of politics is never far from their thoughts. They talk candidly
of Adlai Stevenson, Churchill, John Kennedy, Sam Rayburn, and Lyndon Johnson. (Kennedy is "immature," Nixon, "dangerous," Truman
writes.) Both get "steamed up" over Eisenhower's foreign policy, and
especially during the 1960 presidential election, one feels all the old
political adrenaline rising in them once again.

Another of my favorite observations is one about the preoccupation
with "image" in Washington under the new Kennedy administration.
"This is a terrible weakness," Acheson says. "It makes one look at oneself instead of at the problem. How will I look fielding this hot line drive
to short stop? This is a good way to miss the ball altogether."

Nor does Truman take lightly the increasingly conspicuous role of big money in politics. "I am told that the Dam Democrats at Kennedy's suggestion are putting on a $1,000 [a plate] dinner! If and when that happens we'll quit being democrats with a little d! . . . To hell with these multimillionaires at the head of things."

The kind of money passing about today in politics would have been beyond their imagining, just as it would have been difficult for them to have contemplated a time to come when people would no longer write letters.

There is, to be sure, a gradual change in tone and focus, as age comes on and "the man with the scythe," as Truman says, casts a shadow.

They send each other speeches they have given, report on the birth of grandchildren, write of illnesses and news of the deaths of old friends like George Marshall. "I sat and read it and read it again because my spectacles became clouded the first time," Truman writes.

It is interesting, too, to note what is not to be found in the letters. There is little or no complaining or self-pity, no extensive rehashing of events in order to explain or justify past mistakes, no time taken up with what-might-have-beens.

The last letter in the collection, like the first, is from Truman. "I was greatly pleased by your kind and generous letter on my eighty-seventh birthday," he writes to Acheson on May 14, 1971. "Coming from you, this carries deeper meaning for me."

Truman liked to say that at least fifty years had to go by before a judgment by history can be fairly made, that one had to wait for the dust to settle. It has now been more than fifty years since most of these letters were written, so it is not only high time we have them in hand this way, it is the perfect time.

—David McCullough
April 2010

Affection and Trust

Harry Truman greeted by members of his Cabinet and staff on his return on October 18, 1950, from the Wake Island meeting with General Douglas MacArthur. From left to right: Special Assistant to the President Averell Harriman, Secretary of Defense George Marshall, President Truman, Secretary of State Dean Acheson, unidentified (partly obscured by Snyder), Secretary of the Treasury John W. Snyder, Secretary of the Army Frank Pace, and General Omar Bradley.

1

February to December 1953

A New Outlet for "the Truman-Acheson Front"

*H*arry Truman and Dean Acheson experienced their sudden transition on January 20, 1953, from President of the United States and Secretary of State to private citizens, with some shock. The exercise of power to which they had become accustomed had now to be given up, and revisited only in memory. Their shared sense of loss, together with their friendship, drew them toward each other, and they started writing letters.

Their first letters crossed, prompted only by their respective thoughts of the other. Letter followed letter, the range of subjects grew, and their friendship was recast for this new time in their lives. They shared their thoughts about what the current occupant of the White House and his advisers should be doing. They also sought to be influential by speaking out and writing, and they could do this as a team, as partners attempting to keep the country moving in the right direction, something they felt the new President too often did not seem to know how to do.

Between their forging of a renewed relationship through their correspondence, and their continuing and often coordinated presence in the public-policy arena, the two men carried into the post-presidential years what Acheson called "the Truman-Acheson front." They were still working together—the chief always loyal to and admiring of the brilliance of his adviser, and the adviser always loyal to and admiring of the true heart and true instincts of his chief—just as in the past.

Acheson and his wife, Alice, hosted a luncheon at their home immediately following Eisenhower's inauguration ceremonies, for Harry, Bess, and Margaret Truman and about thirty-five members of his administration. Afterward, the Trumans boarded a train for the long journey back home to Missouri. As the train left the station, Truman waved goodbye to Acheson and the others who had joined him in running the country during some of the most momentous, perilous, and fateful times in its history.

.   .   .

February 7, 1953

Dear Dean:

There are not enough words in the dictionary on the favorable side, of course, to express the appreciation which Mrs. Truman and I felt for your wonderful luncheon of the twentieth. I never have been at a function of this sort where everybody seemed to be having the best time they ever had. We will never forget it, as it is one of the high lights of our trip to "Washington and back."

I hope that we will never lose contact. Should you be in this part of the world be sure and come to see us. You can rest assured that I'll make my presence in Washington known to you if ever I get there, which, of course, I may at some time in the future.

Please express our thanks and appreciation, with all the adjectives you can think of, to Mrs. Acheson.

Sincerely yours,

Harry S Truman

Truman sent Acheson a second letter the same day, this one concerning some last-minute State Department business.

February 7, 1953

Dear Dean:

Thanks a lot for the appointment of Thomas K. Finletter and Adrian S. Fisher on the Panel of the Permanent Court of Arbitration to the Hague Conventions. They are two excellent and able gentlemen and I am sure will make good on the job.

Sincerely yours,

Harry S. Truman

[Handwritten postscript:] Hope you and Mrs. Acheson are having a grand vacation. I've had some sixty thousand letters and telegrams— 99.4% favorable! Believe it or not. You've never seen as much crow eaten, feathers and all.

The favorable letters and telegrams were especially welcome to a brand-new former President of the United States who left office following a presidential campaign in which his administration was tarred with the failure to end the Korean War and characterized in the most strident and acrimonious fashion as corrupt and soft on communism. His approval rating when he left office was a dismal 31 percent.

The Achesons escaped, soon after Truman's departure from Washington, to Antigua, in the British West Indies.

February 10, 1953

Dear Mr. President,

You and Mrs. Truman have been constantly in our thoughts these last three weeks. We see glimpses of you in papers weeks old and read fragmentary reports of you. But you are more vivid in our minds. We have spoken often of that last poignant day together and shall never forget the sight of you on the track platform as the train grew small and smaller down the track. We wish that you would both escape to the peace and privacy for a while of a place like this enchanted and blessed isle, where the sea and air and all around us combine to make rest and relaxation inevitable and delightful. We read and sleep and swim— Alice paints—we keep the world and its doings away from us. But we talk about the great epoch in which you permitted us to play a part and which now seems ended in favor of God knows what.

One of the glorious things which I have read—and which you probably know—is Paul Wilstach's edition of the correspondence between John Adams and Jefferson. If you do not know it, by all means get it. There were two robust old codgers. I think one gets a wholly new affection for Adams.

We are here, I hope, until the end of March. This note brings to both you and Mrs. Truman our devotion and solicitude. I know that these are difficult weeks for you both.

Affectionately,

Dean

Truman's correspondence with Acheson would often be handwritten, as was this letter. Bess Truman, whom Truman calls in understatement "an anti–public office holder," had a moment of softness when she saw the thousands of people who greeted them at the railroad depot and their home. The book deal Truman mentions is for his memoirs. Truman's daughter, Margaret—"Skinny for short"—apparently gave him a full report of a Democratic Party event in New York City on February 14 featuring Adlai Stevenson and Averell Harriman.

February 18, 1953

Dear Dean:

Your letter of Feb. 10th is a jewel I shall always treasure. Never will Bess, Margaret and Harry forget that wonderful afternoon with you and Mrs. Acheson and the official family of a former President of the United States. It was the happiest luncheon I ever had or ever will have.

The send off at the Union Station, the spontaneous meeting in front of your house, the crowds along the line of the B and O—how could any man describe them or want more.

Mitchell, the Porter, stayed up all the night long and reported that at Grafton at 12 midnight, at Clarksburg old Stonewall's birthplace at 2:30 A.M., at Parkersburg at 3 A.M., people wanted a look at the old "ex." All across Ohio, Indiana, Illinois just the same. At St. Louis some three or four thousand on the platform of the Union Station. Same all across Missouri. At the hometown our county police force had expected 300 and there were more than 10,000 at the Mo.P. depot and 5,000 in front of the house at home.

Now why? and again why. Mrs. T. said when we finally arrived inside the house, "Well, this pays for all the thirty years of troubles." Some admission for an anti–public office holder, I'd say.

Dean, if it hadn't been for you and all that official family who were at your house on Jan. 20, it could never have happened.

I've had fifty or sixty thousand letters—99.9% favorable and compli-mentary editorials and columns by the score from terrible papers like the *Cleveland Plain Dealer,* the *San Francisco Chronicle,* the *Los Ange-les Times,* the terrible Knight papers, all eating crow, feathers and all!

Our successors are making hay for the Democrats at a great rate. More power to 'em. I keep still! How can I? But I do. Stevenson made a grand talk in New York on Saturday night and Harriman did a grand job as Chairman. I had a reporter there named Margie (Skinny for short) who gave me the low down and it was all good.

Hope you and Mrs. Acheson are having the grandest time possibly to have, and from your letter I'd judge you are. We are going on a Pacific jaunt beginning March 22 from San Francisco, winding up in Honolulu for 30 days and back here about May 5th.

I'm about to sell out a book for a fantastic sum. It's not worth it but I'm sorely tempted.

My best to you and Mrs. Acheson—and the Boss joins me, may we never lose contact!

Sincerely,

Harry S. Truman

The Achesons were still in Antigua at the time of this letter. Antigua became their favored winter retreat for many years.

February 21, 1953

Dear Mr. President,

Two letters from you came to me today—a record even in the old days. One about our last luncheon. I am glad—very glad—that it gave you and Mrs. Truman happiness. To us it was more moving than I can ever say— To see around you the devotion which you inspired and which had done faithful and good work to the end and could be gay, however heavy the heart was. None of us will ever forget that day—or many others—where you led us to do what did not seem possible to do.

Since I wrote you last, I have gone on with my idle life, mostly reading—with swimming and some moderate use of alcoholic bever-ages. The Thomas Life of Lincoln has impressed me very much. I think you would like it. Most Lincoln books get so bogged down in legend or detail or papers that I have never been able to see what the man was like. What made him tick? Why did he decide this way instead of that way? I used to look at his portrait and wonder what he would have said to me if I had brought him the problems which I brought to you. This book makes it clearer. I begin to feel that I know a little more. But I am not willing to swap chiefs with any Secretary of State before—or since—Jan. 20, 1953.

Alice joins me in affectionate greeting to you and Mrs. Truman.

As always,

Dean

The book that Acheson is talking about below, and which Truman referred to in his letter of February 18, is Truman's memoirs, which would be published in two volumes, in 1955 and 1956.

March 2, 1953

Dear Mr. President,

Your wonderful letter of Feb. 18 has made us very happy. What you say about the luncheon on the Twentieth, the crowds greeting you all the way home, the letters and editorial, and Mrs. Truman's comment on the recompense for thirty years of public life. You ask why. I am sure that I know. It was because the thirty years were years of great public service by a brave and straight shooter and the people know it and appreciate it. You have done what they would like to have done and wanted done.

Your speaking of the *Cleveland Plain Dealer* editorial is particularly interesting. A few days ago I got here a long letter from a linotype operator on that paper, enclosing a copy of the editorial. He wrote that for years the editorials about F.D.R. and you were so bad that he often wanted to chuck the job and be free from having to set them up. This one gave him some sense that it had been worth it to stay on just to say, "I told you so." I have written him to say that the composing room is way ahead of the editorial room.

We are delighted that you and Mrs. Truman are going to have a holiday in the Pacific and know that it, too, will be a triumphal tour. I just hope that people will give you a chance to rest and wish that Margaret could go along to see that you both did rest. We are disgustingly healthy and relaxed.

I am most excited about the book, although I worry when remembering the biblical hope that mine enemy might write a book. Where is it? In Ecclesiastes I think. But there is one book that you have spoken of which I hope you will write—perhaps it will be this one—"From Precinct to President." I see it not as an anecdotal book—which I am afraid the *Life* people will want, and which would stir up controversy (as they would urge it) without shedding light. But it would be built around two central themes. One would be your favorite description of the President's function, to persuade people to do what they ought to do without persuading. This is the heart of the American democratic process. It is an essay in persuasion, not by a dictator with police and guns as his arguments. But by one whom the people are persuaded wants what they want—though they may not always be able to state it in detail, and who must also persuade them that the complicated steps necessary to achieve results in this complicated world are directed to the just satisfaction of the popular wants. This may be pretty much true in other democracies such as England, France, Scandinavia, etc. But we have a further need for persuasion. The division of powers, imposed on us in towns, counties, states and nation, to provide checks and balances, has made government in the U.S.A. a true art and the art of persuasion from start to finish. How all of these problems came to you and were solved by you from Jackson County to the White House would be a great and profoundly useful book to young and old. And your observations on whether the process is flexible enough for the atomic age, for the contest with the monolithic opponent, for the execution of policies with continuity as an essential ingredient, and upon the effects of persuasion à la McCarthy, which is a sort of bastardization of the process & a destruction of it—all of this out of your own experience would be wonderful.

Another theme which goes along with this is the change in the function of government which began towards the end of the last century and came to full flower in the administrations of H.S.T. and F.D.R. The early needs of government were to be policeman, judge, soldier, to provide order, justice, security. But now, with the growth of populations and the complexity of relationships, a managerial element becomes strongly necessary. This emerged when the Granger movement produced the idea of the public utility and its regulation. F.D.R. and you had it in a vast number of fields—the banks, various aspects of the welfare problem, power, mobilization, foreign affairs, where in very truth you were engaged in managing with our friends. The development and strengthening of the alliance of the free.

You may well say, "Whose book is this anyway?" It surely is yours. I am only putting in my plug for the one of yours which I want most. There will be many plugs for other kinds. But I have run on too long. It is the nearest thing to the talks I miss so much. Our deep affection to you and Mrs. Truman.

As ever,

Dean

Acheson was still in Antigua when Truman wrote this letter. The "Canadian Ambassador" is probably Stanley Woodward, who was White House chief of protocol during the Roosevelt and Truman administrations and, from 1950 to January 1953, United States ambassador to Canada. Woodward and his wife would be Truman's traveling companions during his 1956 European trip.

March 6, 1953

Dear Dean:

I can't tell you how very much I appreciated your good letter of February twenty-first. I am glad you received both of mine. I suppose you are having a good time with our Canadian Ambassador at this minute and I wish I could be there too. We are trying to get things in shape so we can leave for Hawaii in a very short time.

I've been reading that Lincoln book you referred to and I like it very much. It seems to be the most sensible one that has come out lately. I am also going to get my hands on the one to which you referred in your other letter concerning the correspondence between Adams and Jefferson. I've read one or two of the letters Jefferson wrote to Adams and one from Adams to Jefferson which, in my opinion, would be difficult to publish in its entirety. They were most interesting.

I hope you and Mrs. Acheson are getting a good rest and I hope you are getting a lot of enjoyment out of what is taking place in Washington. It is very interesting.

Sincerely yours,

Harry S Truman

Acheson refers in this letter to Harry, Bess, and Margaret Truman's journey to San Francisco with W. Averell Harriman (here "Averill") in his private Union Pacific railroad car. Harriman was an influential member of the Truman administration, ambassador to the United Kingdom, the Marshall Plan administrator in that country, and Secretary of Commerce, later governor of New York.

From San Francisco, the Trumans sailed to Hawaii for a month's stay on Coconut Island, which was owned by Truman's friend the California oilman Edwin Pauley.

"Foster" is John Foster Dulles, President Eisenhower's Secretary of State. Eisenhower promised during the campaign that he would bring an end to the Korean War, and Acheson is worried about how he will go about keeping that pledge. Acheson was probably concerned that anxiety for peace might prompt Eisenhower to make unwarranted concessions to North Korea.

The clipping enclosed with this letter is probably Robert Waithman's article, "The Lion Hearted: A Salute and Farewell," News Chronicle, January 17, 1953, which says this: "As for Dean Acheson, a man of scholarship and grace, he was venomously abused by some of his countrymen: he was the object of the cruelest campaign of vilification in modern American memory. We shall remember him in the earlier days, when his irony and eloquence established a wonderful bond between him and the State Department correspondents; and in the later days, when under ferocious and unreasoned political assault he retired into himself, still patient and more resolute than ever, but with the sunlight gone. In these days one after another of the Democratic Party men fell silent, fearing to defend Acheson. But not Mr. Truman. Never once did he equivocate or withdraw an ounce of his support. And Mr. Acheson repaid him with a respect and devotion which it was a most moving thing to observe. A great play should be written, one of these days, around the story of the unblemished and fateful association of these wholly dissimilar men."

April 6, 1953

Dear Mr. President,

Your good letter reached me just before we started home from the West Indies and read of you starting off for your Pacific holiday. Averill came here for lunch last week and made us very homesick by his account of a day's journey with you and Mrs. Truman and Margaret, on your way to the coast. We earnestly hope that Mrs. Truman's hand, which she wrote Alice about and which Averill says was still bothering her, is better and on the mend.

We are most eager to see all of you. I hear rumor to the effect that you might possibly be taking an apartment in N.Y. in connection with your work on the book, etc., and spend some time there off and on.

This would be a great break for your eastern friends, but you will have to discipline us vigorously if you are to get a great deal of work done. It would, I should think, be useful to you to get a different point of view from time to time and see a lot of people without publicity.

The enclosed clipping was written by a good Englishman and so impressed me that I wrote for a copy of it for you. I hope it will please you. He has gotten a view of you which I have seen so often and delight to think and talk about.

Alice and I are loafing at the farm through April and then go back to the law again. I most earnestly hope that Foster and Ike do not appease the Chinese communists to get a truce in Korea. As you know so well, we could always have had a truce on their terms. This new offer does not seem very glamorous to me.

Our most affectionate greetings to all the Trumans.

As ever,

Dean

Truman started a tradition with this birthday telegram, sent on Acheson's sixtieth birthday.

April 11, 1953

HONORABLE DEAN ACHESON
CONGRATULATIONS ON ANOTHER MILESTONE. MRS. TRU-MAN AND MARGARET JOIN ME IN BEST WISHES FOR A HAPPY BIRTHDAY.
HARRY S TRUMAN

Acheson is upset over the misdeeds of the Eisenhower administration. He is concerned about the firing of his close State Department colleague Paul Nitze. He is also referring to Secretary Dulles's practice of dismissing senior staff who had served in the Truman administration. The Wilson he refers to is Eisenhower's Secretary of Defense, Charles E. Wilson. Acheson encloses two articles, by Drew Pearson and John O'Donnell, who had once tormented the Truman administration but were now writing negatively about Eisenhower and his advisers.

Acheson recalls Truman's concern for his older daughter Mary, who suf-

fered from tuberculosis. When Acheson was traveling on State Department business, Truman would call the hospital to get news of Mary and give Acheson daily reports.

"The farm" was the Achesons' farm, Harewood, in Sandy Spring, Maryland, just outside Washington, where they went frequently to escape the city. Mrs. Acheson, an accomplished artist, painted while her husband gardened, wrote letters, or made furniture.

Dear Mr. President:
April 14, 1953

The message from you, Mrs. Truman, and Margaret, as I came around the bend into the seventh decade, touched me and delighted me more than I can ever tell you. It brought back all your kindness and thoughtfulness through so many years. Alice and I shall never forget how you and Mrs. Truman shared with us all our worries for Mary when she was so very ill in 1950.

Well, I am a spry and very lazy lad of sixty summers. After nearly three months off, the very thought of work is repulsive to me. That is, work in an office. Out here on the farm Alice has me painting the porch furniture, plowing the garden, wheel barrowing manure for her roses, building a new wood fence and taking the grandchildren down to the next farm to see horses, cattle, pigs, and puppies. Aside from that I just lie around all day.

I am also getting pretty steamed up about the way the pupils whom you had us teach so carefully are really fouling things up. Two samples are enclosed of men, who used to spend their time making our lives hard, now having a field day with our successors.

So far it seems to me that the worst side of the whole thing has been the terrible retrogression which has taken place in the processes of government and in dealing with the personnel of government. Ike is presiding over something which is corruptive on a really grand scale.

The folly of his supporting Senators and Congressmen who would cut his throat if elected one could put down to total lack of experience in politics and in government. But the studied appeasement of the Hill which is now going on at the expense of the best civil servants we have—certainly in State—is not only criminal but frightening in what it may mean regarding the quality of advice which the Secretary of State, and ultimately, the President, will receive. Just last week Dulles has separated Paul Nitze, the head of the State Policy Planning Staff, who did, as you remember, such fine work on that NSC series under which the rearmament took place and under which Ike himself operated in Europe. I understand that he is being sacrificed to the Hill demand that all who worked with me be changed or fired, and that he may be picked up again by Wilson in Defense.

This seems to me plain cowardice and utter folly. Ike knows better than this. He would never tolerate it for the uniformed members of the armed services. But it is the established policy for all the civilian departments—the exact opposite of everything which you tried to and did bring about.

This brings me to your book, as I long to see it. A book to show how good government is carried on at all levels from the county to the White House. And it is not the way things are being done now.

But I should not disturb your vacation in the quarrelsome way. It is the first time I have blown up in months.

Alice joins me in the most affectionate greetings to Mrs. Truman and Margaret and to yourself.

Most sincerely,

Dean

Although Truman was relaxing on Coconut Island when he wrote this letter, he still worried about what a new former President of the United States should make of the rest of his life. "The 'Boss' " is, in this letter and always in Truman's correspondence, Mrs. Truman. "Gov. King" is Samuel Wilder King, the territorial governor of Hawaii. He was the delegate of Hawaii to the United States Congress when Truman was a senator, and Mrs. Truman apparently knew Mrs. King from this past time. The 74th Club was made up of congressional wives. Admiral Arthur W. Radford, soon to be named chairman of the Joint Chiefs of Staff, was at this time high commissioner of the Trust Territory of the Pacific Islands. "Old man Costello" is probably Frank Costello, a Democratic Party boss from New York City. "C in C" means "Commander in Chief." William Seward was Secretary of State under Abraham Lincoln and Andrew Johnson. "Mr. Republican" probably refers to Robert A. Taft, senior senator from Ohio.

April 18, 1953

Dear Dean:

Your letter was highly appreciated because it is a good letter and because it bolstered my ego! The "Boss" says I already have too much of that commodity and it needs no outside cultivation. Sometimes I'm not so sure.

We've had a grand time here if you can call it a grand time to attain a bad case of Hawaiian fever. It is a worse disease than Mexican Mañana but not so bad as Potomac.

Our first social affair was dinner with Gov. King last Thursday evening. It was a beautiful affair in two sections—the past sixties in the State dining room and the under thirties in the garden. You've been there and know what a lovely place it is. It is suffering from the same debility that affected the White House. The legislators won't furnish the money to rebuild the house. Mrs. King says it will fall down some day. Termites are its trouble. I told her that you and I had trouble with termites in Congress and that Ike seemed to have more of them. She agreed. She and Mrs. T. were in the 74th Club, so we had no political trouble whatever.

Had lunch with Adm. Radford Friday and reviewed the Marine Battalion and Air Force right across the bay from here Saturday morning. The old Marine Lt. Gen. gave me the 21 guns when I appeared. He's from Alabama and his wife is the daughter of old man Costello, who was national committeeman from D.C. when F.D.R. was elected in 1932. I told them that 21 guns for a private in the citizen ranks was going pretty far. Reply was that they wished they had a civilian C in C now!

What shall I do? Been going over a book on what former Presidents did in times past. Maybe I can get some ideas.

Well, the end of the vacation is approaching all too fast but I'm anxious to see and talk to you and some of my other good friends. It looks as if Acheson will be appreciated much sooner than Seward was. I guess if the Fates had us by the hand maybe Ike and Snollygoster [a favorite Truman word, meaning an unprincipled, unscrupulous person] Dulles will help. I read a review of an article by Mr. Republican in *Look*. "Looks" as if he's badly scared, if the review is correct. It makes me want to keep stiller than ever. We just don't need to say a word. Events are taking care of things.

I wish you and Mrs. Acheson were here. What a time we could have! I am hoping to see you not too long after I return so we can discuss things as "nonpartisan" onlookers. Won't that be something.

Bess and Margie join me in the best of everything to you and your family.

Sincerely,
Harry Truman

Truman was upset about Eisenhower too. His and Acheson's letters would often come back to the theme of Eisenhower's poor leadership.

April 24, 1953

Dear Dean:

I certainly did appreciate your letter of the 14th, very, very much. I am sure you do not feel a bit older by being sixty. You are not yet living on borrowed time; in one more year, I will start on that program.

I know just how you feel about going back to work. I hate to see next Tuesday come, when we will be leaving this vacation Paradise.

I am in complete agreement with you about the way our successors are acting. I do not see how it is possible to get things in such a mess as they have succeeded in doing in ninety days. It looks as if the President is giving all his prerogatives away and it will probably in the end appear to be just as well to have a British Legislative Government, although I do not think our country was cut out for that kind of a Government.

I am going to try to arrange that forthcoming book of mine so that we can show what really makes good Government and why it is necessary to have a policy and a program and the nerve to try to put it into effect.

I read the enclosed clippings with a lot of interest.

Tell Mrs. Acheson not to work you too hard; I am afraid she will set a bad example and I, myself, will get into trouble.

All of us join in the best of everything to you and Mrs. Acheson.

Sincerely yours,

Harry S. Truman

The reference to "McCarthy" is to Republican Senator Joseph McCarthy of Wisconsin, the author of periodic accusations of communist sympathy in the Truman State Department. Acheson mentions "the Yale board"—i.e., the Yale Corporation, the governing body of the university. "Mr. Republican" is again Senator Robert A. Taft of Ohio. "Senator Bush of Connecticut" was Prescott Bush, father and grandfather of two Presidents.

May 2, 1953

Dear Mr. President:

Just a note to welcome you home and to wish you the first of many, many free and happy birthdays. Free, because you will not [have] the terrible burdens and responsibilities which you have carried so long and so gallantly. Happy, because you can always know that you performed above and beyond the call of duty. The years before us will bring to all our American people an increasing realization of what they received from you in leadership and steadiness and a human understanding of all the thousands of problems which people in our country have to worry with every day. All of them in a real sense came into your study every day and unloaded these worries on your shoulders. And you picked up the problems and worked them out. You have great causes for peace of mind and spirit and confidence that you have done all in the evil day.

I am delighted that the Hawaiian holiday was so good and restful for all three of you. Your two good letters of April 18th and 24th breathe all your gay spirits when you are rested and loaded for bear. It was a great joy to read and reread them. Your old Marine General who gave you the 21 gun is a man after my own heart. If he were in the State Department, they would probably retire him or send him to Addis Ababa. But the military have a stronger position for which we should be—and I am—grateful.

Alice and I go back to work on Monday—when my address will be 701 Union Trust Building, Washington 4, D.C. We have just had a delightful visit from our Milwaukee daughter, Jane (Mrs. Dudley Brown), who keeps the flag flying in the heart of the McCarthy country and has all the flaming loyalties and prejudices which make a first class human being. She came on to get her batteries recharged, and we all had a great time in the process. She says that all her friends who voted for McCarthy are ashamed but still uneducated. So she returns to the fray with new vigor.

I am most eager to see you and get your views and guidance. My next week-end (May 8, 9, 10) I spend at New Haven, where I have taken up again my duties on the Yale board—along with Mr. Republican and Senator Bush of Connecticut, and fortunately some others. Whenever you are ready for some talk I shall be glad to be available. It is easy to get to New York should you be coming on. It is not a problem to get to Kansas City should you wish to see me there. I am quite sure that you will have lots of work to occupy you when you get home again. But when the time comes that I can be of any use, you have only to tell me when and where.

Alice asks me to get a report from you about Mrs. Truman's hand.

She has worried about it and hopes that the Pacific vacation has been what was needed. She and I send our most affectionate greetings to Mrs. Truman, Margaret and to you.

Again the best of all birthdays.

Most warmly,

Dean

Truman shares some thoughts about the development of historical under-standing. "Our great General" is President Eisenhower. Joe Brown is prob-ably a Kansas City friend with whom Truman sometimes had lunch at the exclusive, and mostly Republican, Kansas City Club. The "All Slops" and "the man who spells Lipp with two p's" are columnists Joseph and Stewart Alsop and Walter Lippmann. Truman also makes some unguarded com-ments about notorious Washington socialite Evelyn Walsh McLean, and about prominent journalist Dorothy Thompson. "His boy" could be John Eisenhower, General Eisenhower's son.

May 25, 1953

Dear Dean:

I have been doing some long range thinking and studying about the future, wondering what the effect of the misrepresentation of facts will be on the history of things.

Evidently you and I have the pathological liars worried. I've seen some Soviet propaganda sheets charging you with certain high crimes and misdemeanors and charging me with murder, rape and arson, all of which has been approved by certain Senate and House Committees.

Our great General, whom you, Roosevelt and I built up to the skies, is about to come down with a dull thud and the apologentia must have a noise to muffle that thud. You and I are the most likely victims. Well, we've licked them time and again and we'll do it for history.

I saw Joe Brown yesterday and he said he'd had a fine visit with you. He is a great admirer of yours.

I'm about to get started on the book. Wish I hadn't signed a contract! I'm getting Mexican or Hawaiian or something lazy in the head. But since this job needs to be done I might as well do it. I expect to stick strictly to the facts and to outline my views on free government gained from experience.

I hope I can do it. May I call on you from time to time for verification of various controversial points?

It looks as if the All Slops and the man who spells Lipp with two p's are in some mental misery. The only man who's been substantially right all the time is Tom Stokes. Did you ever hear Evelyn Walsh McLain's [sic] comment on Dorothy Thompson? She said Dorothy was the only woman she knew who could menstruate in public and get away with it and did! What a gal Evelyn was. She called the boss one night about 12 o'clock and told her all about Ike's feminine affairs in Europe and said she'd sent his boy over to straighten Ike out. But such language. Captain Billy Hayes never had a vocabulary like that!

The vacation did us all a lot of good and made me lazy as hell. I am coming to Washington the week of June 22 and will hope to see you.

Mrs. T. joins me in the best there is to you and Mrs. Acheson. (She hasn't read this letter!)

Sincerely,

Harry Truman

Acheson finds much to worry about. "Ike's abdication" refers to Truman's and Acheson's feeling that Eisenhower did not have a firm hand on the country's helm. "Bob Taft" is Republican Senator Robert A. Taft of Ohio. James E. Webb was director of the Bureau of the Budget and Undersecretary of State during the Truman Administration, and J. Lister Hill was a senator from Alabama.

Dear Mr. President,   May 28, 1953

The well known envelope with your name in the corner and your handwriting on it lying on our hall table always quickens my heart. Yesterday's letter was no exception. It was a delight in itself and because it brought the good news, which I shall treat as confidential until I see it released, that you will be here in the week of June 22 and that I shall see you. You must let me know when you will arrive so that I can have again the joy of meeting you as you step off the train. Will Mrs. Truman come with you?

Alice and I are overjoyed to do anything which will make your visit more enjoyable. We should love to have you stay with us, being emboldened by the knowledge that you do not like air conditioning which we do not have. But we can also understand that you will wish to see many people and that the anonymity of a hotel might be more useful for you and your callers. If so, perhaps Mrs. Truman might wish to escape from your meetings to our house. We can arrange a dinner either at P Street or in the country. Let us know at your convenience and we shall do the rest. Most of all we must have some talk.

What you say about the Great General is frighteningly true. I had a letter from a friend who writes: "I am anxious and worried increasingly from day to day as that fumbling silence in the White House seeps out over the country like a cold fog over a river bed where no stream runs." Ike's abdication has given us that Congressional government, directionless and feeble, which de Tocqueville feared would result from the Constitution. And it comes at the very time when your policy of building strength and unity would have paid great dividends as the Russians ran into the period of weakness and division which the succession to Stalin inevitably created. You remember that we used to say that in a tight pinch we could generally rely on some fool play of the Russians to pull us through. Now that is being exactly reversed. They now have, as invaluable allies, division, weakness and folly. As an example of the latter Bob Taft's latest thinking aloud should get a special prize. It gives one doubt as to his state of mental responsibility.

And it is not only Congressional government, which must always fail because it cannot provide an executive, but Congressional government by the most ignorant, irresponsible and anarchistic elements— anarchistic because their result, if not their aim, is to destroy government and popular confidence in it.

I think that you are quite right that you and I are very likely to be in for another period of attack and vilification. This is also Jim Webb's opinion based upon the belief that Taft will turn McCarthy loose on us sufficiently before the 1954 election to provide distraction, to revive suspicion of the democrats and to get sufficient right wing republicans to free the administration from the need for democratic support and to give Taft the kind of Republican majority which would insist on a policy which Taft would control, and which would make Ike the captive of the right wing. But as you say we have won many fights in the past and need not fear others in the future. It is, none the less, a distasteful waste of time and effort.

As to the book, I shall, of course, be delighted to help in any way you think I can be useful. Call on me whenever you think best.

Lister Hill called me this morning to ask me to meet with a group of Democratic senators to talk about foreign policy on June 8. Unfortunately I have to be in New Haven on that day but said that I would be available at almost any other time. He will let me know. I think the time may be coming when they should keep the record clear that the Administration's words and its acts are not going along the same track, and that the conduct of foreign policy is not a mere matter of words.

I was amused this morning to read the man "who spells Lip with two p's" tell the world how successful were the policies of the past four years. He can't remember who the people were who did these things. The lady you refer to was a fabulous creature. It used to disgust me to see how people who should have known better used to fawn and prey upon her at the same time.

Alice sends her love to Mrs. Truman. We are looking forward to seeing, I hope, both of you very soon.

Most sincerely,

Dean

Charles S. Murphy was Truman's special counsel during the latter years of his presidency. The library luncheons Truman mentions were fund-raising events for his presidential library, which was still in the planning stage.

Dear Dean:
June 8, 1953

I have been quite some time answering your letter and this is not to be considered an answer to it, but merely to inform you of what developments are.

It looks now as if Mrs. Truman and I will drive to Washington. Will probably arrive there on the 22nd and will be there the 23rd, 24th and 25th. Charlie Murphy tells me that arrangements have been made for me to see everybody and I am certainly anxious to have a chance to sit down and talk with you on the situation as it is.

Mrs. Truman and I certainly appreciate your invitation to come to the house but when the staff boys found out I was coming they seem to have filled up every day with something for me to do and I have had little or no control of it. I am enclosing copy of the schedule they have made out for me.

I have to go to Philadelphia on the 26th and New York on the 27th. I am having a Library luncheon in Philadelphia on the 26th and a Library luncheon in New York on the 29th. Averell says he wants to have a luncheon for some Democrats in New York on either the 30th of June or the first of July—then I must start back home.

We will stop at the Mayflower in Washington and the Waldorf in New York.

Sincerely yours,

Harry S Truman

That letter sounds like hell when I read it—but I'll make it look and sound better when I see you. I'm still helpless without an appointment sec.

On June 19, 1953, Truman and Mrs. Truman set off by car for Washington, D.C., and New York. They soon learned that a former President could not easily stay incognito while pumping gas, eating at roadside restaurants, and staying in motels. Truman enjoyed being in Washington again, seeing Acheson and other former advisers, and feeling for a few moments that he once more had a role in shaping world events. "It seemed like a dream to relive such an experience," he later reflected. "For one solid week, the illusion of those other days in Washington was maintained perfectly."

Truman met with Acheson and Averell Harriman about a foreign-policy speech he was planning to make, which he wanted to be important without appearing partisan. His wish to have a bipartisan foreign policy, and his belief that he and others should support the President on matters of foreign policy, was not so strongly felt by Acheson. "Packing of the Tariff Commission" refers to the Republican effort to put trade protectionists on the commission. Senator Walter F. George of Georgia was the senior Democratic member of the Senate Committee on Foreign Relations. "Bad election results in Italy" were the strong Communist Party showings in parliamentary elections, where Italian prime minister Alcide De Gasperi was forced to resign following losses of his Christian Democratic Party in 1953. The MSA was the Mutual Security Agency, which supervised foreign aid programs. "Luce" was Clare Boothe Luce, a member of Congress, wife of the founder of Time *magazine, and recently appointed as ambassador to Italy. Konrad Adenauer was chancellor of West Germany. Repatriation of prisoners of war was a major issue in negotiations to reach an armistice agreement to end fighting in Korea, which ended in a stalemate that still obtains.*

June 23, 1953

MEMORANDUM OF CONVERSATION

Averell Harriman and I had a meeting for an hour or more with President Truman at the Mayflower Hotel this morning.

The President led off by reading us a speech on national defense which he was planning to make before The Reserve Officers Association in Philadelphia on Friday night. After reading the speech, he asked us to criticize it from two points of view:

Was this a proper speech for him to make at this time? He did not wish to attack the President. He did not wish to get involved in partisan politics. He felt strongly that matters were drifting and that a most serious situation was developing, and he felt that the weakening of the defense program at this time was both a most serious aspect of the matter and one on which he could properly speak without getting involved in partisan politics.

Averell and I told him that on the first point we thought that the speech was good, was on a high plane, and should be made.

We then made a series of specific suggestions. We thought that the speech went too far in giving the impression that the Truman foreign policy was in fact being carried out; whereas what seemed to be happening was that the same words were being used but that action was being so weak and confused as to impair the policy itself. We suggested that this might be handled by praising the continuity in the policy, but saying that policy consisted in more than mere assertion; that it required on the one hand strong and difficult action and on the other, consistent and unified negotiation; that Mr. Truman knew very well the difficulties in these fields and that he was prepared to support the President and that he hoped everyone else would when the President asserted his authority in the field of foreign affairs, which must be preserved, and when he took the essential actions which were necessary to put the policies into effect.

The other changes were along the lines of not giving the impression that the President expected an attack upon us or our allies and therefore advised strong defense measures; but that strong defense measures were necessary to keep others from taking actions which might inevitably lead to most dangerous situations and possibly to hostilities.

We then turned to discussion of broader matters. I reported that Lyndon Johnson had told me that he could maintain a very strong group in the Senate to oppose the packing of the Tariff Commission and that this might get to the point of voting against a conference report on the Trade Agreements Act, which had this packing provision in it. Lyndon wondered whether this would be a dangerous action since the Democrats might be accused of defeating the bill. My advice had been that the bill with a packed Commission, together with peril point and other provisions, was worse than no bill, a view with which he said Senator George concurred. I thought that people could understand the Commission packing proposal better than they could complicated fiscal provisions and that it was well to make a fight on this issue. The President strongly agreed.

We discussed trends in Europe. Averell expressed the view that the bad election results in Italy had in his opinion a close connection with the confusion in American foreign policy leadership and with the division between the United States and its Allies. He spoke of a so-called "Crawford Report" of an MSA group which had criticized the Italians, the Luce appointment at this critical moment, and our bickerings with the British. He thought all of this could easily have made the difference in the few thousand votes which prevented De Gasperi from having a strong parliamentary majority. He said that he was fearful that a continuation of the same weakness, together with the uncertainties which a Big Four meeting would inject into European affairs just at the time of a German election, might result in Adenauer's defeat, and that this would put us in a most precarious position.

We also discussed the Korean situation, and at the President's request I explained the similarity between the present Prisoners of War provisions and the December UN Resolution and said that I did not think that the present armistice terms were subject to a just criticism. The President agreed.

He had other matters which he wished to discuss with us, but our time had expired and many other callers were waiting.

Truman's former staff gave a dinner in his honor, at which Acheson delivered a moving tribute.

June 23, 1953

Loyalty . . . is not something which is understood solely by considering those who give it. It requires an understanding of him who inspires it. The finest loyalty is not apt to be inspired by a man unless he inspires both respect and affection. Respect comes for many reasons. It is enough here to say that it springs from the fundamental purposes of a man's life and from his methods of achieving them, his manner of conducting himself in his relations with others. President Truman's fundamental purpose and burning passion has been to serve his country and his fellow citizens. This devoted love of the United States has been the only rival which Mrs. Truman has had. It has never been obscured or deflected by thought of himself, by personal ambition, or desire for position. What he has wanted for the United States is what every decent citizen has wanted for his own family, his own neighbors, his own community and country. It has not been to have it big or rich or powerful for these ends themselves. It has not been to use its power to dictate either to its own people or to other people. . . . He has sought in every way to give full scope for ability, energy, and initiative to create abundance beyond anything we have thought possible. But he has sought to do more. He has sought to make a kind and compassionate country whose institutions would truly reflect, both at home and abroad, the kind and compassionate nature of its people. He has sought to keep opportunity open to all and to mold political and economic life so that the weak and unfortunate are not trampled and forgotten, and so that all who honestly strive to do the best they can may fairly share in the abundance which this country creates. These are purposes which excite the respect and enthusiasm of all who have been fortunate enough to work with him.

Acheson reflects on the meaning of Stalin's death for the United States and its allies. Oscar Chapman was Truman's Secretary of the Interior during the latter years of his presidency. The Washington Post *article he mentions is titled "Writer Finds Mighty Russia Starting to Burst at Seams." Charles "Chip" Bohlen, the preeminent expert on the Soviet Union in Truman's*

State Department, was at this time ambassador to the Soviet Union. Lavrentiy Beria, chief of security and the NKVD, the secret police, under Stalin, became first deputy prime minister after Stalin's death. A member of the Politburo, he was Stalin's much-feared enforcer. The reference is to his sudden downfall, when he was accused of treason at a Politburo meeting, arrested on the spot, and taken away and shot. The book that Acheson mentions, Journey for Our Time: The Russian Journals of the Marquis de Custine, *is the 1839 journal of a French traveler in Russia who generalizes about Russian society and the Russian character in a manner similar to Alexis de Tocqueville's generalizations about Americans.*

The reference to "Stevenson" is to Adlai Stevenson, Democratic nominee for President in 1952, former governor of Illinois.

July 21, 1953

Dear Mr. President:

I am most grateful for the last Cabinet picture, which came to me from you. It brings back the most poignant memories.

All of us here are still talking of your visit. I see the boys from time to time when we meet to discuss Library affairs and last week I had a long and most pleasant luncheon and talk with Oscar Chapman. He is a sound man and most loyal one.

In case you have not seen it, I am enclosing a clipping from last Sunday's *Washington Post.* The story by Eddie Gilmore, who, as you know, has just come out of Moscow with his Russian wife, gives his reflection on the attitudes in Russia since the death of Stalin. I am doubly impressed with them because they accord with many of Chip Bohlen's thoughts.

It is important, I think, not to over-estimate or under-estimate the change which Stalin's death has produced. It does not in any way mean, in my judgment, that the USSR will be any less of a totalitarian, Communist, police state. There will not be any lessening of the danger in the world if the West is foolish enough to weaken itself and make aggression seem the road to profit with little or no risk.

What Stalin did to the Russia of Lenin was to impose upon it a personal, oriental despotism, in which the whims, fears, and ideas of one man and a small coterie greatly enlarged the field for intrigue and the uncertainty of life for everybody from the highest officials to the man in the street. As both Bohlen and Gilmore say, there was almost an audible sigh of relief when Uncle Joe died, and a great yearning for what was nostalgically thought of as "the good old days of Lenin" (which had become somewhat rosy-tinted in retrospect), in which there was plenty of dictatorship and ruthlessness, but in which the government was run by an oligarchy, the head of which had great power but was not deified. This tended toward committee government and greater scope for discussion and greater need for carrying some sort of acquiescence in what was done.

It is Chip's guess—and only a guess—that it was Beria's (the super cop's) passion for intrigue which made him unable to accept the new movement and got him into trouble. The fact that he could be dealt with as he was and that a man who had been in high position for twenty years could be denounced universally as a scoundrel from the start is both very Russian (see the book called *A Journey for Our Time*) and was evidence that authoritarianism has not appreciably declined.

It may be that the Russian leaders will have to make greater concessions to the Soviet and satellite people. If this is so, they will want a period of relaxation in foreign affairs. And if this in turn is so, we may be faced with proposals in regard to Germany and perhaps even Korea and Indochina which may alter some of the factors—i.e., the openness of Russian hostility and willingness to use force against weakness— which have strengthened the allied effort.

But it would be a great mistake, I believe, to think that the essence of the problem is changed. That essence, which influenced the thoughts which you and I have held for so long—that essence is that it isn't merely the imminent threat of aggression from the Soviet movement which causes instability and the danger of war, but the capacity for successful aggression whenever the mood or the desire to engage in it exists. Therefore, our policy was to create strength by binding ourselves and our allies both economically and militarily. It is essential to continue that policy.

I think now that the country is faced with a problem which you and I faced early in 1949, when the Russians raised the blockade in Berlin and asked for a meeting of Foreign Ministers. The first was a gesture toward relaxation, which you and I thought came from a desire on their part to extricate themselves from a failure and a weak position. The great question was how far the Russians were prepared to go. We, therefore, accepted the proposed conference promptly and with an agenda which gave the Russians a chance to show their hand one way or another.

The first week of the conference was devoted to forcing them to expose their hand fully. It turned out that they were not ready to propose anything constructive and in the resulting propaganda battle lost heavily. This, I think, convinced our allies of the true situation more than any amount of speeches and enabled us to go forward together to meet the ensuing danger and hardships with a common appreciation of the facts.

1953 has much in common with 1949. Again it isn't a time for meetings by heads of states, a situation which puts more pressure upon the democracies to have what at least looks like a favorable result than upon the Soviets. But it is a time for a four-power meeting, at which the Russians must be thoroughly smoked out. Much preparatory work should be done with our allies. The White House must discredit the demagogic isolationist wing of the Republican Party which wishes to insult and separate us from our allies.

If the Russians propose nothing which makes a really free unification of Germany possible, I think that again, as in 1949, the Allies can be brought together on a program of building strength. If they are willing to make real concessions, then a most delicate and difficult period ensues. We cannot—and would not wish to—insist upon a continued division of Germany, but we must be very careful about what kind of a Germany we are unifying and what its place in the Western world is. I think this could be handled if there were understanding and wisdom in Washington and if I had any confidence that in the present constitutional and political situation in France that country was able to accept any solution, whatever it was. Since both of these matters are in doubt, I think the future gives rise to real anxiety.

All of this, I know, you have thought of yourself; but it gives me comfort to talk with you in this way.

I have been urging some of Stevenson's friends to get him back here in the near future. His voyaging seems to have been over-prolonged, and I hope that, if he is wise and tactful, he can help bring Democrats of various shades closer together on some lines of policy which will be a little more positive than the Congressional minority has been able to achieve so far. I should hope that you and he would find yourselves pretty close together and that some of us who might be called in a World War I phrase "the old contemptibles" might be of some use.

Alice joins me in the warmest messages to you and Mrs. Truman. I hope that her hands are better and that I am not in her black books.

Most sincerely,

Dean

Truman worries that conditions in Korea and Iran invite Russian adventurism.

Dear Dean: August 18, 1953

I have been trying my best to write you on present day developments but I've had so much business to transact that I haven't had a chance to write you.

Your letter of July twenty-first impressed me immensely. I'd like very much to have your present view on what effect the Armistice has had on our Russian trends and what your guess is for the next strike.

It looks as if the Iranian situation has come to a conclusion where the Russians may walk in and take over. If you will remember, we had things in shape at one time so the Shah could have taken control of the Government of Iran and I think he would have been able at that time to work things out but he balked at the most important point and now he seems to have stepped in in a hurry and has left himself without a throne or a Government. I'd like to have your comments on that also.

I hope, one of these days, to see and talk with you. I have been working like a Turk on the preliminary outline for the book which I contracted to write for *Life* and *Time*. It is a terrific job. If I had known how much work it is I probably would not have undertaken it.

I am enclosing you a letter from Samuel S. Freedman, Chairman, Yale Law Forum. He is inviting me to deliver a lecture before that august body. I wonder if I should consider it. Your advice will be highly appreciated.

Sincerely yours,

Harry

Acheson helped Charles Murphy and others draft the speech Truman gave in Detroit on Labor Day. After Truman left the presidency Acheson continued in his role of foreign-policy adviser to his old boss. Truman, for his part, knew that he still needed help from Acheson and other advisers, such as White House staff members Charles Murphy and David Lloyd, Averell Harriman, and personal advisers William Hillman and David Noyes to formulate and present his ideas. The letter from Acheson to Murphy that Truman mentions offers several revisions to the draft of the speech Truman was to give on Labor Day. Acheson began his three pages of critical remarks by saying of the draft, "It is a very good speech and will have a fine effect."

September 2, 1953

Dear Dean:

I can't tell you how very much I appreciated your interest in my Labor Day speech. Your letter to Charlie Murphy was a jewel. He was kind enough to let me read it. I'll never be able to "square up" with you for all the trouble I've caused you over the last eight or ten years, but I can't say that I am sorry that I did it.

Give my best to Mrs. Acheson.

Most sincerely,

Harry Truman

Acheson helped Truman's speechwriting team write the foreign-policy section of an address Truman gave when he received the Franklin D. Roosevelt Four Freedoms Award at a ceremonial dinner in New York City on September 28, 1953. Acheson is careful to point out to Truman areas where he must avoid appearing too close to some aspects of President Eisenhower's foreign policy, such as "the Dulles liberation ideas," which Acheson believed were impracticable and reckless.

"The Dulles liberation ideas" refer to Secretary Dulles's stated objective of "rolling back communism" in Central and Eastern Europe, which was taken as encouragement by Hungarian patriots in their disastrous revolt in 1956.

September 24, 1953

Dear Mr. President:

Dave Lloyd sent me a copy of Draft No. 2, 9/22/53 of the Four Freedoms Award speech, with the request that I give particular attention to the foreign policy section of it, which I have done. I tried to reach him in St. Louis on the telephone with my suggestions, but have not been successful, so I am sending them to you, with a copy to him here, as I understand that he will be back tomorrow afternoon.

The first suggestion relates to page 5, paragraph beginning "it is not enough to defend our freedoms at home only," to the bottom of the page. I think this part, together with the quotations from President Roosevelt, seems to commit you to an impossibly broad program and one which I am afraid will get you entangled with the Dulles liberation ideas. I do not think that you want to say that it is our task to establish the Four Freedoms everywhere in the world—Russia, China, South Africa, etc.—and that there is no end save victory in this struggle. President Roosevelt may have meant this in the enthusiasm of the war, but I doubt whether he would advocate it today. Therefore, I suggest that this whole section be written as follows:

"It is not enough to defend our freedoms at home only. We must be concerned with a world environment in which free men can live free lives. Franklin Roosevelt knew that we could not exist in an oasis of freedom in a world of totalitarianism or war. 'The world order which we seek,' he said, 'is the cooperation of free countries, working together in a friendly, civilized society.' The Four Freedoms for us, as for all free men, depend upon a world in which peace and justice are maintained by the concerted efforts of the free nations."

My next suggestions have to do with the listing of the foundation of our foreign policy on pages 8 and 9. The first foundation as stated is "a renewed reciprocal trade program." I suggest the insertion after "renewed" of another adjective, so that it would read, "a renewed and reinvigorated reciprocal trade program." The purpose of this is not to commit you to a mere renewal of the act in its present amended and weakened form.

The last suggestion has to do with the eighth foundation. I suggest that it read as follows:

"The willingness, in firm agreement with our allies and from a position of united strength, to seek in all sincerity solutions of our differences with the Soviet bloc through patient and peaceful negotiation."

The first purpose is to fix up the English. As written, it sounds as though we need negotiating differences rather than non-negotiable differences, which clearly wasn't meant. The second idea is to bring our allies into it so that no one would think that you had bilateral negotiations in mind. The third idea is that the purpose of the negotiations is to seek solutions rather than merely to compromise all outstanding questions.

Otherwise, I think the speech is in good shape and I am looking forward to hearing you deliver it and to seeing you in New York on Monday.

I hope Dave showed you the few observations that I am planning to make and that he has any suggestions in regard to them which you might have.

Most sincerely,

Dean

At the dinner, in presenting the Franklin D. Roosevelt Four Freedoms Award to Truman, Acheson said, "I hope that it will never be thought of me that I approach the matter of doing honor to President Truman with an open mind. On the contrary, it is with unshakeable convictions [that I do him honor], one of which is that no honor which can be conferred on Mr. Truman can equal the honor which he has won for himself. . . . I suppose Mr. Truman would like no description of himself better than, in the words of a Seventeenth Century writer, as 'An honest plain man, without pleats.' That indeed he is, but we cannot let him escape with that. In my prejudiced judgment we must bring in a word which is very much abused and which I fear may annoy him a good deal. But he will testify that I have always told him the truth as I saw it—and this is no time to stop. The word is 'Greatness.' "

Truman refers to his regret for not sending a congratulatory cable when Acheson received an award at a Woodrow Wilson Foundation Dinner in New York. Truman also talks of his plans for his presidential library.

October 2, 1953

Dear Dean:

I failed to send you a telegram last night for the simple reason that I was out in the midst of the Caruthersville Fair Grounds making a speech on the educational necessities of the next generation. I left in a hurry to drive eighty miles in an hour and a half in order to catch a train to be home this morning.

I wish I could have been present and would have been had not circumstance prevented me. I don't know of a more well deserved Award than that one. I would have given anything to have expressed my opinion at the meeting publicly in the same manner in which you did to me. I'll never forget that meeting as long as I live. I wish I deserved all the nice things that you said about me and that the other gentlemen were kind enough to say. In fact I was overcome as you could very well see.

I arrived in St. Louis and they had a special session of the Grand Lodge of Masons of Missouri at which I presented them one of the stones out of the White House which had the Masonic marks on it. For the first time in my connection with that organization of some forty-four years, they had an overflow crowd present and gave me an ovation like the one in the Waldorf-Astoria, so maybe we are making some converts.

I am having more interest displayed in the proposed Library than I ever had since it started. Two or three of the great Foundations are now anxious to become interested in it and I am somewhat in a quandary as to just what to do but I guess it will work out all right. The Directors have authorized the construction of the first building, which will be the Archives part of it, and I suppose we will go to work on that in the not too far distant future. I am anxious to get the records of the whole Administration lined up there if I can. I would like, as I told the members at a Cabinet Meeting one time, to have every Cabinet Member make some contribution in papers and documents to that institution.

I had a meeting of the Deans of History and the Librarians in the City of St. Louis while I was at the Grand Lodge. I went to breakfast with these gentlemen of the Universities around St. Louis and was informed by the Dean of History of the St. Louis University that they had obtained permission from the Pope to make photostat microfilms of all the manuscripts in the Vatican—some three million of them—and that those microfilms could be available for my Library on an exchange basis. Something like that has been coming up nearly every day since I have been home from Hawaii. I feel very much encouraged about it.

Again, I can't tell you how very much I appreciated what you did in New York last Monday night.

I have been going down to Caruthersville for twenty or twenty-five years because that southeast corner of Missouri has always been in my corner politically and I went down there this time since I was out of office and not running for office to show them I was just interested in them. I had one of the biggest crowds they ever had when I addressed the meeting and I got a bigger ovation than I did when I was President of the United States. They gave me a great big silver cup engraved— Harry S. Truman. From your friends and admirers in Caruthersville.

They had to take me eighty miles to a city down in Arkansas, Jonesboro, to catch the train for home. There had been no previous announcement that I was to go there but when I got to the station there were two thousand people there. It took two policemen and a

Deputy Sheriff to get me on the train. I don't know what the world is when people in Arkansas and southeast Missouri, which is about the same as the deep South, turn out like that for an Ex-President, who has told them where to get off on Civil Rights. Maybe the world is turning over.

I think I'll put up a tent and charge admission!

Sincerely,

Harry S. Truman

Please give my best to Mrs. Acheson.

Acheson lists several of the Truman-administration veterans who had given generous donations to Truman's presidential library. Some familiar foreign-policy problems from the Truman administration—France, the European Defense Community, Iran—are also on Acheson's mind. Iran was a particularly lively topic at this time. The Iranian prime minister, Mohammad Mosaddeq, had been overthrown by coup d'état in August. Reference is made here to the British Anglo-Iranian Oil Company, nationalized by Mosaddeq and, significantly, not denationalized by the shah when he was restored to power by a CIA-managed coup. David Bruce served the Truman administration as ambassador to France and Undersecretary of State; George Perkins as Assistant Secretary for European Affairs; Stanley Woodward as Director of Protocol; George McGhee as Assistant Secretary of State for the Middle East; Robert A. Lovett as Undersecretary of State, Undersecretary of Defense, and Secretary of Defense; James Webb as Director of the Budget and Undersecretary of State; James C. Dunn as ambassador to Italy and France; Chester Bowles as ambassador to India; and Harold Linder as president of the Export-Import Bank.

October 8, 1953

Dear Mr. President:

Our correspondence has been interrupted for the happiest of all reasons; that I have seen you twice since your letters of August and September. And now I have your letter of October 2 about the Woodrow Wilson dinner in New York, the progress of the library, and the great and deserved ovation which you got at Caruthersville and Jonesboro.

Please do not have the matter of a message to the Wilson dinner on your mind. I knew from David Lloyd what you were up to, knew that you would wire if you could, and completely understood and understand why you couldn't.

The two dinners in New York last week were, I thought, wonderful and happy evidence that what you say in the last paragraph is true — that perhaps the world is turning over and people are understanding better some things which were obscure to them last November.

I am enclosing a copy of the few observations which I made at your dinner and of the speech which I made at the Wilson dinner. The last six months or so I have been thinking a good deal about the essence of the problems which we had to face and the measures which we took to face them. These thoughts I tried to state in a pretty tightly reasoned statement. I hope you will approve of it. In light of what you said on Labor Day and in New York, I think it shows that the Truman-Acheson front remains as solid as it was in the old days.

A few days ago the Republican Policy Committee sent for copies of my speech. The messenger who came for them said they were wanted urgently for a meeting on the Hill. I should like to believe that they were in a mood to learn. The truth probably is that they were to be analyzed for less pleasing purposes. It will be interesting to see what they can do. As I read General Eisenhower's latest speech in yesterday's *Times,* it seemed to me that any shafts which the Republicans loose at you or me may ultimately lodge in the General's palpitating bosom.

I am delighted to hear your good reports about the Library. One of the pleasant experiences which I have had in the last few months is the response of friends with whom I have talked about it.

Dave Bruce, George Perkins, Stanley Woodward, George McGhee, Jim Webb, Jimmy Dunn, Chet Bowles, and Harold Linder have all responded instantaneously and most generously. The other night Bob Lovett sought me out and pressed a goodly check upon me, with the promise of another in a few months. More will come. I am sure the main thing to do now is merely to get a few people in a few cities to raise the matter with your many friends.

As for depositing papers in the Library, I think that so far as the State Department is concerned, you have all the essential papers in your own files. I did not take any at all with me when I left the Department. The real records of our foreign policy are contained, I believe, in the various memoranda which we sent to you for your comment and action and in the detailed reports which went to you every day from the various conferences — four-power foreign ministers, three-power foreign ministers, NATO, the Palais Rose discussions in 1951 and UN meetings. I shall keep the matter always in mind and make available to you anything which I can gather.

In your earlier letter you prod me about developments in connection with the USSR and with Iran. It seems to me clear that whatever inspired the Kremlin to make soft-sounding noises earlier in the year has ceased to inspire them. The recent notes, linking four-power talks with five-power talks at which Red China shall be present and insisting on an agenda for both which puts the most insoluble problems in the forefront, make clear to me that the Russians do not really want meetings except under conditions where we surrender first and talk about details of it later. I think Eden's speech at the Party Conference shows his realization of this.

The French are the troublesome ones, as they always have been. Indeed, French weakness has always been the disease from which our Grand Alliance has suffered. The French appear to be willing to do almost anything to stop the war in Indo-China on almost any terms. I do not see the answer to this, short of a change in the French constitution which will give them an executive strong enough to face up to difficult problems, make decisions, and survive long enough to live with the decisions until the politicians and the public have become adjusted to them. If every one of these decisions, which are always a choice between two difficult alternatives, has to win a popularity contest in the French Chamber, then we will always face governments falling like autumn leaves, the continuance of an inflation which is now thirty years old, and instability of the worst sort in the very heart of Europe.

David Bruce continues to be optimistic about the European Defense Community, but even he says that the decision in favor of it, with the continuance of French weakness, will not solve the problem, although it will be a help.

All of this, it seems to me, makes it clear that there is no sense in and no possibility of a four-power meeting at the level of heads of government. It seems plain that the Russians don't want it. We certainly don't and shouldn't. Churchill, I think, is backing away from it. And only the French would be ready to gamble.

As for Iran, there the Shah's attempted coup, its failure, and the counter-attack and success of Zahedi, together with developments since, show again what we always urged on the British; that so far as relations with the West and the oil dispute were concerned, the problem was deeper than the personality of Mossadegh. The fact that he was impossible made the British believe that somebody else would be the opposite of Mossadegh. I think that this is not true, that Zahedi will be controlled by the same disorderly public emotions to which Mossadegh catered and that any solution of the troubles, if any is possible, will not be very different from the proposals which we made in the last week of your Administration. Details can be changed; a new contract with Anglo-Iranian might take the place of cash compensation, since they are merely different ways of saying the same thing. But I think it impossible that Anglo-Iranian would ever get back in the country on an operating concession basis. And I think that every week that passes it becomes more difficult for Iran to find a market for its oil even through Anglo-Iranian and with the cooperation of the other oil companies. So basically I think the problem remains as tough as ever. Mossadegh's removal is a great help, which means that in working on a difficult problem one does not have to work with a crazy man, but the removal of the crazy man does not change the dimensions of the problem.

This letter, with its enclosures, will already take up most of your working day, so I will only add a plea. Your account of your eighty-mile-an-hour dash at night through Missouri and parts of Arkansas gave me the creeps. Even without the Secret Service to make you behave, you really must be more careful. So please have a heart and remember that the doctrine of chance does not mean that you always win.

Please tell Mrs. Truman from Alice that yesterday the present members and alumnae of the Spanish class were invited to tea at the White House. Alice, on advice—and indeed upon instructions—of counsel, attended. Recalling the days when a certain lady used to chew gum and respond to all questions with a paraphrase of "no comment", Alice discovered that glamour had overtaken this far from perfect pupil. The ushers, however, had not changed and Alice was somewhat embarrassed when they insisted on putting her at the head of the line to be received, taking precedence over her successor. At this point I draw the veil over her comments.

She also sends her love to Mrs. Truman and to you, in which I join.

Most affectionately,

Dean

October 21, 1953

Dear Dean:

   I'll never be able to tell you how much I appreciated your good letter of the eighth. I'll continue to regret that I didn't get to the Wilson dinner and didn't get a message there in time but I told you what my difficulties were.

   I am certainly glad the Republicans had to come to you for information and they will have to continue to do that if they expect to carry on a Foreign Policy that will do the peace of the world any constructive good.

   Your contribution to the Library is wonderful. We are really making progress and before long we will let a contract.

   I think you are entirely right on the four-power meeting. I hope Iran will come out of the kinks. It looks now as if Israel is in for a large shooting war again.

   Sincerely yours,

   Harry

Acheson has just read remarks Truman made at a news conference on December 19, 1950, in response to demands from some Republicans that Acheson be removed from office. "How our position in the world would be improved by the retirement of Dean Acheson from public life is beyond me," Truman said at the news conference. "Mr. Acheson has helped shape and carry out our policy of resistance to Communist imperialism. . . . If communism were to prevail in the world—as it shall not prevail—Dean Acheson would be one of the first, if not the first, to be shot by the enemies of liberty and Christianity. . . . This is a time of great peril. It is a time for unity, and for real bipartisanship. It is a time for making use of the great talents of men like Dean Acheson. Communism—not our own country— would be served if we lost Mr. Acheson."

Bill Benton is probably former Senator William B. Benton of Connecticut, who also served in the State Department during Truman's presidency. The comment about Trieste refers to a running controversy about the future sovereignty over Trieste. Trieste was at this time claimed by both Italy and Yugoslavia. It was occupied by American and British troops, but the two governments had recently indicated that Italian troops would replace their own. Yugoslavia of course objected, and a minor crisis resulted.

Senator Joseph McCarthy was pursuing lower-level staff in the Department of the Army, with—for a limited time—the cooperation of the army.

October 21, 1953

Dear Mr. President,

Bill Benton will be seeing you on November first. I am working on him for the library and he will make a contribution but wants to talk with you first. He will probably not mention the contribution but will undoubtedly raise a pet complaint of his—that the library ought to be in Chicago, where it would get greater use than in Independence (so he says). I think that if he can be reasoned with on this point successfully his contribution will be larger.

My second point is that in looking over the record of developments toward the end of 1950 I read again your wonderful statement to the press in response to the resolution of the Republicans in Congress asking you to remove me. It gave me all the thrills all over again, and makes as clear as day what is now lacking in the White House—courage and leadership. It has every mark of H.S.T. in every sentence. If you look at it again you will see why all of us are ready to go through anything for you. You know how I feel about you, but I want you to know again, because it is a continuing emotion.

Our friend Dulles has landed us in a pretty pickle over Trieste. You remember that we went over this very suggestion from Eden in 1952 & rejected it because we foresaw the position of embarrassment we would get into having started something we could not finish. Why he will not think these things through before he acts I don't know. I'm sure the [State] Department either did warn him or would have, if asked.

Alice is in Milwaukee with our daughter Jane and will bring me the latest from the McCarthy front. Here again the Army seems to be cooperating in building him up and destroying its own morale.

My warmest regards to you and Mrs. Truman,

As ever,

Dean

Truman had to raise private money to build his presidential library, and Acheson helped as much as he could. Truman writes about his meeting with a prospective donor. Tom Evans, an owner of a drugstore chain and a television station in Kansas City, was one of Truman's closest friends. Truman is elated because of strong Democratic results in the off-year elections in New York, New Jersey, and Virginia. The results in New Jersey were par-

ticularly important and were widely viewed as a repudiation of President Eisenhower's policies. Truman often spelled Acheson's name with a "t"— Atcheson—presumably because of the name of the town in northeastern Kansas—Atchison—and of the Atchison, Topeka and Santa Fe Railway Company.

November 5, 1953

Dear Dean:

Your letter of Oct. 21 was very helpful on Bill Benton's visit. I met him at the plane, took him out to Independence for dinner and made him acquainted with the two District Federal Judges and one from the Court of Appeals. You know Dick Duncan, who was on the Ways and Means Committee with Fred Vinson. I succeeded in having Roosevelt appoint him in 1942 and broke all the rules in the Senate getting him confirmed. The other District Judge you don't know. He was a Circuit Court Judge on the Missouri State Court. Was in World War I with me, and when he came home studied law, became a good lawyer, was elected to the Missouri Bench, made a great Judge and I put him on the Federal Court. The Appeals Court Judge you've met, Caskie Collet.

Well, we had a grand time talking about Dean Acheson, the State Dept., Ike and shoes and ships and sealing wax and things.

I let Tom Evans take Bill back to the plane and Tom put in some good licks for the Library—so I guess you can nail him.

Your comments on my statement to the press about you gave me a lift. I hope you'll always feel that way.

There's an article in the last *Reporter* on Trieste which is a dinger. It says if we want a lesson in what not to do diplomatically Trieste is it. Well, if things keep up you and I are going to be tops in foreign policy and everything else.

I've been sailing high since last Tuesday. Nearly all the newsmen called me for comment. All I said was that I was very happy at the endorsement of the New Deal and Fair Deal.

The Madam and I leave for New York on Sunday morning by train— she won't fly. I receive the Stephen Wise award Monday night, address the City College of New York on Wednesday and receive another award from the Hebrew University on Thursday. (Bill Hillman says I should be circumcised if this keeps up!) Well, anyway, I expect about a half bushel of shekels for the Library as a result of these appearances.

Hope Mrs. Acheson had a good time in Milwaukee. When possible

I want to visit with you. The book is fine but what a slave it made of me.

Sincerely,

Harry

Why do I put that T in your name? (Anno Domini?)

Acheson discusses the demagogic tactics used by Eisenhower's attorney general, Herbert Brownell, Jr., who discharged some Department of Justice employees with vague imputations of security risk. Acheson refers to Adlai Stevenson's efforts to position the Democratic Party for a better campaign than that of 1952. Lewis W. Douglas and Walter S. Gifford were both U.S. ambassadors to the United Kingdom during Truman's administration.

Dear Mr. President,   December 3, 1953

I have an unanswered letter from you which came before the Brownell explosion. As that disgraceful episode begins to take on perspective, I think the net result was harmful to all—most of all the country—the Republicans will suffer more from it than we will. This is so, I think, because they have supped with the devil with a very short spoon. Brownell's tactics, as you so well said, were McCarthy's and the latter has grown so great on this food that he now challenges Ike for the leadership. And Ike has responded very feebly. It is here, I guess, that Brownell has sown the dragon's teeth. It is not what pious words Ike utters from time to time which will count, but what he does to assert control and put the fear of God into the sewer rats. I don't see him doing it.

Adlai seems to have done pretty well. The greatest lack I see is the absence of a small able group at the National Committee to keep working on these things, anticipate developments, help to devise a plan of campaign to meet them. I have talked with Charlie Murphy about this and he agrees. But apparently nothing is done. For instance, a theme to be constantly repeated until it becomes a slogan might be "A party which is vigorously and successfully solving the problems of its administration would be talking about its accomplishments."

On our small front the library moves along. Walter Gifford sent me a check for $1000 and a very nice note saying how grateful he was to you for the chance to work with us on the greatest constructive achievement of the country. He is all right—no fair weather sailor like Lew Douglas.

We are all well. Alice has a one man show at the Corcoran in January. Our love to you and Mrs. Truman.

Most warmly,

Dean

Truman frets about partisan press coverage unfavorable to him and his administration. Raymond Moley and David Lawrence were conservative journalists. The "total news monopoly newspaper" he refers to is the Kansas City Star. *"Dulles, Wilson, Humphrey et al." refers to members of President Eisenhower's Cabinet and presumably other members of his administration. Charles E. Wilson was Secretary of Defense, and George M. Humphrey was Secretary of the Treasury.*

December 26, 1953

Dear Dean:

I've been thinking about you and Mrs. Acheson and trying to send you Christmas greetings. You know what hell is paved with—and I've just added another block to that famous pavement. The Boss and Margie and I appreciated most highly your good wishes on the card you sent us.

I've been in debt to you for some time on a communication you sent me—but I had not much to say and wonder of wonders—for me I've said nothing worth repeating.

Conditions are such that Ike can do no wrong and I can do no right. If it weren't tragic it would be the best comedy in history. Ray Moley, Dave Lawrence, the *Herald-Tribune,* the *Star* in Washington, the *Sat. Eve. Post* and the *Baltimore Sun* have had some of the worst editorials and the funniest editorials I've ever seen. I've read the press on Washington, Jefferson, Adams, Jackson, Lincoln, Cleveland, Teddy R., Wilson and F.D.R. and there seems to me to be no parallel. Maybe I'm somewhat prejudiced!

Dulles, Wilson, Humphrey et al. seem to be helping to make confusion thrice compounded and a lot of Republican editors are becoming "mouth pieces" for McCarthy and the Attorney General.

Our total news monopoly newspaper was indicted along with its managing editor, Roy Roberts, some time back. He thought I had something to do with it. I did not but if I'd known about it I might have. Roberts has been writing front page editorials in the *Kansas City Star* and quoting Lawrence, Hearst, *Sat. Eve. Post* and all the rest. Hoping, I suppose, to have his and the *Star*'s indictments quashed. Brownell will probably do it too.

Our Democrats seem to be waking up to the opportunities opening up before them and perhaps will come up with a program. I hope we do just that.

Take care of yourself—we've got a lot of fighting to do in this great period of hysteria.

My best to Mrs. Acheson and all the family.

Sincerely,

Harry Truman

Dean Acheson shakes hands with General Dwight D. Eisenhower on January 6, 1951, as Harry Truman and Secretary of Defense George Marshall look on. Eisenhower is departing for Europe to survey his Atlantic Pact forces.

2

January 1954 to April 1955

Eisenhower's Foreign Policy – Musings on History and Government – Truman's Memoirs – A Serious Operation – The Truman Library – Visits in Kansas City and Washington – Testimony and Tough Political Talk

*E*ven though Truman and Acheson felt that America's former strong position in the world, which they had passed on to the new President, was being dissipated, and their criticism of Eisenhower and his advisers, particularly his Secretary of State, John Foster Dulles, was often harsh, they styled themselves with mock self-deception as "nonpartisan" onlookers of the national scene. Truman enjoyed writing Acheson an occasional "spasm"—an unrestrained outburst—when particularly incensed. Acheson always loved receiving these reminders of his colorful old boss from White House days.

Truman was deeply involved in writing his memoirs by mid-1954. He asked Acheson for help in recovering from memory and from the documentary record the story of the work they had done together in shaping a postwar foreign policy. Acheson traveled to Kansas City in February 1955 to give interviews to Truman's research assistants and to help Truman in other ways. He liked recalling for the interviewers the momentous days of Truman's presidency.

In June 1954, Truman had a gallbladder operation and a bad reaction to an antibiotic, from which it took him months to recover.

In April 1955, Truman traveled to Washington to testify before Congress about the United Nations Charter and to attend a testimonial dinner for House Speaker Sam Rayburn. Although he accepted the role of elder statesman when appearing before Congress, he relaxed at the Rayburn dinner and unleashed a little raw political rhetoric. During this trip he also got together with Acheson for lunch at Acheson's home.

. . .

Despite being an ardent student of history, Truman is having trouble researching and writing about his own presidency. He mentions in this letter a number of people from his administration and the major World War II conferences, except the one he attended at Potsdam, Germany. "Byrnes book on [Yalta]" probably refers to James F. Byrnes, Speaking Frankly *(New York: Harper and Brothers Publishers, 1947). Truman is upset that the Eisenhower administration is adopting a part of his administration's agricultural policy—the Brannan Plan, named for his Secretary of Agriculture—and a part of his national health-care proposal.*

January 28, 1954

Dear Dean:

I have been working on the opening chapter of my purported memoirs. I have tried to place myself back into the position I was in on April 12, 1945. I have read letters to my mother and sister, to my brother and to my cousins. I have read telegrams to and from Churchill and Roosevelt, to and from Stalin and Roosevelt. I've read memos I made of visits to the White House from April 12th back to July, 1944. I've read Ike's, Leahy's, Churchill's, Grew's, Cordell Hull's books. Memos from Hopkins, Stimson, Asst. & Acting Secretary of State Dean Acheson, reports from Marshall, Eisenhower, King, Bradley. Communiqués of Tehran, Cairo, Casablanca, Quebec, Yalta, Byrnes book on it, etc., etc., ad lib[itum], and still I am living today and cussing the budget (Gen. Motors Budget), wondering at the deceit and misrepresentation in the handling of security risks, the adoption of the Brannan Plan for wool— wool of all things, accepting a corner of my health plan.

So you see the past has always interested me for use in the present and I'm bored to death with what I did and didn't do nine years ago.

But Andrew Johnson, James Madison, even old Rutherford B. Hayes I'm extremely interested in as I am King Henry IV of France, Margaret of Navarre, Charles V, Philip II of Spain, and Charlie's Aunt Margaret.

Wish to goodness I'd decided to spend my so called retirement putting Louis XIII, Gustavus Adolphus, Richelieu and five tubs of gold together instead of writing about me and my mistakes. Anyway I made no mistake in my Great Secretary of State.

Hope you're not too bored with this explosion but I had to blow off to you, and you, therefore, are the fall guy. My best to Mrs. Acheson and all the family.

Sincerely,

Harry

Acheson expresses unsentimental views on the importance of power, and balances of power, in world affairs. "Wallace and Hurley" are Henry A. Wallace, Vice President of United States (1941–45), and Patrick J. Hurley, Secretary of War (1929–33), personal representative of President Franklin D. Roosevelt on various missions during World War II, and U.S. ambassador to China (1944–45). The "Berlin fiasco" Acheson refers to is the failure of a recent meeting in Berlin of the foreign ministers of the four occupying powers in Germany to reach any agreement regarding the unification of Germany. The so-called New Look in American foreign policy, which Acheson derides, was announced in a speech by Secretary of State Dulles on January 12, 1954. It was based on "a great capacity to retaliate" with atomic weapons. The EDC is the European Defense Community, a plan, never ratified, to create a single military organization composed of forces from the continental-European NATO member countries, including, most important, France and Germany.

February 5, 1954

Dear Mr. President,

What a joy your letter brought to Alice and me! I took it home and read it to her. Right at the start we stopped at "Charlie's Aunt Margaret." I, in my ignorance, claimed that it was a general expression for anyone not involved in your memoirs. Alice said, Not at all—that you knew, and when you said his Aunt Margaret, you meant it.

So down came the *Britannica* and, sure enough, there she was—the daughter of the Emperor Maximilian and Charlie's aunt all right. I have been trying her out on some of my high brow friends, and their degree of error is very comforting to me.

From the whole letter we could picture you full of energy and eager to get your hands on the work of building for the future with all your resources of knowledge of the past and understanding of the present. Whenever you want to blow off steam, we claim priority on being blowee, as the lawyers would say.

I know how bored you get in concentrating upon your own actions years ago. In a way I have been doing the same thing in these group discussions at Princeton and I do find that one can only do about so much a day—to do too much at a time gives me a strange dreamlike sensation of living in two periods almost at once.

As I look back over your administrations I do not see much to regret in any of the great decisions, but do see many, many times when I am amazed at the boldness, courage and insight of decisions. Comparing those years with the present, I am amazed too, by the way in which we assumed that vigorous leadership was just normal and how in the face of the most awful brawls with the hill you made the Congress do things which the present crowd would not dream of attempting.

The problems which tended to defy solution came, I think, from an erroneous decision which you inherited, and from another which you were swept—almost forced—into making or agreeing to in 1945.

The inherited error was the total destruction of Japanese and German military power and, in the case of Germany, of any German state at all. This completely withdrew all local containing power on both sides of Russia. Our own great power might have acted in large part as a substitute if we had not dispersed that in 1945–6.

Power is at the root of most relationships—by no means the only factor, but one of vast importance. A balance of power has proved the best international sheriff we have ever had. Many of our troubles—or perhaps better to say, many troubles—came from the dissolution of our power and the destruction of any balance capable of restraining the Russians from acts which weakened the West greatly, although we did deter them from direct attack on us or Europe. This is an interesting field to speculate about. For instance, how much did Stalin change his plans about China and Korea when, to what must have been his utter amazement, our army, navy and air force simply melted away. Crooked as he was, I think his talks with Wallace and Hurley must be read in the light of our power at the time he was talking—not that he was sincerely adopting a line of action on which any one could or should rely, but I doubt whether he believed that we would permit him to adopt any other course and then we had the power to make our will effective without the necessity of using the power.

These thoughts I write during a day spent without food or water having my insides X-rayed. This leads to contemplation but not to powerful flights of imagination. I hope this is to be the wind-up of almost a year of trying to get rid of some amoebae that I collected somewhere probably in Africa or South America.

When this Berlin fiasco is over—and it seems to be following the exact pattern of the Paris meeting of 1949—some attention ought to be given to the "new look," that precious intangible—"the initiative", which, believe it or not, is exercised by "retaliation", etc., etc. This is in reality the policy we had to follow before you began the rearmament in 1950—and at a time when we had the monopoly of the atomic bomb.

I should think it unwise to raise the matter strongly while Berlin is still going. Partly not to attack a man who is representing us abroad, and partly because Dulles may well be crawling out of this speech now if he really hopes to get the French and Italians to ratify the E.D.C. Also I am not sure that people's minds generally would be as open to an analysis by you or me, as they would to some one who would not be charged with responding to defend their own work against direct action. If Stevenson would do it and stay on the line he would get a real audience and then Senators and Congressmen could pick it up. Sam Rayburn would be an ideal person to do it.

Our trip to Antigua this January, although shorter, was in some ways more fun than last year. We felt better and we had our daughter Jane Brown from Milwaukee with us, who is a pretty good vacation just in herself. We had a great time swimming, eating, laughing and drinking some good rum together. Everyone returned brown and happy.

Our deepest affection to you and Mrs. Truman. We hope her hand has recovered and that all is well. I wish I were seeing you in N.Y. tonight.

Most sincerely,

Dean

In 1954 Eugene Meyer bought Robert R. "Bertie" McCormick's Washington Times-Herald *and merged it with the* Washington Post. *"Snyder" is John W. Snyder, Secretary of the Treasury. The Tenth Inter-American Conference, held in Caracas, Venezuela, was in progress at this time. Sullivan & Cromwell is the New York City law firm where John Foster Dulles was a partner before he became Secretary of State. "Puck's exclamation" in Shakespeare's* A Midsummer Night's Dream *is "Lord, what fools these mortals be!"*

St. Patrick's Day, 1954

Dear Dean:

Well, here you are due for another explosion. I've read your good letter of February 5th time and time again. It gave me a lift and as a result I've become more philosophical about my situation. Maybe I should go on a fast as you had to! Hope they caught that bug.

I was thinking of history and government when I wrote you before and I still spend time thinking about both. Our fatal instinct has not been eliminated by science and invention. We, as individuals, haven't caught up physically or ethically with the atomic age. Will we?

Let's hope our grandchildren do catch up. That's a hypothetical statement on my part but not on yours.

Can you imagine old man Dulles trying to make Berlin and Caracas great and statesmanlike victories? Wish old Ben Franklin were alive. He'd give John Foster the Poor Richard treatment—and that is what he needs.

Ike's rich-man-tax-bill speech was a jim dandy for the Democrats. You see what political and legislative inexperience can do for an amateur—a general! Until he learns how to fight with Congress and beat them to the punch, what chances he had, to take all the fire out of the dragon by tax reductions, foreign affairs. But he let the snollygosters tell him what to do. And I have to keep my mouth shut and use all the effort I have to keep from exploding publicly—hence you are the victim.

The tone of my mail has changed completely. It still comes in by the bushel but there's hardly a mean one in two hundred and it has been as high as five in one hundred. Most of the mean ones quote Bertie McCormick's editorials and cartoons. How in the world are you and I to survive without the *Times-Herald* in Washington? Somebody will have to give us hell or we'll be off the front page for good.

What pleases me most [is] that the alibiers for Ike are having one hell of a time keeping the policies you, Snyder and the former President put into operation under wraps. They can't play both sides of the street much longer.

What did you think of Caracas? Did we help or hurt ourselves?—Or did Sullivan and Cromwell win a victory for the United Fruit Company and the Bolivian Tin Trust? How has Guatemala been able to keep its monetary unit at par with the dollar when no other country but Canada has? I'm not so sure that dollar diplomacy hasn't come back into its own.

Please tell Mrs. Acheson that there are a lot of girls in the history books who've been overlooked along with Margaret of Austria, Eleanor of Aquitaine, Justinian's Empress to name a couple. We hear a lot of Elizabeth I, Catherine of Russia, Isabella of Spain, and Cleo of Egypt and the Medici. I like to read of them because they made Puck's exclamation in *Midsummer Night's Dream* so true. Hope you're well entirely. The Boss and I will see you we hope about May 4th.

Sincerely,

Harry

Acheson enclosed with this letter an article about the New Look foreign policy to be published on March 28, 1954, critical of Secretary of State Dulles. It is titled " 'Instant Retaliation': The Debate Continued," regarding the Dulles policy of arming Taiwan against China and encouraging rebellion in Soviet-occupied Europe. "Mr. Hull" is Cordell Hull, Franklin D. Roosevelt's Secretary of State from 1933 to 1944.

March 26, 1954

Dear Mr. President,

This is only an interim reply to your good letter which delighted me and made me feel that we had had a good talk. I am looking forward to a real one in May.

The enclosed is my only departure from the quiet and happy obscurity of our private life. I became too worked up over the fraud of the New Look to be quiet any longer. This piece does not deal in personalities or quibbling over words but tries to lay out the skeleton of our international situation so that the reader can see what we are talking about and what we must talk about. These facts of life can't be made to disappear by slick talk. Dulles may fool the people by the unleashing of Chiang, the liberation of the East Europeans, and the new look—all bare faced frauds—but he can't fool the fates. The mills grind on.

Poor Mr. Hull. I have just learned of Mrs. Hull's death and go to her funeral tomorrow. How the old man can go on I don't see. He depended on her for everything.

Our most affectionate greetings to you and Mrs. Truman.

Most sincerely,

Dean

Acheson sent Truman a two-page memorandum, dated April 7, 1954, about agreements between the United States and the United Kingdom on the use of the atomic bomb. Truman presumably needed this information for his memoirs.

Truman visited Washington in May 1954, had dinner with the Achesons, and spoke, on May 10, to the National Press Club. His theme was the need for a bipartisan foreign policy or at least a clearly defined foreign policy. This letter includes a "spasm." Truman is worried that the Eisenhower administration wants to intervene militarily in Indochina. France had just been decisively defeated by the Viet Minh communists at the Battle of Dien Bien Phu. Arthur W. Radford was a U.S. Navy Admiral and Commander in Chief of the Pacific Fleet during World War II and at the outbreak of the Korean War. General Douglas MacArthur, supreme commander of Allied forces in the southwest Pacific during World War II, was in charge of U.N. forces helping South Korea during the Korean War. Admiral Forrest Sherman was Chief of Naval Operations from 1949 until his death in 1951.

May 28, 1954

Dear Dean:

Now that the smoke has cleared away somewhat you are in for another spasm. To start with, your dinner was quite the most enjoyable event to Mrs. Truman and me, of the whole visit.

Our conversations with Gen. Marshall gave me a great kick—and by the way, he sent me a grand memo on China which with your White Paper makes a complete and factual record of what took place.

I've been working about seventeen hours a day on the book, the mail and the customers who come to see me. We are going over the Potsdam Conference and some of the happenings are fantastic to say the least. On the second day there was an argument about Franco and the German Fleet's disposal. I finally became exasperated and told Churchill and Stalin that I hadn't come to Berlin to try Franco although I thought no more of him than Stalin did. If we'd come to Berlin to run a police court, I'd go back home because I had plenty to do there.

When my outburst was translated to Stalin, he roared with laughter and suggested we talk of Poland or some other internationally tough subject. I'd forgotten the incident but Ben Cohen recorded and Jim Blair, now Lieutenant Governor of Missouri, was in to see me and repeated the story to me as I've set it down here. Jim was a Lt. Col. in civil government in Italy—I guess it was military government, at the time. I'd sent for him to come to Potsdam and offered him a ride home with me. He refused the ride because he could go home sooner on orders. When Jim arrived at the Little White House, I was having a conference with all the high military—five star generals and admirals, not one there with less than three stars. I invited Jim in and introduced him to Marshall, Leahy, Eisenhower, King, Patton and the rest and while that was going on I told him that I'd just appointed his pet political enemy to a job back in Missouri. He stopped and ripped out a paragraph of swear words (no one has a better vocabulary) and wound up by saying "for God's sake Senator what in hell did you do that for." The high brass almost fainted. I knew what Jim would do and I told him that good lie so he'd blow his top.

In the campaign of 1940 the Missouri politicians had a breakfast for Henry Wallace in St. Louis at which I was present. Our candidate for Governor at that time was Larry McDaniel, now dead. Larry lost the election because he told off color stories from the platform. He was to ride from St. Louis to Jefferson City with Wallace, and Wallace's secretary cautioned him about his demeanor with Wallace. Larry had nothing to talk about when his stories were shut off so he slept all the way to the Missouri capital. After the luncheon they went on to Kansas City for a dinner. Jim Blair rode from Jefferson City to Kansas City in the front seat and regaled Wallace by damning Republicans and his personal Democratic enemies and telling Wallace a dozen dirty stories. When they arrived and were getting out of the car Henry turned to Larry McDaniel and said "Who did you say that fellow is? He's the most interesting man I've met on this trip." Larry was fit to be tied because he thought he knew more and better stories than Jim did— without the swear words.

Now look what I've done—got off on a side issue instead of what I started to write you about. I believe the reaction to the trip east was good, thanks to the help and good advice I received from you and the boys. The McCarthy side show is causing a lot of shame to our Republican friends. Even the old *Saturday Evening Post* with its 1896 political background and philosophy "has enough."

I'm worried about our world situation. We are losing all our friends, the smart but inexperienced boys at the White House are upsetting NATO and throwing our military strength away. Yet they seem to want to intervene in Indo-China. Radford is a MacArthur policy man and always was. That was why I wouldn't make him Chief of Naval Operations when Sherman was appointed. Let me know how you feel on this subject please.

My best to Mrs. Acheson.

Sincerely,

Harry

The "first class disaster" at Hanoi is the dénouement of the war of liberation against the French in Indochina, leading to the creation of independent Vietnam.

June 16, 1954

Dear Mr. President,

Some day I must meet Jim Blair, get some of his stories and particularly get him to talk about you. That I think ought to be good and would come in handy the next time you offer me into bondage as an advisor to Foster Dulles. Not that he doesn't need a whole company of them, he most certainly does. But his trouble is that he won't listen to those he has already.

You are quite right to be worried about the world situation. It does not seem possible that a spendthrift crew could dissipate their inheritance as this Administration has done. In eighteen months we have gone from a position of acknowledged, gladly accepted and successful leadership to a position of impotent sulking while our alliances—and, indeed, some of our friends—disintegrate. And the trouble centers right where you said it did in your press club speech—in the White House. The other day one of my Republican friends said to me:—

"I want to apologize to someone and you'll have to do. I just didn't realize how much we had when we really had a President."

The next few months can really be bad. If things go on as they are now going and we have no plans or leadership, and if about October the French have a first class disaster at Hanoi with large scale local desertion of local troops and the rest of the army pinned to the beaches at Haiphong, and Congress campaigning—then what? Ted White has a first class article on Indo-China in the last *Reporter* which is worth your reading.

Even at this late hour it would be possible to work out a policy designed to regroup, hold, and reconstruct. But it requires some basic decisions and a real show down to determine who is boss in the present

Administration. The decisions are (1) whether our Alliances are or are not the foundation of our policies, if so they have got to be restored, particularly our understanding with the British, and (2) what is our purpose in South East Asia. Is it to save it, or as much as possible, from Communism? Or is it to try to destroy with arms the regime in China. If it is the latter—or rather unless we make it clear that it is not the latter, we shall get no help, our alliances will further disintegrate, and if we try it alone we may blunder into World War III. This, I think, is the heart of the matter and our people are getting very badly confused. "New Looks"—which are not new and look about as far as an ostrich with its head in the sand—, "United Fronts" without knowing with whom or about what we want to be united, intervention, alone one day, and the next only on conditions as long as a life insurance contract & involving no American boy anywhere on his own feet—these shifts, twists and turns have people groggy. And the grog is that prohibition hooch which makes some people go crazy and blinds others.

In the meantime we have added another grandson—my son David's—to the roster. He came into the world sooner than he was supposed to—either because he didn't know what he was getting into, or because he thought he could vote this fall.

We are so happy that you enjoyed the evening with us. It was a great one for us. Our warmest greetings to Mrs. Truman and yourself.

Sincerely,

Dean

On the evening of June 18, 1954, while waiting backstage to appear as himself in the musical Call Me Madam, *Truman suffered a violent seizure and was taken to the hospital, where his gallbladder and appendix were removed. Acheson provides a whimsical diagnosis for the cause of Truman's difficulties. Dr. Wallace H. Graham was Truman's personal physician during and after his presidency. "A certain general" is the occupant of the White House, President Eisenhower.*

June 21, 1954

Dear Mr. President,

Country bumpkins like Alice and I did not know of your illness, I think happily, until we knew also that you were sitting up perkily and doing well. It is a mean operation you had and will take you quite a while to be really your old self. I doubt whether anyone knows whether you will be a good patient, probably not, because you don't know what it is to be ill. If Mrs. Truman needs any help—which I also doubt—all she has to do is to call a special Cabinet meeting and we shall all be there prepared for once to lay down the law.

When papers tell us that you had a gangrenous gall bladder, I was at once prepared to tell Doc Graham how you got it. It comes from reading the newspapers. No one can escape some malady from this cause. With me it has taken the form of an attack of gout, probably from a suppressed desire to kick some one or more person or persons unnamed but not hard to identify.

For your convalescence I have asked the book shop to send you Cecil Woodham-Smith's *The Reason Why,* a really superb account of the Sebastopol campaign. When you get acquainted with Lords Raglan, Cardigan and Lucan you will be reminded of a certain general we both know. It will take your mind off the present and give your secretions a chance to adjust.

Our most affectionate greetings go to Mrs. Truman and to you. Get well quickly but get active slowly. You will be all the more powerful for the rest and quiet.

Most sincerely,

Dean

Truman suffered an allergic reaction to an antibiotic following his operation.

June 27, 1954

Dear Mr. Acheson—

Harry deeply appreciated your thoughtful telegram and one morning when I came in I found him reading the book you so generously sent him, Thank you loads and loads.

We are still remembering the delightful evening in your home—it was one of the *very* happiest we had while we were there.

We are really having a battle now to whip this wretched terramycin and I am definitely worried.

Sincerely,

Bess

[Postscript by Bess Truman:] Am in one of those [word indecipherable] writing stages again but not much use telling you that!

Rose Conway was Truman's personal secretary and administrative assistant from 1945 to 1972.

June 30, 1954

Dear Mrs. Truman:

It was very good of you in the midst of your worry and vast load of messages to write me. Since Sunday the reports have given us some comfort, as did my talk with Rose Conway. I hope your anxiety is lessened. It is touching the way so many people—elevator boys, our cook, taxi drivers, people on the street—keep asking me about the President. He is deeply loved—even by the Press. We are earnestly hoping that from now on all goes well.

Mr. Churchill, whom I saw yesterday, asked most warmly about him and said that he would like to fly out to Kansas City before going home. But Mr. Truman's recent set back made that seem a bad idea. The old gentleman is in good shape and felt that his trip here has been very necessary and successful. Eden was also looking very well indeed.

Please, under no circumstances, answer this note. It merely carries an extra greeting and word to you both.

Most sincerely,
Dean Acheson

Acheson refers to Joseph M. Jones, Special Assistant to the Assistant Secretary of State for Public Affairs, 1946–48. Jones published The Fifteen Weeks (February 11–June 5, 1947) *in early 1955. Main Duck Island in Lake Ontario was Secretary of State John Foster Dulles's favorite vacation retreat.*

September 21, 1954

Dear Mr. President:

. . . I am delighted to hear from Charlie Murphy that you are improving daily. I hope that you will take it easy and not be drawn into making a lot of speeches in the campaign. You like to do this, but it really takes a good deal more out of you than you think, and this seems to be one year when you can let some other Democrats take the burden.

A man named Joseph Jones has talked to Dave Lloyd and has written or will write to you asking permission to look at some of your files for the first half of 1947 and, if you have time, talk with you briefly. The latter you need not feel any obligation to do unless you happen to feel like it at the time. But I do hope that you will both let Joe look at the files he has in mind and ask Bill Hillman and the others to be a little cooperative with him, since they can help him greatly and he can help not only them but the whole cause.

Joe is writing a book called *Fifteen Weeks,* in which he is developing the thesis that in the time from the end of February, 1947, when the British Ambassador notified you that the British were withdrawing from Greece and Turkey, and the middle of June, you had made the most far reaching decision in foreign policy which laid the foundation for everything which has been done since. Joe worked for me at the time. He is a professional writer, an economist, and can do the job well. I do hope that you can let him get a look at the material which he needs.

I trust that the check arrived in time for you to buy the property fronting on the Library site. The obligation of the highway commission to take it off the Library hands looks a little tenuous from this distance, but we are counting on you to save the day.

There are two cracks of my son's which I must pass on to you. He says that Christian Dior has brought great trouble on the Administration. First he designed the New Look, and the Administration designed a foreign policy after it. Now he comes out with the flat bust and so does the Administration. His other observation is that there really is a basis for a deal with the Communists. We will give them Duck Island and they will give us Formosa.

Our warmest greeting to you and Mrs. Truman.

Sincerely yours,

Dean

This is Truman's first substantive letter to Acheson since the onset of his illness in mid-June. He refers to Acheson's article in the March 28, 1954 New York Times *and to one in the autumn 1954* Yale Review *titled "The*

Responsibility for Decision in Foreign Policy." He mentions the only speech he made during the 1954 campaign.

October 14, 1954

Dear Dean:

I am very sorry to be so long telling you how much I am in your debt for letters, for the article in the *New York Times Sunday Magazine* and for the *Yale Review* piece on Responsibility for Decision in Foreign Policy.

You've no idea how heart warming it is to this still controversial former President to have the people who actually knew the motivating facts, tell what those facts were. No one knew the travail we went through in those years from Apr. 12, 1945 to Jan. 20, 1953 as did you, Gen. Marshall, John Snyder and Charlie Brannan. As you know those decisions had to be made and as you also know they were based on the facts presented by the most reliable men a President ever had to give him the facts.

Dean, I've had a hell of a time since June 19th. Went to our outdoor theater in Swope Park to see *Call Me Madam* which I've never seen (and don't want to) and didn't see that Friday night. A pain overtook me which I couldn't stop with all the will power I could exercise and the "Boss" drove me home. It is fifteen miles and I thought we'd never arrive. Wallie Graham was in the back yard and went upstairs with me. Saturday was a blank. I guess he gave me knockout drops. Went to the hospital Saturday night and after some consultation Doc told me that the white corpuscles were increasing at the rate of a 1000 an hour and that a little butchering would be necessary. I wrote a codicil to my will and went out—I mean out.

Well, Doc did a fine job and gave me a fancy hem stitched sewing up. They gave me about five or ten gallons of antibiotics by sticking needles in veins. But they just couldn't kill me. Only when I was seasick on the *Zeppelin* coming home from France in 1919 did I feel worse.

You know so many flowers came to the hospital that I supplied every customer from the basement to the seventh floor. In addition to that five or six bushels, a hundred thousand cards and letters came asking me to get well. I just had to accommodate 'em.

Bess says I'm worse than a Bridge Club Lady—talk about my operation and bore people to death. That's what you get for being my good friend. I was very sorry about the Jones affair. But he was not very courteous and I'm afraid of breaking my contract, so I told him to wait until the manuscript is in the publisher's hands on my book and then we'd go on from there.

I'm only making one political speech and for me it's on a very high plane. I can see your grin on that one. It will be broadcast at 9:30 P.M. our time on the American Network—no television thank goodness.

On Nov. 6 we are having a Library dinner here and do you know believe it or not they've sold 387 tickets at $100.00 a piece and no invitations are out yet. The room only holds 600 and they say that you won't be able to get 'em in. Now what about that prophet in his home town?

If you and Mrs. Acheson will come out I'll furnish you tickets and free room and board at our house. Anyway I want to put you on the witness stand for the book if you come. Marshall, Snyder, and Charlie Brannan and Oscar Chapman have all been through the ordeal and not one has been indicted for perjury—so surely the greatest lawyer of them all should [not] be afraid of a Truman Grand Jury! Dean, I am anxious to talk with you about the main theme of the book because I have the utmost confidence in your judgment.

My best to Mrs. Acheson—Alice.

Answer this in person Nov 6!

Sincerely,

Harry Truman

Truman's lingering convalescence from his operation in June prevented him from taking a substantial part in the 1954 election season. He did no campaigning and made only one speech, at a Midwest Democratic Rally held in Kansas City on October 16, which was carried on national radio. Truman began the speech by saying that some had advised him that, after eight years as President, he should now be an elder statesman "on a high and mighty plane and say nothing except the nicest things," that he "speak softly and not in what they call the whistle-stop technique." Truman couldn't take this advice. "The whistle-stop technique," he said, "is the very heart of American political debate and political frankness in this free country. Again tonight I intend to be myself and speak plainly on the issues." For half an hour, he attacked the Republicans in his plain-speaking style. "I cannot see where there is any leadership among the Republicans to deal with the great needs of this country," he insisted. "On the contrary, what I do see is a hopeless drifting and a gradual surrender to selfish interests at home." Once or twice he found his typed speech too tepid and decided to say something stronger. The typed copy read, "I have not tried to single out all the mistakes that have been made—the list is very long." Truman, not satisfied, wrote in, "It would take all night and all day tomorrow to list them." Again, where the speech talks about economic problems brought on by the Republicans, Truman adds: "If the Republicans had controlled the government for the 20 years after 1932 you'd have no job, no farm, no business to lose in 1951."

Acheson listened to Truman's radio address. Philip Jessup was Truman's delegate to the United Nations in 1951.

Dear Mr. President,   October 19, 1954

It was a great joy to see the familiar handwriting again and to hear once more on Saturday night the well remembered voice. Phil Jessup, Alice, and I listened to you together. You came through very well indeed. We were all so excited and delighted that we all had another drink which we did not need. Alice said that just to hear your strong healthy straightforward talk regardless of the arguments, after these studio trained swoon boys, made her sure that everything was all right somehow or other. We all agreed and I know a great host of listeners did also.

I am sorry that we could not have helped with the text but somewhere the signals got mixed up. David and I wrote a thirty minute speech in which we had some pretty good touches. Then David got word to cut it to 12 minutes. So the good touches went out. But you spoke for a full half hour and timed it beautifully.

It was fine, but that is enough for this campaign. You must take it easy for a while longer.

Contrary to Mrs. Truman's prediction your report on your illness was most eagerly read. I had known from her letter that you had been very ill indeed and that for a while it was touch and go. Your account has made it vivid and brought home how lucky we all were that your number was not up. I'm glad too that you had a chance to see the deep affection which the country has for you. At one time I thought that we would have to go to New York to comfort the editor of the *Times* who was almost in a state of collapse.

Please don't worry about the Joe Jones affair. He managed it very badly and although he is a good man and will do a good book for your administration he is not tactful or courteous and does get excited.

Dave and I should have paved the way with a careful explanation of what he wanted so that you could have considered it carefully and in advance. I do not think that he would have led to any trouble on the contract—which could not be risked at all. There is really only one fact which he needs to ascertain and should be shown in a document which General Marshall and I brought to you and you approved on February 26, 1947. He does not need to quote it at all. Perhaps some time you and I can talk about it.

This brings me to the sad fact that, although Alice and I would dearly love to do so, we cannot accept your most welcome invitation to be with you on November 6th. I have to speak at Cambridge, Mass., on the 4th, attend a Yale Corporation meeting at New Haven on the 5th and 6th and argue a case in the Supreme Court on the 8th. But I hope that this does not rule us out forever and that you and Mrs. Truman will let us come later on at some time when you have an open date. Probably I will not be much use on the book but it would be great fun to talk it over with you, and the greatest joy to see you both.

Bob and Adele Lovett will be here with us this weekend and we shall talk a great deal of you as we did when we stayed with them last summer. Both of them were ill last winter and spring (Adele had her gall bladder out) but they are fine now. Bob finds private life as dull as I do—and, I suspect, you do, too. It has its compensations but they are not in the field of absorbing interest.

All our children are flourishing. David has presented us—or rather his wife has—with a fifth grandchild. Time marches on! What I hear and read of Margaret is full of happiness and success in her work.

With most affectionate greetings to Mrs. Truman and yourself.

Most sincerely,

Dean

Truman is looking forward to getting Acheson's critique of the draft of his memoirs. The book Truman refers to, Civilization and Foreign Policy *(1955), is by State Department official Louis J. Halle, Jr.*

January 11, 1955

Dear Dean:

You were right about Louis Halle's book, if I may pose in my stuffed shirt capacity as a "judge."

That inscription to me and the Introduction by you would make it a great book for me if nothing else were between the covers. But I have certainly enjoyed reading it.

You know, Dean, I think you and I will live to see what we tried to do appreciated for what it is. Not many who have had our positions lived to see what they'd done appreciated.

I hope you and Alice, if she'll allow me to call her by the first name, had a grand holiday season and I hope 1955 brings you everything you want. Bess and I had a happy time because "Miss Skinny" was at home. You know I called her "skinny well fed" as she grew up because I didn't have a boy. But I wouldn't trade her for a house full of boys although I always wanted a couple and another girl. It didn't happen and I'm amply compensated!

We are going great guns on the book. I hope you and Alice can come out and spend a few days with us so I can put you under the cross examination with no "objections" allowed.

The damned thing is turning out much better than I thought it would but I need your opinion badly.

My best to you, Mrs. Acheson and all your family. Say hello to the gang.

Sincerely,

Harry

Acheson's comment about Milwaukee refers to the fact that Senator Joseph McCarthy represented that district of Wisconsin. Acheson refers to political commentator Walter Lippmann's book Essays in the Public Philosophy *(1955), also published under the title* The Public Philosophy.

January 20, 1955

Dear Mr. President,

I am so glad that you liked the Halle book. It seemed to me really first class, laying out, as it did, the problems we faced both abroad and from the very nature of the American public, what the choices were and what the right choice was and is. I wish everyone could and would read it, including Mr. John Foster Dulles.

Alice and I are off tonight for Pittsburgh where I speak on Friday—not on public matters—to the Pennsylvania Bar Association. Its members ought to be a fine lot of McKinley conservatives if the term

"Philadelphia lawyer" describes them. But I am to talk on legal subjects. I am fooling them by reminiscing about the old Supreme Court and when I went to work for Justice Brandeis thirty-six years ago. If the speech gets printed I'll send you a copy.

From Pittsburgh we go on to Milwaukee to see our daughter, Jane, whose place I have never been to. While we were in office Milwaukee did not seem the most ideal spot in which to relax. We shall be there over the weekend. Then Alice goes on to Michigan to get her nephew married and I come home.

We would love to come to Kansas City to see you and Mrs. Truman. Our last opportunity in November ran into all sorts of Court and college engagements. So you name the most convenient time for you and we will bend our lives to suit. It would be better for us if it could be after the middle of February and not the weekend of the 25th, 26th and 27th when we have guests on our hands. My engagements in the office are so flexible and light that I can arrange to get away at almost any time. The week of Feb. 7–12 I am spending at Yale where I have taken on a heavy schedule of lectures and seminars for undergraduate and graduate students. The two weeks before I had better spend on preparation, but if sometime in those weeks were much better for you please let me know. And whenever we come do not let us be a burden on Mrs. Truman. You will know how to avoid that and our earnest desire [is] that it should be avoided.

Walter Lippmann has a new book out in which he makes the amazing discovery that the weakness of the democracies today comes from encroachments on the executive power, by legislative bodies pandering to an ignorant and volatile public swayed by mass media of communication. If he had known this and used his power—which isn't much but something—to support the executive when we really had one instead of joining the chorus of misinformation, I could read him with more patience. One of the editors of a great weekly told me the other day that the feather bed which the whole press and radio, TV, etc. put under this administration was quite unbelievable. He said that if we had done one quarter of the fool and other things which this crowd has our great free press would have gone utterly crazy with denunciation. Perhaps some day the populace will see that the king has no clothes on.

Our most affectionate greetings to you both.

As ever,

Dean

Truman suggests the Muehlebach Hotel's Presidential Suite as a place where Acheson might stay when he comes to Kansas City. During Truman's presidency the suite served as his headquarters when he and his staff came to town. Barney Allis was the hotel's owner.

               January 25, 1955

Dear Dean:

As usual your good letter gave me a lift. When I hear from you I always feel better.

I am anxious for you to come out and discuss parts of the book. If you and Mrs. Acheson (Alice) can come out Feb. 16th and stay with us the rest of the week or as long as you feel you can we'll be delighted and I'll make you believe you had a real "one man grand jury" session!

We'd love to have you and Alice stay with us or if you prefer "great eastern" style I'll have Barney Allis put you in the Presidential Suite at the Muehlebach Hotel.

Sincerely,

Harry Truman

Walter George was the senior senator from Georgia, often supportive of the Eisenhower administration, and chairman of the Senate Committee on Foreign Relations from January 1955 to January 1957. Acheson feels that the administration is being played for fools by Chiang Kai-shek.

               January 31, 1955

Dear Mr. President,

I shall set my plans for Kansas City Wednesday, February 16th, with great joy. I ought to get back here by Saturday, February 19th. Alice would love to come, but is doubtful whether she can. She has just been away for ten days during which the cook has collapsed with various ailments. So that department is in disorder. Then next week she has to be away again with me. So she is breathless at the moment and unable to be clear about the future. She wants you to know that she would love to see you and her beloved Mrs. Truman.

I should, of course, love to stay with you and have no longing for the Muehlebach's Presidential elegance, which I know. But above all I do not want to bother Mrs. Truman by adding to household cares.

Until the 16th! What a magnificent mess these people are making of the Far East. And our Democrats are not very bright, particularly Walter George who gets committed when he doesn't know the play.

Yours,

Dean

February 4, 1955

Dear Mr. President:

This is just a note to you before I leave for a week at New Haven, to tell you our plans for coming to you.

As Alice has written Mrs. Truman, to her great joy she has gotten things straightened out so that she will be able to come with me. We are planning to arrive at 12:15 p.m. on Wednesday, February 16, via TWA, Flight No. 1. And we have gotten reservations to return on a TWA Flight which leaves Saturday morning at 8:30 a.m.

If these plans can be changed in any way to be more convenient to you, we shall do it as soon as you tell us how. Miss Evans will take care of everything here while I am away.

We are looking forward to our visit like children to the holidays. Alice saw Margaret yesterday and reports that she was (1) very well and gay, and (2) prettier than ever. She gave her consent to our visit.

Most warmly,

Dean

February 5, 1955

Dear Dean:

I was pleased no end when yours of Jan. 31 came. Margaret saw Mrs. Acheson at the reception and told us that both of you were coming. I'm glad you'd rather stay at our small town residence than at the Presidential Suite of Barney Allis' hotel.

I'm so anxious for your comments on what I say about Korea, MacArthur and the Employee Security Program that I'd do most anything to get them. Let me know your time of arrival on the 16th so I can meet you. I have no Secret Service, no Intelligence Service. So you'll have to tell me.

Sincerely,

Harry Truman

February 9, 1955

HONORABLE DEAN ACHESON
YOUR TIMING IS PERFECTLY ALL RIGHT. MRS. TRUMAN AND I
WILL BE LOOKING FOR YOU AND MRS. ACHESON TO ARRIVE AT
TWELVE EIGHTEEN FEBRUARY SIXTEENTH. WE ARE EXCEED-
INGLY HAPPY.
HARRY S TRUMAN

February 19, 1955

THE HON AND MRS HARRY S TRUMAN
SAFELY HOME WITH THE HAPPIEST MEMORIES AND DEEPEST
GRATITUDE FOR THE BEST VISIT EVER
AFFECTIONATELY
ALICE AND DEAN

*Truman met the Achesons at the Kansas City airport and drove them to a
luncheon at the Muehlebach Hotel, where they gave a press conference.
Among the luncheon guests were the small staff who were assisting Truman with his memoirs. Much of Acheson's time during the next three days
was spent giving interviews to Truman's three main associates on the
memoir project—journalist William Hillman, advertising executive David
Noyes, and University of Kansas professor and chief writer Francis Heller.*

February 21, 1955

Dear Mrs. Truman,

What a glorious visit you gave us! We delighted in every minute of it.
Even when the three man grand jury had me under examination I was
reliving days which were the best and fullest I have ever lived. It started
with the very first moment when we came out of the plane and saw you
and the President and Margaret waiting for us at the bottom of the
steps. That nearly did us in. But I think the greatest joy came in seeing
you three all so well and so happy, in your own home, and surrounded
by the affectionate devotion of your own community. It was so right
and sound and inspiring. It made us feel all over again the strength and
grandeur of the fabric of this America of ours.

And what luck for us that Margaret was at home with you at just this time. Not only because she is the greatest fun in her own right, but because, too, the Trumans reach their highest form in trio. Each one eggs on and complements the other two. If she had not been home I should never have seen—and participated in—the overpowering of the President's curiosity by the new guitar.

We came home refreshed and happy with new memories to add to the volumes that we have of you—the evening at home, the evening in the railway car, the evening at the ballet. During the drives with the President—whose prowess behind the wheel I slandered shamelessly last May—we had more concentrated talk about events and people than we could have packed into a whole year of our Monday and Thursday meetings.

It was great happiness for us. I only hope that as we took off into the rain, which stopped a little East of Chicago and is catching up with us now, we did not leave you exhausted by your kindness to us.

My newspaper friends say that under the President's expansive influence the Kansas City press got more out of me in a few minutes than my friends here have been able to get in two years. The morning mail brings demands for a TV interview.

We are grateful and happy. These are the messages which go to you from us.

Most affectionately,
Dean

Truman is looking forward to his next meeting with Acheson in Washington in April, at a testimonial dinner for House Speaker Sam Rayburn.

March 7, 1955

Dear Dean:

I haven't yet fully believed that grand visit of yours and Alice's really took place. It was just too good to be an actual fact—but it was and how happy it made Bess, Margaret and me.

Bess has a letter, later than yours, from Alice about a luncheon or a dinner at your house while we are in Washington for Sam Rayburn's dinner. If Sunday luncheon after church (the Boss wants to go to church) will suit you that will be all right for us. Then we can go to the station and catch the train for home as we did on another occasion.

You've no idea how much good and what a life saver you did and gave to me. When I see you we'll go into detail. You'll probably have another spasm at length from me soon.

Sincerely,

Harry Truman

Acheson recalls in a telegram the so-called Truman Doctrine speech to Congress. The President had decided to provide economic assistance to Greece and Turkey, because Greece was pressed by communist elements and Turkey by the Soviet Union.

"I believe that it must be the policy of the United States," President Truman told the Congress on March 12, 1947, "to support free peoples who are resisting attempted subjugation by armed minorities or by outside pressures. I believe that we must assist free peoples to work out their own destinies in their own way."

March 12, 1955

Telegram for Harry S Truman, Independence MO

EIGHT YEARS AGO YOU ANNOUNCED A GREAT AND GALLANT DECISION

IT WAS ONE OF THE TURNING POINTS IN HISTORY

TODAY YOU AND IT LOOK BETTER THAN EVER

OUR LOVE

DEAN

Truman has been asked by Senator Walter F. George to testify on April 18 before the committee about proposed revisions to the United Nations Charter.

March 29, 1955

Dear Dean,

I am enclosing for you a copy of a letter from Walter George, together with a copy of my reply to him and a copy of the note which I have sent to Dr. Wilcox.

I shall appreciate it most highly if you will make some suggestions to me as to what sort of statement I should make to the committee on Foreign Relations.

I am perfectly willing to appear because I want to show the country

that when an appearance is in the public's interest and for a real purpose I am more than happy to appear.

   We are looking forward to a grand time with you and Mrs. Acheson.

   Sincerely,

   Harry Truman

You are due for a hell of a long hand letter one of these days!

*Acheson worries that Republican senators on the Committee on Foreign
Relations may ask Truman questions about difficult current foreign-policy
problems when he appears before the committee. William F. Knowland was
a Republican senator from California.*

March 31, 1955

Dear Mr. President,

   I shall try to be helpful about the U.N. Testimony when I get back
here from a journey to New Haven and Albany which starts tomorrow
and runs until Wednesday.

   I am sorry you got let in for this, because Knowland and Co. may try
to get you into Formosa and a lot of things and there isn't much that
one can or should say about U.N. Charter revision now. But we shall do
our best and hope the Committee can't meet on the 18th after all. We
can have some talk about it when you are here.

   All is set for a big welcome for you and Mrs. Truman here and in no
spot is it more eagerly expected than at 2805 P St. I also look forward to
the letter, but save that for a time when we shall not have you yourself.

   Our warmest greetings.

   Most sincerely,

   Dean

*Truman arrived in Washington, D.C., on April 15 and attended a formal
dinner in his honor that night. The next day he lunched with members of
his Cabinet and White House staff and attended a formal dinner in honor
of Speaker of the House Sam Rayburn. At that dinner he lashed out at the
Eisenhower administration: "This administration has been playing partisan politics with our security," he said in his strongest whistle-stop style;
"this administration has been playing partisan politics with our foreign
policy, this administration has been playing partisan politics with our
Civil Service, this administration has been playing special privilege partisan politics with our nation's resources. I regret to say that we have not*

seen such cynical political behavior *in any administration since the* early twenties." *The* Chicago Sun-Times *the next day ran the headline, in their largest font,* TRUMAN OPENS FIRE ON IKE AS DEMOCRATS EYE 1956. *A former member of Truman's Cabinet who heard the speech, Wilson W. Wyatt, wrote to Truman, "Now that you have led the way I hope that all of our Democratic speakers will be willing to tell the simple Anglo-Saxon truth about the Eisenhower myth." The day after the Rayburn dinner, April 17, Truman and Acheson shared a private dinner at 2805 P Street, and the next morning, Truman testified before the Senate Committee on Foreign Relations about the importance of the United Nations.*

Truman refers to Republican Senator Homer E. Capehart of Indiana and Alben W. Barkley of Kentucky, Truman's Vice President (1949–53), who had been reelected to the Senate in 1954.

April 20, 1955

Dean:

What a time we had in the capital of the United States! The Boss says she had the best time she's had in years. Your luncheon was the highlight even if you did make me cry. You know I'm a damned sentimentalist but I hate to show it!

That appearance before the Foreign Relations Committee was something to write home about. Thanks to your good advice I don't believe I made any major errors. The attitude of the private citizen respectfully appearing before the august high committee of the Senate of the United States seemed to please them. Even the Republicans asked friendly questions, including Knowland but for one. Only Capehart tried to be a smart-aleck and Barkley said he got his tail in a crack and that it was still there when the Committee quit business.

All of them paid tribute of the highest order to the statement. I am eternally indebted to you for your help, criticisms and suggestions.

Now I'm feeling much better after exploding at the Rayburn dinner. Of course I'll catch hell for that and be right in my element. I don't want to be an "elder statesman" politician. I like being a nose buster and an ass kicker much better and reserve my serious statements for committees and schools. But I had a grand time, only not enough time, with you.

Sincerely,

Harry

Acheson regrets that he will not be present at the groundbreaking ceremony for the Harry S. Truman Library on May 8, Truman's birthday.

April 29, 1955

Dear Mr. President,

Your notes and Mrs. Truman's brought joy to Alice and me. We had such a glorious time at our Sunday lunch for you that it was doubly satisfying to know that you did too. I had not intended that my words to you should be anything but gay, like the occasion. But it is too hard for me to speak about you without going beneath the surface where emotions and affections run deep. I must discipline myself more strictly.

Your testimony on the U.N. went very well indeed. I was too full of worries about it and should have known that you would take care of yourself perfectly. It was particularly good coming before Mr. Hoover's and drawing a comparison. Poor Mr. Hoover! His latest idea of giving the parcel post back to the express company was the perfect expression of his attitude.

For your birthday we send all good wishes. Our especial wish for you—long years of health and happiness—seems to be in fair way of being granted already. I have never seen you so well and so blooming with happy vigor. I wrote a good friend the other day that none of us here were able to keep up with you on this last visit. You left us convinced that you not only enjoyed jet assistance on the take-off, but that after the take-off it continues from your own self-generated power. This suggests, as I remember the plans for the library, that there may be a duplication in them. One room is called "power plant" and another marked President Truman's office. Perhaps these two should be put together.

Alice and I hoped that we could arrange our commitments so as to be with you on the eighth of May to celebrate your birthday and to see you put that gold plated spade into the ground to start the library. Even if it is gold plated you will still call the spade a spade and use it as such. Please leave something for the bulldozers. Our own plans, as they so often do, have become entangled again with Yale where I am committed to speak. But our disappointment is mitigated by selfish considerations. We shall look forward to another visit to Independence when we can have you more to ourselves without the competition of great events. But you will know that both of us will be thinking of you and talking to you on this day to which you have looked forward so long.

With our heartiest congratulations on breaking ground for the

Library and our most affectionate greeting to you on your birthday and to "the boss" for preserving you from the last one to this one, a great feat.

Most sincerely,
Dean

Harry Truman sits in a limousine with Dean Acheson in Washington, D.C., on December 28, 1951, upon the President's return after spending the Christmas holiday in Independence, Missouri.

3

June to August 1955

A Blunt Critique of Truman's Memoirs

In June and July 1955, when Truman's deadline for submitting his memoirs to his publisher was drawing near, he asked Acheson to review the second draft of the work—1,775 pages bound in four thick books, two books for each of the two memoir volumes. The first volume would be titled *1945: Year of Decisions* and the second volume *Years of Trial and Hope, 1946–1952*. Acheson set energetically to work, scribbling corrections, changes, additions, and comments within the text and in the margins, and he drew his ideas together in six letters totaling forty-five pages of typescript. The annotated manuscript and letters together constitute a sometimes shockingly blunt critique. Truman, though, expressed gratitude for "the ideal help I've had in the form of an intellectually honest Secretary of State." Truman considered every suggestion Acheson made, adding his own marginal comments on the annotated drafts. He then turned over the manuscript and Acheson's letters to his assistants to make revisions in response to Acheson's comments.

. . .

Truman's first memoir volume, 1945: Year of Decisions, *covered his early life, his political career before becoming President, and the first year of his presidency.*

June 7, 1955

Dear Dean:

I am sending you the draft of the First Volume of the book I have been trying to write. There is a preface that goes with it but I have not yet prepared it.

The book will be in two Volumes and will be called "Memoirs" by Harry S. Truman. The First Volume will be called "Year of Decisions," and the Second "Years of Trial and Hope."

This is next to the final draft but it will have to be back in my hands in time to make any corrections suggested so that I can get it off by June 30th. After June 30th, *Life* and Doubleday will be reading for corrections so that in that period there will be another opportunity to correct any errors. There will also be a chance to correct galleys and final proof.

I hope you will not be overwhelmed by my request that you go through this Volume very carefully and make any suggestions you feel should be made. Do not spare my feelings in the matter. What I am trying to do, as you know, is tell the truth and the facts in a manner that people can understand and in my own language.

The Second Volume will be sent along in a couple of weeks after I return from Portland, Oregon, but it will not be published until February or March of next year.

Sincerely,

Harry S. Truman

"My best to Alice."

In this letter Acheson's penchant for accuracy and honesty of exposition is cleverly coupled with tactful arguments for the revisions. He comments on Truman's account of, among other things, his first days as President, his early life, his service in the Senate, his selection as vice-presidential candidate in 1944, his termination of lend-lease, and President Roosevelt's "Supreme Court packing proposal" of 1937. Truman gave this letter to his chief writer, Francis Heller, who marked it to indicate revisions in the memoirs manuscript in response to Acheson's comments.

June 21, 1955

Dear Mr. President:

I have read with great interest the first of the two manuscript volumes which you sent me, containing pages 1 through 442. I think it is a fine job. It gives the reader a real feeling of the kind of man you are and it holds his attention.

As a general observation, which may be useful when you come to editing and cutting down, the material is more interesting and gripping when you are talking about your own life and your ideas than it is when you are giving lists of callers at the White House and the activities of the Truman Committee which do not reveal much about you as a man. I know these latter things are necessary, but I think they can be shortened and I will make specific suggestions as we go along. Now for specific and sometimes minor points:

Page 6, line 1. Bishop Atwood was the former Episcopal Bishop of Arizona and not of Washington. [Truman staff marginalia: "corrected."]

Page 8, line 11. Do you really doubt that FDR made any major political decision without consulting Mrs. Roosevelt? As you say later on, I think, she was useful to him in getting, through her, impressions of public opinion; but my guess would be that he did not consult her much or rely on her judgment in making decisions. [Truman staff marginalia: "same comment made by SIR (Samuel I. Rosenman)—slight change made in wording."]

Page 8, last line. Couldn't you put stars instead of the word "Wisconsin"? Certainly Senator [Alexander] Wiley [R., Arizona] is and was a windy senator, but he stood by us pretty well, and I think this reference would unnecessarily hurt him. [Truman staff marginalia: "recommend be done."]

Page 9, line 7. I make the same suggestion about your reference to [Senator Pat] McCarran [D., Nevada], but for different reasons. I just don't think it accomplishes much to leave the reference specifically identified. [Truman staff marginalia: "should be done."]

Page 14, line 9. Shouldn't it be "There *are* bound to be some changes," etc.? [Truman staff marginalia: "corrected."]

Page 36, last paragraph. You say that during your meeting with Byrnes on April 13, "I had told Byrnes that I was thinking of appointing him Secretary of State after the San Francisco Conference." This raises two questions. One is that, although I looked for it later on, I never found any point where you actually asked him to be Secretary of State. The second is that one wonders why you told him you were thinking of making him an offer rather than either making it or not speaking of it until you were ready to make the offer. I seem to recall that you told me once that you actually made the offer to him on the train coming back from the Roosevelt funeral. (Please read here the post script to this letter.) [Truman staff marginalia: "except for the point made in the final sentence of this paragraph (which check w/HST) this requires no correction. I have checked p. 535 and see no inconsistencies."]

Page 37, middle of the page. You say, "I felt it my duty to choose without delay a Secretary of State with proper qualifications." Wouldn't it be better to add to the end of the sentence, "to succeed, if necessary, to the Presidency"? Otherwise, it seems like quite a crack at poor Ed Stettinius [Secretary of State from 1944 to 1945]. [Truman staff marginalia: "this insertion has been made."]

Page 45, two lines from the bottom. You refer to Blair House as the official guest house "for heads of state." A small matter—but shouldn't one say "foreign dignitaries"? [Truman staff marginalia: "correction made."]

Page 47. The inclusion of this conversation with John Snyder and Jesse Jones [Secretary of Commerce under President Roosevelt] seems to me rather pointless. John is being modest about his qualifications, but he says he might be "accused of being a Jesse Jones man." Why, the reader wonders, is that the subject of accusation? I would suggest merely recording that you talked with John, offered him the position and that he accepted it.

As a matter of English, in the middle of the page, shouldn't it be "I don't think you ought to appoint me *to* that job," rather than "for that job"? [Truman staff marginalia: "this change made."]

Page 59, last sentence. This one-sentence reference to the press, I think, should come out. If you are going to attack some section of the press, it has to be done more fully and with some more proof and power. This one sentence seems to me weak and sounds a little querulous.

Page 68. In the middle of the page Sam Rayburn says, "Just a minute, Harry." I seem to recollect at some earlier page, after you had become President, somebody else called you "Harry." This I don't like, and I don't like to see you quote it as though it were of no moment.

Why not just leave out the "Harry"? [Truman staff marginalia: "This is a matter of record—should stay as is—"]

Page 114, line 3. You use the cliché, "striped pants boys in the State Department." I should like to see you change this to "people in the State Department," not merely because the phrase is tiresome, but because it gives quite a wrong impression of the tremendous support which you gave to the career service and for which they will be forever grateful.

Page 147e. This page is very confusing, as undoubtedly the transcript of the conversation was. From the middle of the page down, Churchill is reading a telegram which he proposes to send. This is not at all clear from the text, and the confusion is not clarified until one comes to the bottom of 174f. Here the same telegram is read again. I think that some editing would be useful here to keep the reader on the track. [Truman staff marginalia: "suggest a footnote on 147 to remind reader that this is exact transcript—with asterisk for names not understood and some garbles. Addition (made) of interior quotes helps this →"]

Page 147g. At the end of the first paragraph, the word "oration" with a question mark appears obviously to be a garble. I wonder if editing couldn't make the real meaning clearer?

Page 150. Are you correct about Frances Perkins's title? I always thought she was called "Miss Perkins" or "Mrs. Wilson." [Truman staff marginalia: "checked and correction made."]

Page 151, line 2. The name of the eating place on 17th Street is the Allies' Inn. [Truman staff marginalia: "checked and correction made."]

Page 151, last paragraph. You refer here to three agencies which you did not want cut down "because of their importance in the prevention of inflation." Two of these are the Petroleum Administration for War and the Foreign Economic Administration. I did not understand that these two had anything to do with the prevention of inflation.

Page 153, line 7. You speak of apprehension "that the isolationist spirit might again break out into the open." Is this the phrase that you want? It would seem to be a good idea to get it into the open. Weren't you apprehensive rather that the isolationist spirit might again become an important political factor?

Page 154, second paragraph. You refer to Harold Smith's report of our bad administration of relief in Italy. It isn't at all clear what Harold was talking about; whether this was relief distributed by Military Government or UNRRA; nor is it clear what the British were doing which seemed undesirable. Furthermore, you say that you accepted this "as probably an accurate report" and asked the State Department to correct the situation. I don't think you ever did accept a secondhand report as probably accurate. Finally, although it may be that the State Department had some control over the situation, I cannot quite see now what it could be. These two paragraphs, on page 154 and the top of 155, seem to me most obscure, and I suggest their elimination.

Page 158, middle of page. Will Clayton at this time was Assistant Secretary of State, not Under Secretary. [Truman staff marginalia: "checked and corrected."]

The progress of the narrative up to Chapter 8 has followed the method of taking the reader with you through each appointment and through the various documents laid before you in the days immediately following your assumption of the Presidential office. Up to Chapter 8 I think this has served as a useful method. It makes real to the reader the exact nature of the responsibilities which suddenly devolved upon you. No general description would convey this the way your hour-to-hour and visitor-by-visitor method has done. But I think this method can be overdone and I think that beginning with Chapter 8 it is overdone. It starts out with the problem of Germany and McCloy's report. On page 164, we get into specific callers again. And so it continues. I would suggest in editing Chapter 8 that it be made the dividing line and that you no longer give us a detailed list of callers but dwell on the main problems with which you had to deal.

Chapters 9 and 10 about your early life are well done and most interesting.

Page 229 and 236. On both pages you use exactly the same words in describing Carl Hayden as "one of the hardest working and ablest men in the Senate." [Truman staff marginalia: "correction made."]

Chapter 11, which deals with your first term in the Senate, is interesting at the beginning and at the end. But there are about ten pages in the middle which I think should be approached from a different point of view.

These are pages 238 to 248, which deal with the various votes you cast. In these pages you have short paragraphs dealing with the views you held on matters, many of which are of the greatest historical importance. These comments give an impression of a man quite contrary to what you are. They are brusque, didactic, and in one instance, which I shall specify, superficial. I should like to see these pages reorganized so that you concentrate on two or three important measures, giving your own feelings in more than a short paragraph about them; and, as for the rest, saying that your general point of view can be gathered from the measures for which you voted and against which you voted, and then merely enumerating each. I urge this, not merely from the point of view of reader interest, but so that you will not give what I think is quite a wrong impression about yourself.

One of these measures you discuss in eight lines on page 245. This is the Supreme Court packing proposal of 1937. The discussion of it seems to me so inadequate as to be almost irrelevant. You list the different numerical relationships [Truman staff notation: "relationships" crossed out and "memberships" substituted] of the Court throughout the years, say that you saw no reason why it should not be increased in 1937, making reference to the new Court building, and suggesting that you thought that [the purpose of] the whole bill was to get enough judges to keep the Court's work up to date.

This does not do justice to you but does you grave injustice, and I think will do you harm. The Court proposals of 1937 had nothing to do with appointing enough justices to do the Court's work. They were directed toward reversing the current majority and changing the current interpretation—which I believe was wrong—of the commerce clause and the Fifth Amendment, which interpretation has since been changed. The proposal did not purport to do this openly and frankly but through a most cynical subterfuge. This attack on the Court and the counter-attack on the President, I think, damaged both irreparably. It was a tragic episode; made even more tragic by the lack of necessity; for within four years, time had given the President the majority which the Congress denied him. There were grounds on which legislators might honorably, though I think mistakenly, support the proposals— grounds based upon action both taken and threatened in England to reduce the power of the House of Lords. But all of these involved a grave constitutional crisis, as grave a crisis as was involved in General MacArthur's challenge to your authority in 1951.

The paragraph on page 245 gives the impression, which I know is erroneous, that you were wholly unaware of any of these considerations, and that the whole question was that, having built a large court house, we should have more judges. I do not think that it is necessary or desirable for you to re-argue the Court proposals, and I would strongly urge that you do not, but merely list your vote along with the others to show that which, so far as the history of your life is concerned, is the important thing; that is, the loyalty with which you stood by President Roosevelt. I know that you will not be offended by the frankness with which I have written. I do it because of the grave injustice, as I have already said, which this paragraph does you.

Page 249, line 2. The discussion of your opposition to the $500,000,000 cut, I do not think, enlightens the reader, nor do I think you will want to leave in the ad hominem reference to Harry Byrd. If my suggestions above of merely listing the bills is a useful one, this would not be necessary.

Page 260. Your story about Jim Wade is a good one, but I ask you to reconsider the last sentence, that adds to it that later on, when you were President, you made Jim Wade Collector of Customs in St. Louis. This is the only reference you make in the volume which I have read about minor appointments. It would give the uninformed reader the quite unjustified impression that political patronage and the reward of political supporters was your major consideration in making appointments. This, of course, is not true. When you compare the impression which this leaves with your discussion on page 262 of your concern about special interests, inside influence, etc., there is a very sharp contrast. I suggest you drop the last sentence on page 260. [Truman staff marginalia: "done."]

Page 268–269. Can't the material from the middle of page 268 through the first full paragraph of page 269 be greatly compressed? The recitation of these formal appearances slows the narrative and delays your getting into the major work of the Truman Committee.

Pages 260–300. These pages cover a discussion of the Truman Committee's work. I think that these pages need editing, both to shorten them and to concentrate them on the main achievements of the Committee and to correct some erroneous impressions which they leave. Wouldn't it be well to start out with a better orientation of your approach and that of the Committee? This might be done by bringing out more fully than you do your tribute to the great part played by the industrial organization and power of the United States in winning the war and to the vast majority of patriotic industrialists, both those who stayed with their factories and those who came to Washington, who transformed American industry for war production. It could be brought out that this produced, inevitably, confusion and duplication and waste, and that the Committee's purpose was to help in overcoming these quite inevitable evils as quickly as possible. Since you have to talk about errors and mistakes which were made, you have to avoid giving the impression that everyone except the Committee and its staff was stupid or venal. Of course, you do not mean to give this impression, but it emerges, and I think could be easily remedied by having your staff go over these pages with a red pencil.

Page 302. In the second paragraph, I think the specific reference to [Senator Owen] Brewster and [Senator Arthur] Vandenberg should be removed or elaborated and proved. Couldn't this sentence be altered to say that, whenever any member of the Committee showed signs of yielding to the temptation of bringing Congress into control of the conduct of the war, you were able by private talks to get the work of the Committee back on the rails without any crisis arising?

Page 307. Here you are again talking about your votes. Again I suggest the same treatment discussed above of listing them for the purpose of indicating your general point of view. For instance, in the paragraph toward the bottom of the page, where you discuss a bill of 1941 exempting taxes on income from state and city bonds, I do not think that the analogy to federal bonds is relevant in this discussion. The question is whether the federal sovereignty can tax the bonds, or indeed the salaries or other property, of the various state sovereignties, or vice versa.

Page 312. I suggest leaving out the last sentence of the second paragraph. In the preceding sentence you record that FDR has asked Frank Walker [Democratic National Committee Chair from 1943 to 1944] to notify Byrnes of his decision that he wanted you as Vice President. You then say, "I believe, therefore, that Byrnes knew that the President had named me at the time he called me in Independence and asked me to nominate him at the convention." The narrative does not need this sentence, and I think that it makes a specific and unnecessarily bitter accusation against Byrnes. If Frank Walker had notified him, then he knew, if Frank Walker had not done so, perhaps he didn't know. Is it necessary for you to take a position?

Page 314. Is my memory correct that you once told me that after the telephone talk with President Roosevelt you then had a talk with Jimmy Byrnes and told him what the President had required of you. If this is so, it is an important fact which should be included. But I can easily be wrong about this.

Page 324, 5th line. In the fifth line you refer to the President functioning as "Commander-in-Chief of the United States." I think ill-disposed persons might have some fun with this reference. Section 2 of Article II of the Constitution says, "The President shall be Commander in Chief of the Army and Navy of the United States, and of the Militia of the several States, when called into the actual Service of the United States."

Page 327. Has your reference to "Mussolini's puppet Socialist Republic" been checked?

Page 328. At the bottom of the page you refer again to the Himmler proposal, which is discussed in a good deal of detail on pages 147(d) and (e).

Page 342 and 343. This is very good, and exactly the sort of exposition of your own wisdom and views which I hope to see more of in the next volume.

Page 345 et seq. I suppose that this narrative of your discussion with Churchill about the differences of opinion as to the course of American military advance after the collapse of the German Armies has been carefully checked with Churchill's last volume. As I recall it, he makes quite a point of this, and I only suggest it to be sure that nothing has been overlooked.

Page 371. In talking about the decision to curtail lend-lease presented to you by [Leo T.] Crowley and [Joseph C.] Grew, is it necessary or excessively honest [Truman staff annotation: "ly" crossed out, "y" added to "honest," thus "excessive honesty"] for you to say in the last sentence of the second paragraph, "I reached for my pen, and without reading the document, I signed it."? I suppose the answer turns on whether Crowley and Grew had already fully explained to you the contents of the document. If they had done so, and I am sure that they would do so honestly, then is it necessary to say that you did not read the document? Perhaps the real heart of the matter lies not in not reading the document, but in not taking more time for reflection and for discussion with others, who might have presented different views. If I am right about this, I think you could quite properly leave out the phrase, "without reading the document."

On the rest of this page and on the next page or two you give the impression that the real impact of your decision was on the Russians, and that if more time had been taken it would not appear as if somebody had been deliberately snubbed. It seems to me that the real impact of this was on the British, and that a great many of their later financial troubles came from the very severe foreign exchange pressure which the curtailing of lend-lease placed upon them at a time when they were unable to revive their exports. I think it would be wise to reconsider this and perhaps rewrite these pages from that point of view. So far as the Russians were concerned, I think the trouble was merely a matter of appearances. So far as the British were concerned, it went to the very heart of their economic life.

Page 396. In the middle of the page please eliminate the words "native governments" and substitute "national governments." These people resent the word "native."

Page 400. Is the third paragraph about Churchill's motives correct or necessary. I do not remember the situation, but from the preceding narrative it does not necessarily appear that he was motivated in the least by the desire to maintain British influence. It seems rather that he was urging that action should be taken in the Adriatic before the situation got out of hand. The narrative seems to me somewhat better without this paragraph in.

All of these pages of criticism must give you the impression that my whole attitude is critical. This it most certainly is not. I think the book is good, interesting, and, as I said before, will give vast numbers of people an understanding of you which they could not have in any other way. I have necessarily directed myself to things that seem to need change.

I am now at work on the second volume. I find much less to comment on, and shall hope to get something off to you about it by the end of the week.

With warm regards.

Most sincerely,

Dean

P.S. Since writing the above, I have come across two matters in the second volume which relate to the first one.

First, I note that on page 530 in listing the Cabinet you refer to Miss Frances Perkins, which supports my theory as to her proper title.

Second, on page 535 you mention the appointment of Jimmy Byrnes. In the third paragraph of that page, talking about it, I think what you say is inconsistent with what you say on page 36 of the first volume. Page 535 seems to support my recollection set forth above regarding what you told me. I think you will want to read these two pages together and bring them into harmony.

Acheson continues his critique of Year of Decisions, *the first volume of Truman's memoirs. His reference to "the second volume" indicates the second bound portion of the* Year of Decisions *manuscript.*

June 24, 1955

Dear Mr. President:

I have now read the second volume through Chapter 28, that is, through page 758. I am getting off this letter to you today so that you will have most of my comments on the two volumes well before June 30th. In fact, on the second volume I have very few comments. It is most interesting and well put together.

On this volume the main concern which you might have is one on which I can not be of any help. This is whether you have taken into account the other material in the field, such as the books of Byrnes, Churchill, and Eisenhower, as well as the voluminous documents which you yourself have and many of which you quote.

Page 487. You begin again the discussion about the withdrawal of our troops to their zone of occupation and the difference of opinion with Churchill which arose about this. A good many of the telegrams on this subject appear in the first volume of the manuscript, which I have now returned to you. I think you will find these on page 345 and the following pages. Without the first volume before me, I cannot recall whether there is a sound reason for dividing the discussion and the documents in this way. Might it not be better to bring all of the earlier discussion into Chapter 19?

The discussion in Chapter 19 then proceeds to the settlement or lack of settlement of our rights in Berlin and thus involves, although it does not discuss, the reasons and responsibility for the nebulous situation which resulted, and which later somewhat obscured the legal questions involved in the blockade of Berlin. It may be that this question of who should have done what and when about our rights of access to Berlin is still up in the air where perhaps it has to remain. At any rate I did not get any new, clearer ideas about this from your narrative in Chapter 19. I think to the reader of this narrative Churchill seems to come off best. He appears to have sensed the need for maintaining our forward positions and of [for] delaying the fulfillment of our obligation to retire to the zone of occupation until the Russians had fulfilled their obligations and made satisfactory arrangements. Our position impresses the reader as being somewhat rigid—that is, we had agreed to retire and, therefore, we were going to retire—without full consideration of the necessity for reciprocal fulfillment of obligations on the other side. I have no suggestions to make about this, because I do not know enough about the facts. From Marshall's telegram on page 501 it looks as though Eisenhower did about what he was directed to do. But again I do not know. I merely think that this should be noted and perhaps carefully reviewed by your staff and you.

My remaining comments are few and minor.

Page 532. Here you recount your first meetings with Miss Perkins at the time you were presiding judge of the Jackson County Court. I think you have already done this at about page 150 of the first volume.

Page 538. You say that today "there are nine members of the Cabinet." Isn't it true that the addition of Health, Education and Welfare brings the number to ten?

Page 539. It seems to me that the second paragraph on this page rather over-simplifies your relations with Cabinet members and gives the impression that "everything" was put on the table at Cabinet meetings. Your main point on this page is the difference between your practice and that of President Roosevelt, and this is very true indeed. But I think it might be well to expand this paragraph, to make the reader aware that many important questions were thrashed out at meetings of less than the full Cabinet; for instance, in the reprint of my *Yale Review* article of October which I sent to you, in discussing the NSC, I point out that this is not an operating agency with powers of decision, but is merely a meeting of the President with certain selected members of the Cabinet whose functions relate more particularly to national security. This same method of discussing matters with selected members was frequently employed by you.

One outstanding example, which you will undoubtedly come to later, was in the relief of General MacArthur, where you selected Marshall, Harriman, Bradley, and me for that discussion. The fact remains, as you well bring out, that in all these cases the decision is the decision of the President, the Cabinet officers acting merely as advisers.

Page 561. On the third line from the bottom, in referring to the people with you at the table at Potsdam, you mention "Davies." I suggest that you identify him as Joseph Davies, the former Ambassador to the Soviet Union.

Page 712. In the last half of the last sentence of the second paragraph, you say "and the American people, their President included, wanted nothing more in that summer of 1945, than to end the fighting and bring the boys back home." This seems to me an unfortunate sentence. You do not mean it literally. As this whole part of the book brings out, there were things which you wanted more than to end the fighting and to bring the boys back home. These were to end the fighting under proper conditions and to do your best to bring about a stable and just peace. Might it be better to say "and the American people, their President included, were unwilling to engage in new military operations unless the national interests of the United States clearly demanded them"?

These are all the suggestions which I have up to Chapter 30. I shall finish the volume over the weekend and write you on Monday as to whether or not I have any further suggestions.

Let me say again how much I like this second volume. All involved have done a very fine job indeed in writing it.

With warm regards.

Sincerely yours,

Dean

Acheson concludes his critique of the second portion of Year of Decisions. *At the end of this letter he congratulates Truman on his June 24 speech at a commemorative session of the United Nations at the Opera House in San Francisco, where the United Nations Charter had been signed ten years earlier. "The United Nation," Truman said, "is a beacon of hope to a world that has no choice but to live together or to die together."*

June 27, 1955

Dear Mr. President:

Over the weekend I finished the second manuscript volume of your book and continued to think that it is a very good job indeed. My comments are very few and only one of them seems to have any real importance.

Page 776. The last paragraph at the bottom of the page. Wouldn't it be better to eliminate the first two sentences of this paragraph and begin with the third sentence, starting "Winston Churchill had on several occasions, etc."? The first two sentences say that part of the British economic difficulties came from the fact that they had come to depend on lend-lease and that it was a very painful operation to sever this tie. The British had come to depend on American economic assistance because they had to. The war had cut off their exports which were their principal earning power. If Britain were to play her essential role in the Grand Alliance, she would have to have assistance until she could reconvert from war to civilian production and regain her export markets. As you point out, the British loan was a recognition of this and the Marshall Plan later on was an even greater one. The two sentences which I criticize give the impression that the British found it more convenient to live on our help and that it was painful to them to cut it off. I think that it was really more painful to receive it than to cut it off, and these observations have nothing to do with the story which the remainder of the paragraph and the following pages bring out.

Page 785, second paragraph, last two sentences. Here again, wouldn't it be better to eliminate these two sentences and join the first sentence of this paragraph with the last paragraph on the page? The first of these two sentences is not very clear, because I do not know just what you mean by the sterling area resuming "trade on a multilateral basis." The sterling area was conducting trade within the area on a multilateral basis. The difficulty arose in trade between the sterling area and the dollar area. Here the sterling area had to limit dollar purchases to the most important items and this, of course, resulted in discriminations. The dollar loan eased this situation but did not eliminate it, as the last sentence in the paragraph seems to suggest. In fact there were specific provisions in the loan agreement which permitted the continuance of discrimination under certain circumstances. It is true, and I think the last paragraph brings this out, that the dollar loan was intended to ease the situation and to enable the British to move gradually towards its total elimination, a condition at which they have not yet arrived.

Page 798. This page raises a delicate situation, which I mention with hesitation, but I know you will not take offense. Any autobiography necessitates the continual use of the first person pronoun. It is worth some ingenuity to reduce the occurrence of this, and through a large part of the book it isn't noticeable at all. This page, however, brings the problem out rather forcibly. The pronoun occurs eleven times on this one page. I mention this not for this page alone but in order that you might have it in mind when you have a final review of the whole manuscript for style.

Page 808. On line four the Brookings Institution is referred to as the Brookings Institute.

Page 898–902. These pages contain the crucial part of the crisis with Jimmy Byrnes over the Moscow Conference. At the bottom of page 898 you refer to the substance of the errors which Byrnes had committed at Moscow, and this begins with Rumania and Bulgaria. "We had agreed," you say, "to sit down with Rumania and Bulgaria to write peace treaties," whereas they had violated all decent standards about elections. Again you say, "Yet Byrnes had agreed to let the Russians have their way about peace settlements with these nations." Later on you mention his failure to take a vigorous attitude in regard to Iran.

Now it seems to me that in regard to Rumania and Bulgaria you are not on very strong ground and that it may be well to leave that with the reference which occurs in your contemporaneous letter and not mention Rumania and Bulgaria as a count in the indictment on pages 898–899. I say this because your complaints against Jimmy Byrnes seem to me to be proved and to be strong when you talk about his failure to keep you advised, resulting in the troubles with Vandenberg and the misunderstanding of what he was doing on atomic energy. They also seem to me strong when you talk about Iran. But the record on Rumania and Bulgaria is not so good. In the first place, it does not seem fair to say that Jimmy had agreed to let the Russians have their way. The Communique establishes a Council of Ministers on which Harriman was to sit, to provide for free elections, civil liberties, and matters of that sort; and the recognition and peace treaties were to come after that. Of course, the Russians did not live up to their agreements, but nevertheless on February 5, 1946, the Government sent a note setting up the substance and procedure for the Council of Ministers (which is reported in *Department of State Bulletin,* XIV, page 256) and on February 15 we recognized the Rumanian Government, as appears on page 298 of the same volume. Later on notes of protest were sent. While I have not looked up a record on Bulgaria, I imagine it was about the same. So far as the peace treaties were concerned, the Moscow Agreement merely said you would write the peace treaties, not what they should contain.

So I think, with this record of action taken in February, presumably under your direction, Jimmy Byrnes, who is both able and consistent, can tear your account to pieces on this particular item. With this in mind, the paragraph beginning on page 898 and the following paragraph on page 899 should be revised, eliminating Bulgaria and Rumania and making more of Iran and the embarrassments caused to you in connection with atomic energy by your complete lack of information from Moscow.

My congratulations on the book. I hope it isn't taking too much out of you. Surely, if you need a little more time for polishing, the *Life* people after they see the text should be so pleased with it that they will be amenable.

I have heard from Charley [Murphy] and Dave [Lloyd] excellent reports about your reception and speech in San Francisco. It is wonderful that everything went so well and it must have made you very happy.

With affectionate regards.

Most sincerely yours,

Dean

Truman refers here to the actual second volume of his manuscript, Years of Trial and Hope.

June 30, 1955

Dear Dean:

I am eternally grateful to you for your comments on the manuscript which we have sent you.

I am sending you the second volume and while the turnover has been made corrections will be possible before the books are published so if you can take time out to get back to me as quickly as possible it will be a very great accommodation.

I am in debt to you eternally, as I said before, and you will have a long "sob sister letter" as soon as I can get around to it.

Sincerely yours,

Harry S. Truman

Truman sends Acheson a copy of a letter he'd sent to Joseph Jones, former State Department official and author of The Fifteen Weeks. *Despite earlier problems with Jones, Truman liked the book. "I have only one statement to make," Truman wrote Jones, "and that is that you are entirely too kind to me." He was pleased with Jones's treatment in the book of Acheson and George Marshall—"two wonderful men."*

July 6, 1955

Dear Dean:

I am enclosing you a copy of a letter which I have written to Joseph M. Jones.

As soon as I can manage it, I will sit down and write you a long letter, which you are due to receive, and I hope, in spite of the fact that it may be too long, that you will read it.

Sincerely yours,

Harry

My best to Alice. You've no idea how you helped us.

His work on the manuscript finished, Truman celebrates with a few caustic remarks about Eisenhower and Dulles. But Truman still wanted Acheson's review of the draft of the second volume of the memoirs. Wilmer Waller was treasurer of the Truman Library. "Foster" was President Benjamin Harrison's Secretary of State, John W. Foster, who was also John Foster Dulles's grandfather. Wayne Morse's joke about General Grant was that Eisenhower was such a bad President he made Grant look good, Grant being the notoriously worst President in U.S. history because of venality and corruption in his administration.

July 9, 1955

Dear Dean:

I'm sitting here in this Shah carpeted office in the Federal Reserve Bank Building after finishing an answer to the last accumulated letter. Those letters piled up to three or four feet and they worried me no end and you know that I'm a hard one to worry.

The damned book or the cussed manuscript has been accepted by the contractor (Time, Inc.) and I've paid [Wilmer] Waller the note which you witnessed in the National Bank of Washington. Now I've employed Peat, Marwick and Mitchell to see that Brownell and Humphrey et al do not send me to Leavenworth or Atlanta. I sort of wish I'd let the history of the period lie dormant because when these two volumes of mine come out, Ike, Stevenson and several others are going into conniption fits and I'm going to Timbuktu or Bali. I really believe I'll take Bali in spite of my seventy-one years!

I'm eternally grateful to you for your suggestions and corrections. In fact, never can I meet the obligation I owe you for recent actions and for what you did as Asst. Sec. of State, Acting Sec. of State and the greatest Secretary of State of them all. And, Dean, I know the history of every one of them from Jefferson in Washington's cabinet to date. Even including an old man named Foster, who served nine months & five days with old Ben Harrison. His grandson is having a hard time living up to grandpa's no reputation with another Ben! I fear that he'll make a statesman out of old Dan Webster or Jim Buchanan. You know what Wayne Morse said on "Meet the Press" when asked Ike's most outstanding accomplishment. He said Ike had made a great President out of General Grant. I'm in agreement on both propositions and can make a G.E.D. on either one. I've made up my mind to accept Lord Halifax's invitation to Oxford.

So you're elected for another U.N. suggestion. Wish you could have been in San Francisco. You'd have thought I'd been nominated by another Democratic Convention. They gave me an ovation when I came in, another one when introduced and wouldn't quit when I came to the end of the speech. Dulles and Molotov held their hands behind their backs. Mrs. Henry Grady was watching both from the gallery. But Molly came to the U.N. reception for the foreign ministers for me— and Dulles didn't! Lodge came to the reception but yawned every time he had to stand for me! What a show! I watched both Molly and Dully during the delivery but I couldn't see 'em when they were supposed to stand. Spectators reported their actions.

I read Joe Jones galley proof. It is a dandy and I so wrote him. I told him he gave me too much house and you not enough. He really gave Hull and Byrnes their comeuppance!

You've stood enough. My best to Alice. Wish you both would come and see us again. That was a most pleasant occasion for the Boss & me.

Sincerely,

Harry

Acheson begins his critique of the second volume of the memoirs, titled Years of Trial and Hope. *The McMahon Act he refers to is the Atomic Energy*

Act of 1946, which, among other things, forbade the sharing of atomic secrets with other nations and spurred the United Kingdom to develop its own atomic-energy program.

July 11, 1955

Dear Mr. President:

I received last week the first manuscript part of Volume II and this morning the second part. I am putting as much time as I can in on them, but other matters press on me and I am not as free as I should be for so large a task as over 800 typewritten pages. Could you let me know what the time schedule is? Whatever I do will have to be finished, I presume, before the 15th of August, when Alice and I go off for a month or six weeks visiting in Europe. Would it be useful for you if I send back, say, two hundred pages at a time with some suggestions noted on the manuscript and a covering letter? Or do you want me to wait until I have read through the whole second volume? For instance, in Chapter 1 of Volume II the "I" problem becomes rather acute. I have gone through making suggestions for solving this problem. I could continue doing this in other chapters, which would take a lot of time. Perhaps, with the suggestions I have made, someone in Kansas City could go through, adopting the same technique. What is your wish about this?

I also note in Volume II, Chapter 1, that on page 26 the story of our discussion with the British about cooperation in atomic energy breaks off right in the middle. Perhaps it is resumed later on. If so, I have not come to it. At any rate, it seems to me that at this point it should be carried at least to the point where the matter became more or less settled in accordance with the inhibitions placed upon us by the McMahon Act. This would involve the modus vivendi worked out by Bob Lovett about December '47 or January '48, the attempts to carry on cooperative exchanges within the McMahon Act, which broke down in 1948 or early 1949, and the final effort, which I think was in 1949, culminating in the Blair House meeting and the blow-up of the joint Congressional committee to get some amendment to the law to permit real cooperation. The result of our inability was to start the British on their present atomic energy work. Whether this is good or bad from the point of view of the total effort, I don't know enough to say. It is certainly the direct result of the McMahon Act.

Something along this line should be introduced at the end of Chapter 1, which now leaves the whole matter hanging.

I also have a general comment about Chapter 2 and another about Chapter 3. Both of these chapters seem to me pretty heavy going and in neither case does the heavy going end up by rewarding the reader as much as it might.

For instance, in the last part of Chapter 2 there is a running account of the back and forth battle which you waged for price controls immediately after the war. In and of itself, no one cares much about this, and the text does not give the reader any reason why he should care. But, if it is true, as I think it is, that the greater part of the inflation arising out of World War II came in these postwar years and if it came in whole or in part as a result of your losing this battle with the Congress, then this story is very significant to the average reader, because it explains why his dollar is worth only from one-half to two-thirds of what it was before. I don't know enough economics to know whether what I say is right or not. But, if it is right, this ought to go in at the beginning of the price control section to make the story much more significant than it now is. If what I say is not true, then this story is not very significant anyway, and it should be greatly cut.

Chapter 3 on the budget, I think, is too long and rambling. I haven't any specific suggestions as yet and perhaps will not have, because this is not my cup of tea. Somehow I don't think that a general exposition of budgetary principles adds a great deal to your autobiography. I merely raise a red flag about this chapter now.

I am so glad that you found my earlier comments on Volume I useful.

With warm regards.

Most sincerely,

Dean

Acheson continues his critique of the second volume of the memoirs. This is his most blunt and negative letter about Truman's memoirs, in particular his comments about Truman's account of the recognition of Israel. He rebuts Truman's linkage of the Balfour Declaration, which stated the British government's support for the establishment in Palestine of a national home for the Jews, with the principle of self-determination as put forward by Woodrow Wilson. Acheson wanted Truman to eliminate this idea from his memoirs. Truman rejected this recommendation. "I discussed the nature of [Acheson's] criticisms with the President this morning, July 21st,"

Truman's chief writer, Francis Heller, recorded, "and he confirmed once again his firm belief in the principle of self-determination and in his belief that the Balfour Declaration was a manifestation of this principle." Heller thought Acheson's comments reflected a "pro-Arab point of view."

July 18, 1955

Dear Mr. President:

First of all, thank you very much indeed for your grand letter of July 9th [*sic*]. It took a little extra time getting to me, and for a rather interesting reason—the special delivery stamp. This short-circuited the Georgetown branch post office, which knew we were not at P Street and has been forwarding mail to the office. So your letter was dropped through the door of an empty house and stayed there for several days. That only increased our pleasure at its contents.

Secondly, the book I have finished the first manuscript volume of Volume II and am mailing it back to you today. In this volume I have written a host of suggestions onto the pages of the manuscript and will here only mention those that don't lend themselves to this treatment or which need explanation.

The comments, outside the manuscript, on Chapters 1 and 2 are in my letter of July 11. They still seem sound to me. I have only one other minor one.

Page 8. Here there are three numbered paragraphs in your letter to Senator McMahon. These paragraphs are almost identical—the points made in them are identical—with the similar paragraphs on pages 5 and 6, in your memorandum to the Secretaries of War and Navy. A suggestion which you might wish to consider is eliminating the three numbered paragraphs on page 8 and inserting a note reading as follows: "(The letter then set forth in the same order the three points made in the foregoing memorandum to the Secretaries of War and Navy, in approximately the same language. It then continued:)"

Chapter 3. I wish that this could be cut, but don't feel qualified to try. 22 pages is too much for this material. Much of it seems elementary and does not sustain the reader's interest. For my own taste the explanation of what a budget is, the procedures, the importance of it, etc., could come out. How you got your special interest as a hobby, almost, is interesting and the actual results of your budgets, important. Couldn't it be reduced by, say, seven pages and still say everything needful?

Specific suggestions:

Pp. 50–51. The marked sentences I would leave out. It raises the whole question of corruption, influence, mink coats, etc., and contributes nothing. As for "experts" being in charge of law and finance, the Department of Justice was the weakest spot in the Democratic administrations for twenty years, and my guess is that it was under Bob Hannegan in the Bureau of Internal Revenue, that so much of the monkey business, for which you paid later on, got its start. The sentences marked ask for trouble without settling it.

P. 62, first paragraph. I just don't understand what is meant by this. Other readers may be in the same fix.

P. 69, bottom. This is a puzzling explanation. The Treasury furnished the money to the R.F.C. [Reconstruction Finance Corporation]. If it competed with banks, so did the Treasury regardless of where the R.F.C. was located on the chart of organization. The idea of R.F.C. loans was that it did not compete with the banks because it made loans which were needed but which banks would not and could not risk.

P. 93, bottom. I don't think this is right. The effect a policy is likely to have is an inherent part in devising and recommending the policy. The C.I.A. is not the Presidential adviser on the effects of policies. This is the State Department. The illustration does not illustrate; it confuses. It ought to come out, leaving the exposition solely on Intelligence.

Pp. 95 and 97–98. The paragraphs are duplicates. The later one can well come out. Anything not in the earlier one can be there.

Pp. 104 and 113. Was the final meeting with Marshall re China on December 14 or 15? My recollection is the latter and the letter handed to him is dated December 15.

There is a story that after this meeting Marshall stayed behind when we had gone and asked you whether his instructions meant that when the chips were down we were for Chiang and would support him, and, so the story goes, you said, "Yes." Is this true? If so, it is of some significance, possibly that he thought the written instructions were equivocal. Marshall never mentioned this to me, and I only heard the story a year ago from Herbert Feis. Where he got it, I don't know.

Somewhere in the chapter on China, perhaps on page 103, where you say, "China appeared now to be headed for more trouble," it might be helpful and revealing to the reader to bring in General Wedemeyer's recommendations made in November 1945—shortly after V-J Day. They are, I believe, printed in full in the China White Paper and are summarized on pages 8, 9, and 10 of my little pamphlet, which you have, "American Policy Toward China," dated June 4, 1951. These bring out very clearly the limitations and conditions of the Generalissimo's capabilities. It was his failure to realize these which brought about his downfall; and when General Wedemeyer states them, we really have the opposition speaking.

On page 116 I have made some notes on the manuscript which I expand here. The first paragraph is a puzzling one as it is written. The fighting in China was clearly the result of the political differences. To say that Marshall's view of his mission was to bring the fighting to an end and yet avoid political matters is a non sequitur. Wasn't his view rather that his best chance of effectiveness was to restrict his mediation to those matters which could be said to have a military aspect? The truce was one of these, so was the vital politico-military question of how the military forces in a united China should be organized; what their size should be, and what should be the Nationalist Communist ratio. This was highly political and went to the very root of power. I think it would be well to spell out the substance of his suggestion here, since it was a most important one. If adopted, it would have carried out vast reduction in men under arms, would have created a military power five-sixths Nationalist in composition, the command of which would have been in a government headed by Chiang Kai-shek. These talks were great and delicate ones, and I believe that General Marshall felt that all of his good will would be used up in accomplishing this and that his best chance for agreement on other political measures was, not through mediation, but through encouraging the two major parties and the independent parties to compromise.

The last paragraph on page 116 also bothers me. It raises the question whether Marshall agreed with the Communist appraisal of the situation. My guess is that he did not because, if he did, he was playing into their hands.

My worry would be eliminated if the middle of it read: "And it was his impression that the Communists were more ready to take their chances in a struggle conducted in the political arena than were the Nationalists. The Nationalists so it seemed to Marshall, appeared to be determined to pursue a policy of force which he believed would be their undoing."

Chapter 7. Pages 148–149. The first paragraph and the first sentence of the second bother me. In the first place, are you sure of the facts? Was such a message sent to Stalin? If it was, and since you quote other important messages, I think you should quote this one. If you do not have the message, do you know that it was sent and, if so, what it said? Unless your anecdote about the message can be supported one hundred percent by documents, I strongly urge leaving it out. It gives an impression of impetuous and not too well considered judgment. Would we really have moved into Iran and, if so, with what? What would the United Nations have said, and how would this square with your support of the UN? What would our allies have said? Furthermore, was Stalin a man to respond to messages of this sort? I should not have thought so. Please reconsider this paragraph.

At the bottom of page 148 and on page 149, you jump from Iran directly into the delivery of the message to Congress on Greece and Turkey on March 12, 1947. As a literary device, this seems to me a mistake. It gives the impression of a two-gun man in the White House shooting with both hands in all directions at the same time. You tell Stalin off at the top of the page. You are on the rostrum of the House, intervening in Greece and Turkey, without any explanation at the bottom of the page. Things didn't happen that way and you didn't decide things that way. I think these paragraphs, as indicated in the manuscript, should come out, and you should go along more calmly with the development of the Greek-Turkish story. Perhaps the transition could be something like this: "It was not long before the same issue was presented to us again in the same part of the world." And then pick up the story at the bottom of page 149.

Page 151. In the middle of the page you mention the Turkish request for advice when they received the notice from the Soviets on the Straits, and say, "I instructed Acheson to inform the Turks, etc." Again this does not do you justice. It sounds as though you read the telegram and barked out the orders without more ado. It was in fact far more complicated, and an example of the very thorough governmental administration which you conducted. The whole story is spelled out in Joe Jones's galley proof. What you did was to direct State, War, and Navy to study the matter. This was done smoothly and quickly and resulted in a unanimous recommendation which was brought to you at a meeting where the Secretaries of the three departments and the Chiefs of Staff were all present. General Eisenhower was Chief of Staff. It was all thoroughly discussed with you. I remember your pulling the big map out of your desk drawer and entering in a most impressive way into the discussion of the strategy of power in the Middle East. You approved the recommendation. We then coordinated our views with our allies and ended up with a strong position, which was communicated to the Turks. At the same time they received similar views and support from the British and French. This is a much more impressive story than what appears on page 151.

Page 155, last sentence of next to last paragraph. You say that the British note on Greece and Turkey stated that they would take all their troops out of Greece. My rather clear recollection is that this is not right. I think again you will find this discussed in Joe Jones's galleys. My recollection is that the note was silent on this point and that Marshall took it up personally and orally with the Ambassador, who reported that the British were planning to take their troops out as soon as this could be conveniently done and that, after some talk back and forth, we got them to delay it for a considerable space of time.

Page 189, first paragraph. This discussion of the currency problem does not seem right, and this is important, because the currency problem was pretty close to being the heart of the Berlin issue at the outset. In other words, although the Russians undoubtedly had embarked upon a program of making our occupation of Berlin difficult by harassments, it was the introduction of our currency into West Berlin which really produced action on their part. You give the impression that the row arose because the Russians were counterfeiting our money and did not want to stop. It may be that the trouble over the plates continued until 1948, but it was my recollection that we had stopped that some time before by changing the plates. I think that the real difficulty was much deeper. The reformed West German currency was good currency; the Eastmark was not. Since the Eastmark would not be legal tender in West Berlin, everybody wanted the good currency, which was ours; and this was producing difficulty for the Russians, both in East Berlin and in East Germany. The blockade was their first response to this economic threat. After it had started, I think their ideas grew and they began to see the possibility that the blockade might get us out of Berlin altogether. But the beginning of it was economic and I do not think this has been adequately explained at the point noted.

Page 191. For the reasons given immediately above, your explanation of the reason for the blockade of Berlin seem to me incorrect. Again you oversimplify. I think the Russians blundered into the blockade, rather than choosing it as their counter-attack.

Page 201, bottom. It is a small point, but as I recall it, [Howard] Kingsbury Smith had written out the questions which Stalin answered, or questions something like them, quite a while before and had left them with the Foreign Office. I do not think that the interview was by telegram. The practice which I have suggested would, of course, have been a good one with the Communists, since, by it, they always had questions on hand which they could answer when it suited them to do so. I assume that, if they changed a question a little, the favored correspondent would not complain.

The paragraph beginning at the bottom of page 202 condenses some protracted negotiations, and I think condenses them incorrectly. As I recall it, one of the principal items in the reply by [Jacob A.] Malik [Soviet representative to the United Nations at the time of the Berlin crisis, 1948–49] was that the West should call off its actions to create the West German Government. I can look this up if you want me to, but I remember my conferences and standing very firm on this issue.

Chapter 10. I shall restrict comments on this chapter, because I never was enthusiastic about the policy and, therefore, am not a sympathetic critic. Some things, however, seem clearly wrong.

Page 206. You say that the Balfour declaration has always seemed to you to go hand-in-hand with the noble principles of Woodrow Wilson, especially with the principle of self-determination. It seems to me that if there was one principle in the world which was absolutely and directly violated by the Balfour Declaration and the resulting policy it was the principle of self-determination. Self-determination, I believe, would entitle the Arabs living in Palestine to decide whether they wanted to be inundated by Jews. Instead, what was done was to bring the Jews in over the objections of the Arabs. However noble the policy may have been, it certainly was not one justified by self-determination. The whole sentence, which I have noted, could be profitably eliminated.

Page 208, next to last paragraph. Here self-determination crops up again. Isn't it enough that commonsense and fairness required that the Arabs, as well as the Jews, should be consulted, without [b]ringing in self-determination?

In the last paragraph on this page and several times thereafter you say that you believed the solution in Palestine should be reached peaceably. Looking at this from the point of view opposed to yours, the statement has a sanctimonious ring. Of course you wanted the solution to be peaceably reached, but you insisted that the solution should be the immigration of Jews. This was what the Arabs were not prepared to accept peaceably. Therefore, what you are saying is that you thought the Arabs should surrender rather than fight for what they regarded as their country. I think you can make a good enough argument for your case without this sort of assistance. Therefore, I am for eliminating your hopes for peaceable solutions of an issue where the line of policy precluded it.

Page 242. On this page, again, we have American policy designed to bring about by peaceful means the establishment of the promised Jewish homeland. This occurs in the second paragraph and it occurs in the next to last paragraph. The next to last paragraph really shocks me, and I hope it can be eliminated. You say the simple fact is that our policy was an American policy. The reason that it was an American policy was that it was aimed at a peaceful elimination of a world trouble spot. Really this seems to me to go too far. Advocacy is one thing, but this is not advocacy. Would this policy, which you say was American policy, have been ours if there were no Jews in the United States? Please leave out these instances when you protest too much.

Page 254. The last sentence of the first paragraph I hope you will take out. I know the officers who worked on the Palestine question and can honestly say that I do not think that they were anti-Semitic. They were irritated just as you say you were, at the Zionist pressure tactics and blew up about this from time to time. A part of the pressure was to insinuate that those who advised contrary to Zionist wishes were anti-Semitic. But it seems unfair to them to add the great weight of your authority to the charge.

Chapter XIII. Here, Mr. President, I shall try your patience and good nature. The part up to and through page 277 should—I strongly urge—be wholly re-written. To me it does not ring true at all. The very opening words are all wrong—"If I had consulted my personal impulse . . . I should have made plans to leave the White House at the end of my first term." This is not the fighting man that we all loved and love and who led the damnedest knock-down and drag-out in political history. The first thirteen pages do not impress the reader as Harry Truman speaking but as someone writing what Horatio Alger might have said under the circumstances.

I don't believe your "impulse"—what one of my partners calls your "gut reaction"—was concerned with F.D.R.'s unfinished business, or the danger from reaction, or the state of world affairs. These were, of course, the important background. 1948 was not 1924. But all of these intellectual considerations were applicable also in 1952, when your decision was different.

The truth seems to be nearer this: Your first term was brought about by the accident of death. You had never sought the job, you didn't want it. You hadn't been elected to it. But you had it and you tackled it as hard and conscientiously as you tackled everything. After a brief honeymoon, the tough boys wrote you off as of no account. They flouted your policies and began to reverse FDR's as hard as they could. They won the Congress in 1946. They overrode your vetoes. The press belittled you. The pollsters said you hadn't a chance. Many of your own party went back on you. Reaction seemed to them to be in full swing. It was all personified in the 80th Congress.

You have never run from a fight in your life. You knew damn well that the everyday American believed in what FDR and you had stood for. Your Dutch, or Irish, or Missouri was up. You believed Americans would respond to fighting leadership and to the facts stated simply and powerfully. If the tough boys wanted a fight—and they didn't even believe there would be one—you would give them the goll-darndest fight they had ever had. You might get licked—you didn't think so, but you might—but, if you did, the other guys would go to the Inaugural Ball with the biggest pair of shiners seen around these parts since Old Hickory put away his shillelagh.

This sounds like you and like the truth. What has been written does not. It is too rational, too reluctant, too pious. The "I never struck a blow except in defense of a woman" sort of thing. And the historical business on pages 268, 269, seems dragged in. You would have fought in '48 as no President ever had before.

Much of the stuff on the later pages about the press, Congress, etc., is usable and good, but in a more fiery setting. However, the statement on page 277 that your trip was not meant to be political; but nonpartisan; you were not even a candidate, will seem to the reader insincere. Even in professional parlance, it squeaks by on the narrowest and most technical definition of "political." You were not on a lecture tour and you were running in the way in which at this stage a shrewd candidate had to run.

Please put away the club you have out for me and rewrite these pages.

If you do, then the latter part of the chapter about the impending splits in the party by which you lost your right and left wings can be pointed up to their important and great significance. They were infinitely more courageous decisions for a man who was going to pay the price for them and who wanted passionately to win, than they would have been for a retiring President or for a man who had no realization of their political consequences. It took cold nerve to do what you did, as you show later on by the fact that Ohio had the deciding votes.

Chapter XIV. There are minor notes on the manuscript.

Pages 292–29L as marked. I would omit this. Almost everyone has become familiar with the workings of national conventions through television. These pages slow the story.

Pages 294–5. 295–6. I strongly urge the omission of these conversations with Douglas, instead merely stating that you made him the offers and that, after considering them, he decided to remain on the Court. It is bad for the Court and for you to have reported this sort of back and forth between a President and a Justice. It will offend many people—it gives me a shudder—and it does no good.

Pages 298–326. Here again I am going to step on your toes. These pages ought to come out. I do not think they are good either as a literary device by which you review your predecessors, or on the merits. And they slow up the story.

As a literary device they strain credulity. It may be that with a critically important speech to make from notes only, you did not think about it, but reviewed in detail the fortunes of every President of the United States. I am sure no one will believe it. Every few pages you have to reassert the improbable fact that you did (pp. 298, 304, 308, 309, 310, 317, 319, 323, 325). The effect is forced, like someone trying to entertain [at] a dinner when the guest speaker is late or the hour for radio has not arrived.

On the merits, the material is open to the criticism that there is very little of your own views and opinions, which a reader would want to know, and a good deal of elementary history—that Washington presided over the Constitutional Convention, etc.,—which everyone knows. Nor does all of this historical review lead anywhere; no conclusions emerge. The reader feels stuck on the fly paper for thirty pages.

My suggestion is this: Take these pages out of the book. They don't belong here at all. Save them, and later on, when your income tax is not so much of a problem, do them over into articles—"Harry Truman Sizes Up His Predecessors." This would take a little more work than you [have] done on these thirty pages, but ought to make at least three good articles for which you should be well paid.

Don't give the customers too much in this book—which is about you and not your predecessors.

Pages 342–357. The Vinson "Mission" to Russia. [Truman had planned to send Chief Justice Fred M. Vinson to Moscow as his personal emissary to Stalin to break the deadlock over Berlin, but the mission was halted.] These pages do not—to this reader—come off. They seem disingenuous, not wholly frank, unconvincing.

The theme is that the Vinson mission had nothing to do with politics, was a good idea as foreign policy, and was spoiled by misunderstanding. Is this supportable?

In the first place, no one will believe that it had nothing to do with politics. If, in fact, it did, why be ashamed of it? The present meeting at the summit had everything to do with politics. Winston proposed it on May 11, 1953, as an answer to the Labor Party's charges of war mongering. He completely spiked their guns by his speech, and the Conservatives probably won the election by ensuring that it would take place.

If Wallace's attacks were giving liberals and middle-of-the-roaders the idea that you would not negotiate, a gesture to prove them wrong would have been perfectly proper politics.

So why defend ground which is nearly indefensible and unnecessary to defend?

Second, as to the mission, I did not understand it at the time, and the account does not help me. The issue in the autumn of 1948 between the Russians and us was Berlin. What was Fred [Vinson] to do about that and what effect would the proposal of the mission have upon the firmness of our position? Not a word is said about Berlin. The "big" issue you speak of on pages 341–4, 347 is control of atomic energy. That was a pretty sick issue by that time.

The analogy of Lord Reading has, to be sure, one similarity—he was Chief Justice of England. But England was not blockading U.S. forces, and the problems between the two countries were susceptible to method in a way which was not true of USA-USSR relations. I don't think an analogy helps when it suggests more differences than similarities.

Finally, in this text your relations with Marshall on the proposal are not clear. On page 350 you were going to talk with him on "Monday morning before we do anything further." But on Sunday you reached agreement with Vinson, alerted the networks and Lovett. Then came a leak. On page 351, "I had another talk with Secretary Marshall and found him upset over the misrepresentations by other delegates of the purpose of the mission."

One wonders what happened at the first talk and what he thought of the mission apart from misrepresentations.

Might it not be better to cut the whole story down to cover very briefly your purpose (which must I think have taken Berlin into the picture), the political situation, Fred's willingness to go, Marshall's concern, your very proper consideration for that and the abandonment of the idea—say less than half the length it now is?

Page 358. I have suggested a way out of the mixed metaphor of the "ground swell in the grass roots."

Page 362. At the very top of the page, as indicated, the meaning of the sentence is not apparent. How small states get an "equal voice" I don't understand; nor, how the electoral system "saves a lot of trouble" in "abnormal" situations. If this is useful here, it ought to be cleared up.

Pages 379–381. Point 4 is presented in these pages as a capital investment program. But on pages 383, 384, 386, 390, and 393, both the discussion and the appropriations asked for and given concern a technical assistance program. The capital asked for was small, except in India at the end, and was to build pilot or demonstration plants.

Page 380. I suggest eliminating the part about colonialism. Point 4 was not an attack on colonialism and did not operate in colonial areas. What you say on pages 380–1 will only cause hard feelings.

These are a lot of tough criticisms, not calculated to endear the critic. But they call attention to what seem to me to be errors which will harm you. The story except for Chapter III and part of Chapter II is a fine one and holds the reader.

I have almost finished the last volume, pages 396–858, and will start a letter in a day or two.

Most warmly and faithfully,

Dean

P.S. This letter though begun on the 18th is finished and mailed today July 20. D.

Although Truman had already turned over the memoir manuscript to his publisher, he tells Acheson he can still make changes on the galleys. He looks forward to receiving Acheson's comments on the final part of the second volume.

July 19, 1955

Dear Dean:

I found your letter of the 11th on my desk when I returned from Chicago and I certainly do appreciate very much your generosity in helping me polish up this second volume.

I am hoping that if there are any errors of fact you will point them out, and if my recollection of the meaning of the facts at the time they took place has gone askew I know you will set me straight.

I am going over the second volume as carefully as I can but I had to make the turnover on June 30th. We will still have time to make corrections on the galley proofs.

If it is convenient to you to send in the installments of 200 pages, or groups of chapters, that will be very satisfactory to me.

I sincerely hope that you and Mrs. Acheson have the grandest time in the world on that European trip. I'll be in touch with you right along.

It is almost as much satisfaction to get this *Time* contract behind me as it was to get out of the White House and I want to say if it had not been for the help which you and John Snyder, and one or two others, gave me I don't believe I would ever have been able to get it done. Of course, Bill Hillman and Dave Noyes really did a yeoman's job on putting this material together.

Sincerely yours,

Harry S. Truman

You are just too good and too patient.

July 25, 1955

THE HONORABLE HARRY S TRUMAN
AM SENDING YOU TOMORROW A LONG LETTER WITH SUGGESTIONS WHICH I HOPE YOU CAN CONSIDER THE LAST 400 PAGES OF MANUSCRIPT, WHICH I AM ALSO MAILING TO YOU
DEAN ACHESON

Acheson's comments on the last part of Truman's second volume of memoirs deal with General MacArthur's deployments in the Korean War, in violation of orders, which brought in the Chinese intervention and greatly damaged the Truman administration's standing in public opinion. The

"Wake Island meeting" refers to a flight Truman made to Wake Island, in the mid-Pacific, to meet with General MacArthur about the conduct of the Korean War.

July 25, 1955

Dear Mr. President:

I have now finished reading your manuscript and return the last volume with my suggestions.

This manuscript flows along more smoothly than the last one and is most interesting. I congratulate you on it. For your generous references to me, I am profoundly grateful.

My comments are divided into two groups:—minor and stylistic suggestions; and, suggestions going to substance.

The former do not require comment and appear as interlineations on pages 396, 401, 402, 403, 405, 414, 417, 418, 421, 425, 435, 438, 478, 479, 488, 489, 492, 494, 496, 510, 512, 515, 516, 521, 524, 529, 547, 576, 579, 591, 607, 626, 683, 684, 685, 688, 693, 696, 697, 698, 699, 700, 701, 703, 704, 712, 713, 714, 720, 721, 776, 794, 820 (Edward VIII killed that phrase), 821 (unnecessary and meaningless sentence), 828, 838, 841–2 (in the last sentence on the page running over something is left out).

Suggestions dealing with substance:

P. 406. The second paragraph as written seems to contradict the first paragraph. I have made on the page a guess as to what Bevin said.

The last paragraph, as it runs over on 407, can well be cut. It sounds like one of Bob Lovett's more involved efforts and really says nothing. The same is true of the rather trifling and desultory discussion reported on p. 408. What really happened appears at the bottom of 408.

P. 415. It is often and erroneously said that under our constitution the nation cannot commit itself in advance to go to war under specified circumstances. Unless Mr. Bricker changes things, the U.S.A. has in foreign affairs all the powers of sovereignty and can bind itself in any way it chooses. [Senator John W. Bricker sponsored the Bricker amendment limiting treaty power.] The changes indicated save this point without raising the argument.

P. 451. Question: Isn't the reference to parities being forced down inconsistent with what you have said above about the Brannan Plan? For the first time, the Brannan Plan became clear to me in your explanation. But this sentence mixed me up again.

P. 470. I suggest that in view of the Supreme Court's decision in the

Peters case [*Peters v. Hobby,* 1955] you leave these two paragraphs out. The Court decided that under your order the Loyalty Review Board had authority only to review an appeal by the employee. It would be a mistake to cause any new confusion as to what the order provided.

P. 487. The slogans indicated do not seem to me to be "similar" to the others which appealed to intolerance. Shouldn't they come out?

P. 497. I don't understand the last sentence on the page. Shouldn't the sentence read: "How else could you have known that it should not be brought before your Committee unless you saw it and formed your own judgment?" And yet do you mean to imply that in all such cases chairmen of committees should see secret papers? Perhaps the best course is to leave out your reply.

P. 513. Is this classified information? It may now be public knowledge; but I cannot recall reading anywhere the method by which we learn about atomic explosions in Russia.

P. 514. I would leave this out. There is evidence that the Russians are pretty good in scientific development.

P. 525, top. Was the first test thermonuclear shot in March 1951? I had thought that it was still unproven until the November 1952 test.

Pp. 554–557. Blair House meeting on Korea, June 25, 1950. The best account of "Why We Went to War in Korea," is in the *Saturday Evening Post* of November 10, 1951, by Beverly Smith. He wrote it after, by your orders, he had seen all our notes and papers. You should read it and then revise these pages which are skimpy on the greatest story of the 1949–1953 Administration and sometimes not altogether accurate.

To begin with, method—which was one of your strong points—is wholly left out of your story. It was this: Louis Johnson [Secretary of Defense, 1949–50] and Bradley were away, flying back from Tokyo on that Saturday night. Over the phone you told me to get together with the Service Secretaries and the Chiefs of Staff and get working parties started getting recommendations for you when you got back. These obviously could not be cleared with Louis and Brad and so the first order of business after I reported on the state of affairs was to lay out the recommendations for discussion. They formed the framework of the whole evening. It was not, as would seem on page 556, a series of off-the-cuff, disjointed observations.

One other preliminary observation. You did not permit any discussion until dinner was served and over and the Blair House staff had withdrawn. Then you asked me to report on the situation and recommendations. This I did first before anyone made any observations.

The situation report is what you have up to the top of 556. Then I reported the following recommendation for immediate action:

1) That MacArthur should evacuate Americans from Korea—the dependents of the Military Mission, etc.—and, in order to do so, should keep open the Kimpo and other airports, repelling all hostile attacks thereon. In doing this, his air forces should stay south of the 38th Parallel.

2) MacArthur should be instructed to get ammunition and supplies to the Korean army by airdrop and otherwise. [Truman staff marginalia: "That the Seventh Fleet should be ordered into the Formosa Strait to prevent the conflict spreading in that area."]

3) The Seventh Fleet should be ordered from Cavite north at once. We should make a statement that the fleet would repel any attack on Formosa and that no attack should be made from Formosa on the mainland. (At this point you interrupted to say that you agreed that the fleet should be ordered north at once, but that you would sleep on the statements until the fleet was in position. You expressed no opinion on them on the merits.)

4) The situation was not clear enough to make any further recommendations that night.

After this report you asked each person in turn to state his agreement or disagreement and any views he might have in addition. Two things stand out in this discussion. One was the complete, almost unspoken acceptance on the part of everyone that whatever had to be done to meet this aggression had to be done. There was no suggestion from anyone that either the United Nations or the United States could back away from it. This was the test of all the talk of the last five years of collective security. The other point which stands out in my mind from the discussion was the difference in view of what might be called for. Vandenberg and [Admiral Forrest] Sherman thought that air and naval aid might be enough. [General J. Lawton] Collins [army chief of staff, 1949–53] (and I think Bradley) were clear that if the Korean army was really broken, ground forces would be necessary. But no one could tell what the state of the Korean army really was on Sunday night. Whatever the service estimates might be everyone recognized the situation as serious in the extreme.

After listening to the discussion, you directed that orders be issued carrying out the recommendations as modified by you.

Louis Johnson has said that he and I had a debate on Formosa that night; he for protecting it, I against. That is completely untrue.

P. 559. Throughout Monday the situation in Korea deteriorated rapidly. You called another meeting at Blair House Monday night. The same persons were present, except that Assistant Secretary of State [Elbert G.] Mathews took Rusk's place and Secretary of Navy [Francis P.] Matthews was not present. The decisions taken that night were announced by you the next day, Tuesday, June 27th. The draft was prepared by me and adopted by you with minor changes. They were:

1) U.S. air and sea forces to give Korean force cover and support.
2) Seventh Fleet would neutralize Formosa.
3) Our forces in the Philippines would be strengthened.
4) Aid would be accelerated to Indo-China.
5) Senator [Warren] Austin [U.S. ambassador to the U.N., 1946–53] was to report all this to the U.N.

Meanwhile the Security Council of the U.N. met again and adopted the Resolution (on June 27th) calling on all members of the U.N. to give assistance to South Korea. That morning you met with the Congressional group.

P. 564. On Thursday (our time) MacArthur made an air reconnaissance of Korea and during the night on the wire with Collins asked for permission to move in a regimental combat team as the beginning of a two division force since the Korean army had dissolved. Permission was given, and later general agreement with your action was voiced by the NSC and a meeting of Congressional personnel.

The clear skeleton of this story of progressive decisions as events called for them does not come out clearly in these pages which are interspersed with too much conversation about who said what. The important thing is to get the bones in—because they are glorious bones—and let the conversational flesh come along afterward. [Truman marginalia: "Correct as hell is hot."]

Pp. 581–588. Harriman's Memorandum of his talks with MacArthur.

The inclusion of this memorandum raises serious questions. [Truman staff marginalia: "HST says go ahead."]

First. This should not be published without W.A.H.'s consent—and he should know the dangers to him as pointed out below. The literary rights in this memo belong to the writer and not the receiver. While you might have published it for governmental purposes while in office, you now have no official right to do so. [Truman marginalia: "Correct."]

Second. The memo will bring attacks and recriminations on W.A.H., who is in active politics and will want to run for Governor, or President, or to be Secretary of State some day. The memo, particularly the part of p. 583 which makes such a fool of MacArthur, will arouse his friends. [General Matthew] Ridgway and [General Lauris] Norstad will be drawn into the row to say whether things were or were not said. Then on page 585 MacArthur "thought it might be a good idea to let him [Chiang] land [on the mainland] and get rid of him that way." This will be furiously denied. [Truman marginalia: "Will it?"]

Then Averell says, "I explained in great detail why Chiang was a liability," etc. Dewey can ring the changes on this to Averell's great embarrassment. [Truman marginalia: "Can he?"]

I think it very bad business to print the memorandum. You can go through it and say that Harriman, who kept notes of his talk with MacArthur, told you that _____ and then paraphrase those portions of the memo which relate to the real point, which is that Averell explained the policy to MacArthur who said that he would, of course, loyally support it. [Truman marginalia: "Let's look and see if this may be right."]

P. 590. Your description of the meeting is not as I recall it. My notes of it are: "When we came into his office the President had in his hands some yellow sheets of newsticker paper. He told us to sit down. He was obviously angry. He read aloud to us the whole MacArthur letter, his voice getting harsher as he read. He said that this letter had been sent by MacArthur to the Veterans of Foreign Wars over the open telegraph; it was now on the AP ticker. He didn't see how this could be done without somebody in the U.S. government knowing about it. He was going to ask each one of us in this room whether we had anything to do with it, whether they knew anything about it or were in any way whatever involved in it. He pointed at each person in turn around the room. Each answered, 'No, sir.'

"By the time the President got through it was a pretty thoroughly intimidated group. He turned to Louis Johnson and said, 'I want this letter withdrawn. I want you to send an order to MacArthur to withdraw this letter. That is an order from me. Do you understand that?'

"Louis said, 'Yes, sir, I do.' The President said 'Go and do it. That's all.' Everyone went out and disappeared very fast."

Pp. 599–600. This is a very important and critical point in your relations with MacArthur. There is more to the matter of orders violated than you make clear—as I recall it. But my recollection and notes should be checked against the papers you have.

I was in New York on September 28, at the U.N. You sent for me to return to Washington. I got there that evening. The next day, Friday, September 29, after a cabinet meeting, General Marshall and I went to Blair House to lunch with you. When lunch was over and the luncheon things cleared away, an officer came in with a large map on which were the troop dispositions. General Marshall explained the military situation. He said the North Korean army was dissolving. The question was what orders should MacArthur be given. He told us of a tentative order sent by the Joint Chiefs to MacArthur for comment on, I think, the 27th. He now laid it before the President. The idea, as I recall it, was that MacArthur by amphibious and other operations would occupy, fortify, and hold the line Pyongyang-Wansan, running southwest to northeast across Korea. North of that line only Korean troops might operate.

This was discussed by the three of us. All the points which later became important were considered; i.e., as we might move north of this line, our supply line and air support would become longer and more difficult, the enemy's easier and shorter. The danger of Chinese intervention would increase. We came nearer to the Soviet border which would involve greater risks. The President concluded,—General Marshall and I were in complete agreement—that MacArthur should stand on the line mentioned and not go further north with U.N. troops—only Korean units might be used for policing and pacification if that proved possible.

I do not have and cannot find in the hearings before the Joint Congressional Committee the directives of September 27 and September 30, although they are discussed and certain portions of them are quoted in the Hearings before the committee by General Collins on pages 1216, 1230, and 1239. I believe that my recollection of what they contain is correct, but it would be most important to have this verified. They came up a month later, as I point out below, when on October 25 the Joint Chiefs protested against the general advance order which MacArthur had issued without consultation with them on October 24. This is a very important matter, because it was this advance, which, according to my recollection, was contrary to his directives, which brought about the disaster in North Korea. I think it now seems plain that, if MacArthur had kept his army where he was told to keep it, in a strongly fortified position, it would not have been disorganized and routed by the Chinese intervention.

Then following the Wake Island meeting: on October 15th MacArthur told HST that 60,000 men could not possibly get across the Yalu.

On October 24, 1950, without consultation with Washington and contrary to the order of September 30, MacArthur ordered a general advance of all his armies to the north. His dispositions were amazing in view of the possibility of Chinese intervention. The 8th Army and 10th Corps were separated. Then the 8th Army was divided into four or five separate columns out of touch with one another. The 10th Corps was divided into three widely separated forces.

On October 25th the Joint Chiefs protested against this departure from the September 30th order. MacArthur replied that "military necessity" required his actions; that he did not read the September 30 telegram as an order but as advice; and that the Wake Island conference had covered the situation.

The Joint Chiefs and Marshall fumed, saw the danger involved, but, in view of the tradition since Grant of the authority of a theater commander, were not willing to order MacArthur back to the September 30 line. They thought they were too far away. (There was also MacArthur's prestige.)

Now this was a critical point in history. The defeat of the U.S. forces in Korea in December was an incalculable defeat to U.S. foreign policy and destroyed the Truman Administration. If we had had Ridgway in command this would not have happened.

The extraordinary stupidity of MacArthur's action is shown by chronology. This divided, seven pronged advance was ordered by MacArthur on October 24.

October 26, first Chinese prisoners taken.

November 4th, MacArthur reports Chinese intervention distinct possibility in an intelligence appreciation.

November 5th, in special communiqué to U.N. MacArthur says North Korean forces have collapsed and "the most offensive act of international lawlessness ever known in history" has occurred in Chinese intervention in power into Korea.

November 6th, MacArthur in special report to U.N. complains of Chinese intervention. This was debated in the U.N. on November 7th and 8th. (But the advance north continued.) We in State were almost wild by this time because in our meetings at the Pentagon no one could explain what MacArthur was thinking of.

By this time, unknown to him, MacArthur had over 100,000 Chinese in his rear. See S.L.A. Marshall, *The River and the Gauntlet.*

November 8th. The vote to put Chinese intervention on the U.N. Security Council agenda was 10 to 1, Malik voting no. The Red Chinese were invited to appear and rejected invitation on November 11.

Meanwhile we met frantically at the Pentagon and with you—November 2, November 6, twice, November 13, November 14, November 17, November 29, December 1, December 2, December 3, December 4, etc.

November 21. 7th ROK [Republic of Korea] division reached Yalu.

November 21. MacArthur flew to Korea and announced on November 24, general assault which would end the war.

By November 28–29–30, 8th Army and 10th Corps were in headlong retreat. This was the worst defeat of U.S. forces since Bull Run. The generalship was even more stupid.

MacArthur's true nature was never plainer than in defeat. He first lost his head and the game was up, and then started to blame his government for his own assininity.

December 1st, MacArthur replied to a telegram from *U.S. News & World Report* that the limitations imposed on him were an enormous handicap, unprecedented in military history. On [the] same day he telegraphed Arthur Krock speaking of odds unprecedented in history.

December 6th. President sent his directive to submit statements.

December 11th, MacArthur made a statement that UN command was in fine shape having carried out "tactical withdrawals."

You have this in the text of his telegrams on (a) extending the war and (b) being unable to defend Korea and Japan.

Collins and Vandenberg went to Korea and Ridgway took over in place of [General Walton H.] Walker. By January 17 the situation had improved.

While we were approaching the 38th Parallel for the second time and discussing policy with our allies, MacArthur, I think in February, issued a statement that from a military standpoint we must materially reduce the existing superiority of our Chinese Communist enemy engaging with impunity in undeclared war against us, with the unprecedented military advantage of sanctuary protection for his military potential against our counterattack upon Chinese soil, before we can seriously consider conducting major operations north of that geographic line. This was open defiance again of the Government's position.

On March 7th, he said: "Vital decisions have yet to be made—

decisions far beyond the scope of the authority vested in me as the military commander, decisions which are neither solely political nor solely military, but which must provide on the highest international levels an answer to the obscurities which so becloud the unsolved problems raised by Red China's undeclared war in Korea."

In other words: war against China.

Then came the episode of the President's proposed statement and MacArthur's interference. (Your text, page 722.)

Another order to MacArthur to make no statements.

He immediately made one to the effect that he had ordered the army to cross the parallel at will. This brought violent reaction from Nehru and others.

Then the letter to Martin, released April 5th. At the same time the *Daily Telegraph* published an interview with the British General H. G. Martin, who quoted MacArthur to the same effect.

Senator Ferguson proposed that a congressional committee go to Tokyo to learn from MacArthur his views on how war should be conducted. Smith of New Jersey supported him.

P. 738, et seq. I have made some notes on the margin of your account of the meetings preceding MacArthur's relief. The following is an account put together last year by Averell and me from our notes and recollections.

Pursuant to messages received from you on the afternoon of Thursday, April 5, there met with you in your study from 11:30 to 12:30 Friday morning, April 6, following the Cabinet meeting, General Marshall, General Bradley, Harriman, and myself. We discussed the question for an hour, and it was apparent that everyone took the most serious possible view of the situation. It was apparent that General Marshall had not come to a conclusion and wished to reflect further; also that General Bradley would have to confer with the Joint Chiefs of Staff. I believed that General MacArthur should be relieved, but thought that it was essential that you should act, if possible, with the unanimous advice of your military advisors—General Marshall, General Bradley, and the Joint Chiefs. Therefore, at this meeting, I analyzed the situation, without stating any other conclusion than that it should be thought over very carefully because it was a matter of the utmost seriousness. Harriman argued very strongly for the relief of MacArthur.

The next morning, Saturday, April 7, at 8:50 a.m., the same group met for a short further meeting with you in your office. At that time you requested General Marshall and General Bradley to confer with the Joint Chiefs of Staff and be prepared on Monday to make a final recommendation to you. On Sunday, the 8th of April, you sent for me to come to Blair House, discussed the matter briefly with me, and told me that you had consulted Snyder and, I think, Vinson. You said that you would be prepared to act on Monday when Marshall and Bradley made their report.

We met in your office at nine o'clock on Monday morning— Marshall, Bradley, Harriman, and I. Bradley reported that the Joint Chiefs had met with him on Sunday, and it was his and their unanimous judgment that MacArthur should be relieved. General Marshall said that he had come to this conclusion. I said that I agreed entirely, and Harriman re-affirmed his opinion of Friday, to the same effect. You said that your own conclusion was the same and you directed General Bradley to prepare the orders and confer with me, since the office of Supreme Commander, Allied Powers, was also involved. The same group returned to your office at 3:15 on Monday afternoon, April 10, with drafted orders, which you signed. It was decided that the notification of these orders should be given to General MacArthur through [Frank] Pace [Jr., Secretary of the Army, 1950–53], who was then in Korea, we thought at 8th Army Headquarters. You directed me to send the orders with a message also prepared, to Pace, through [John J.] Muccio, directing him to go to Tokyo at once and convey the orders. Our message was delayed in reaching Pace, both through mechanical difficulties in transmission and because Pace was not at Headquarters but was at the front with Ridgway. About ten o'clock Monday night I was informed that, due to this delay and to the fact that Bradley had reported the rumor of a leak, you had thought it best to send the message also by direct Army wire to MacArthur. I was then instructed to, and did, inform Congressional leaders and also got Dulles to come to my house, telling him of what had occurred and asking him to go to Japan to assure the Yoshida Government that the change in commander would not in any way affect our policy of pushing the Japanese Peace Treaty to a speedy conclusion. This Dulles agreed to do.

This is the story according to the best recollection of Harriman and myself. I think it important that you should have it because it differs in some respects from the account which appears in your manuscript. Both Harriman and I were convinced then and now that your mind had already been made up, but it seemed to us then and now that you acted very wisely in not expressing your opinion to anyone until you had the views of all, which happily turned out to be unanimous. This proved to be a very strong point in the hearings which later occurred before the joint Congressional committee which investigated the MacArthur relief.

Pp. 629–630. Suggest cutting out the paragraph at the bottom of the page. It is very speculative. I doubt whether there was a master plan there. We also tend to attribute too much of this to the Russians.

I have not made detailed notes on your manuscript of the MacArthur story. It would help it a lot to pull it into sharper focus along the lines of my outline. Emerson said to Holmes after reading his critical essay on Plato—"If you strike at a king, you must kill him." MacArthur can be shot right through the heart. I do not believe this text does it.

[Truman marginalia: "Something to that. Let's shoot him. God knows he should be!"]

P. 658. Verbal change.

P. 666. The statement attributed to me is quite contrary to what I have said. Wasn't it, rather, that, if while we were so heavily engaged in Korea we permitted Formosa to be attacked and fall, we would raise the gravest dangers in Japan and the Philippines which were the bases from which our operations were being conducted and upon which our whole Pacific position rested? [Truman marginalia: "This is true."]

Pp. 721 and 722. Verbal.

Pp. 737–8. I would omit this which seems to me untrue.

Pp. 738–40. Please see my notes above on MacArthur's relief.

P. 677, 2nd line. This specific reference will embarrass Attlee and should come out.

P. 686. You never can support the charge that MacArthur *wanted* war. His argument is that there would have been no war. You can win on the charge that he was willing to *risk* war when it was neither necessary nor warranted to do so.

P. 689. These two sentences I would leave out. The first is garbled. The second seems very strange to me. I thought our Kansas line was about the strongest position in Korea. These southerly lines were so impractical anyway that even reference to them will give the idea that you or Bradley were contemplating them.

P. 719. Please cut out marked paragraph. MacArthur's generalship in Korea was awful and his leadership worse. Have you read S.L.A.

Marshall's *The River and the Gauntlet?* Don't go down in history as authority for this dreadful endorsement. [Truman marginalia: "Let's look. I'm in doubt."]

See also comments noted on pp. 744, 751, 755. Are these instructions declassified? Is it necessary to print them?

Pp. 763–4. I suggest cutting the marked paragraphs and substituting the short suggested conclusion. These paragraphs add nothing to the story already told. Furthermore, the word "unthinkable" drives me wild. If something is unthinkable it is unwritable too, or ought to be. Unthinkable is a new kind of superlative which has been downgraded to mean that almost everyone has already thought the unthinkable thoughts. My favorite sentence would be "to implement the over-all, unthinkable picture."

P. 786. Isn't it poor taste to designate your own lawyers as "distinguished" men while your opponents' are "high powered corporation lawyers"? They were all lawyers and like Senators, they are all "distinguished" or "eminent." Let's stick to tradition.

P. 792. This should come out. The sound rule is, never argue with the court that decides against you. It impresses no one. You have made all the arguments in the foregoing pages. This hurt you much more than it does the court.

P. 797, 1st paragraph. The first sentence is not correct. It would be if rewritten: "The off-shore oil and mineral resources from low water-mark to the three mile limit fall, as the Supreme Court has held, within the full 'dominion' and 'power' of the United States Government. From the three mile limit to the end of the continental shelf it is the policy of the United States Government, in the words of a proclamation which I signed on September 28, 1945, that they are 'appertaining to the United States, subject to its jurisdiction and control.'"

I would also eliminate the paragraph at the bottom of the page. The claims of Texas and Louisiana vary from time to time. But the point is not that federal control is the only logical position. The other positions are logical enough, if that matters at all. The point is the federal control is the right answer.

P. 810. The marked sentence is a bad one. It is wrong for a man on the court to have further ambitions. It is Douglas's curse. If Hughes "used" the Court, that is no reason why Fred [Vinson] should. But Hughes didn't. In his case it was a draft, as it would not have been in Fred's.

In view of the fact that Fred's heart we now know was in poor shape in 1952, I would leave out the last sentence on this page. It sounds a little as though you were callous about his survival and you have already expressed your opinion of his qualifications.

P. 822. I would leave out this paragraph. In the first place, I don't think that the phrase, "The mess in Washington," was Adlai's at all. So he did not waste his gift for phrasing. He quoted the other fellow's question in answering it. This may have been a mistake. But it was like the attack on you for the "red herring" sentence which was not yours but your questioner's.

In the second place, it may or may not have been a mistake for any candidate not an incumbent President to say that if there were any corruption around he would be twice as much against it as the other fellow. The alternative was to deny that there was any and get on the defensive at once.

This paragraph doesn't sound well coming from you. In fact, I would be just as happy, indeed more so, without any discussion of Adlai's mistakes.

P. 829. The sentence at the top of the page has no verb. This sentence and the next paragraph I would regard as really saying nothing, but leaving a disparaging atmosphere about Ike which is a little small. If you leave the paragraph, "in the first instance," etc., in, the last sentence needs something. Is that cloak worn by all politicians, including you, or only bad politicians? I am for cutting the whole business out.

These suggestions were written under great pressure for time and are not very tactfully put. I hope that they won't offend you. The book is a fine job. It ought to be sound as a bell on every point, and is on most of them. My points are intended to raise a few points which I hope you can consider when you go over the galleys, though this may be difficult. I did not realize that you were so far along until your last letter. When my work was nearly done. So I send it along anyway.

Our most affectionate greetings.

Most sincerely,

Dean

Truman expresses gratitude for Acheson's comments on his memoirs, especially those pointing out errors.

Dear Dean: August 12, 1955

It was a great treat to me to talk with you the other day. To learn that my mysterious $5,000 Library contributor is a friend of yours made the contribution twice as valuable to me.

I am still reading proof and correcting errors and misstatements. It is certainly surprising what can creep into a simply common sense statement of what is supposed to be fact. Someone who doesn't know his Scripture has quoted old man Job as saying, "Oh! that mine enemy would write a book." Job didn't say it in his book, but it's a good quotation anyway. I've been told or read it somewhere that Herodotus said that "the man, the event and what happened hardly ever arrived at the same place at the same time, but a good historian would take care of that."

Well, I guess that's a good idea but I've tried to avoid it in my effort, thanks to the ideal help I've had in the form of an intellectually honest Secretary of State. There have been some others too who have said plainly and bluntly that my memory is at fault. And, Dean, I like it. There's nothing worse for a man's character than friends who tell him always how good he is.

May you and Alice have a wonderful trip. I hope Bess and I may have the good luck to see you when you return.

Most sincerely,

Harry

The Achesons left for a lengthy vacation in Europe, stretching over two months, sometime in August.

Dean Acheson and Harry Truman with Winston Churchill aboard the presidential yacht, the U.S.S. Williamsburg, *during Churchill's brief visit to Washington on January 5, 1952. Also pictured is Sir Anthony Eden, British Foreign Secretary.*

4

August 1955 to September 1956

The Potsdam Papers – "Intellectual Prostitutes" –
Margaret Is Married – A Trip to Europe

*B*y the fall of 1955, with the presidential election about a year away, both Truman and Acheson were getting involved in politics. Acheson found himself thrust into the role of Democratic Party spokesman, largely because of the considerable success of his book *A Democrat Looks at His Party*, an excerpt from which was published in the press in September.

Aside from politics, many subjects found their way into the letters between the two men. Margaret Truman married in April 1956, and the Trumans traveled to Europe during most of May and June. Truman was awarded an honorary degree from Oxford University during that time. Acheson wrote a draft of an important address that Truman gave in London.

Acheson asked Truman to allow State Department historians to see Truman's papers relating to the Potsdam Conference, where Truman had met with Winston Churchill, Clement Attlee, and Joseph Stalin in July 1945. Truman wanted to grant Acheson's request, but he was, then and for the rest of his life, very reluctant to let anyone see what he regarded as his most sensitive White House papers.

.   .   .

August 21, 1955

Dear Mr. President,

You sent us off with a real start. As soon as we reached our cabin we found the warm note from you and the flowers from Mrs. Truman and you which have kept us company all the way to the Irish coast. You gave us a warm glow of happiness.

You and Mrs. Truman must do this soon. And when you do, take one of these slow boats in the off season where you can poke along in comfort, have plenty of elbow room and find comparatively few autograph seekers and no jazzy life at all. Alice and I have never had such rest even on the beach at Antigua.

On my way through New York I found Harpers enthusiastic about my little book. It will come out about the middle of November under the title *A Democrat Looks at His Party*. It gives my ideas about the problems of our day and why the old Party is the only one equipped to deal with them. You will have your own specially inscribed copy.

Our most affectionate greetings to you and Mrs. Truman.

Most sincerely,

Dean

While visiting former adviser and now New York Governor Averell Harriman in Albany, New York, Truman made a statement to the press praising Harriman's qualifications for the presidency and distancing himself from the 1952 Democratic nominee, Adlai Stevenson.

October 14, 1955

Dear Mr. President:

I was glad to see the Truman family reunited on the front page of the *New York Times* a few days ago. You all looked very well and very happy to be together again.

In your own phrase, you certainly "stirred the animals up" with the press conference in Albany. People can no longer complain that the pre-campaign period will be dull or cut-and-dried. I just hope that our boys don't get into a throat-cutting competition and am counting on you to not let the rivalry go to lethal consequences.

I have had [a] telephone call and a letter from Arnold Heeney, the Canadian Ambassador, enclosing a copy of his letter to you of October 13 and his letter to the *New York Times* of October 12. These are the letters in which he refers to installment twelve of your Memoirs published in the *New York Times* of October 7, in which you refer to Canada as one of the countries whose soldiers were equipped by lend-lease means during World War II. This, of course, was an inadvertence which I should have caught and regret very much that I did not. I told the Ambassador that you were counting on me to pick up things like this and that to my great sorrow I failed you on this occasion. He is not at all worried about it; but, since the Canadians are, as you know, hypersensitive, he is anxious that this be corrected when the Memoirs are published in book form. I told him that you would be most insistent upon having errors corrected and that I was sure that this one would be in the definitive text. I don't think there is anything that you need do about it now, except assure him directly that this is the case.

The advance copies of my own book should be coming along in the next week. I shall send you one as soon as I can get my hands on it.

Alice joins me in the most affectionate greetings to you and Mrs. Truman.

Sincerely yours,
Dean

Truman mentions his daughter Margaret's debut hosting of a radio show in New York.

October 17, 1955

Dear Dean:

I certainly appreciated your letter of the fourteenth. It was my intention to stir up the animals when I went to New York, and I believe I succeeded.

Margaret and the "Boss" and I had the time of our lives together in New York. I tried my best to bring Margaret home with us, but her new contract was to start right away. She'll be on the air four hours a day with her own show. Beat that if you can!

I hope that you and Alice are in the best of health and that everything is going as it should with you. The only thing we missed on our trip east was an opportunity to see you in Washington.

The error concerning Lend-Lease to Canada was found and corrected in the book galleys but was missed in the *New York Times* proofs. I am very sorry about it, and I will appreciate you telling the Ambassador that it was an unintentional slip.

I have found several errors in the book. It seems that no matter how closely you read and re-read and edit a publication of this kind, errors are bound to slip in. For instance, I had Sam Rayburn presiding at Roosevelt's first meeting with Congress after his return from Yalta when, actually, it was John McCormack. All these will be corrected in the next edition. After you have had a chance to calm the Canadian Ambassador down, I will write him a letter of explanation.

I am most happy that you helped me with the editing; it gives me a wonderful chance to be a buck-passer.

Sincerely yours,

Harry Truman

[Handwritten postscript:] What's this I hear about *A Democrat Looks at His Party*? I must see that.

A prepublication excerpt from Acheson's book had appeared in Harper's Magazine *in November 1955. The article and the book helped make Acheson a Democratic Party spokesman in the upcoming presidential campaign.*

Ivan Miller's letter, which Truman mentions, invited Acheson to speak on December 7 at a dinner sponsored by the Cleveland Bar Association. Edward Hayes wrote Truman to ask his help in persuading Acheson to accept the invitation. Truman agreed to "go to work" on Acheson.

October 18, 1955

Dear Dean:

I am enclosing a copy of a letter I received from Edward J. Hayes. He also sent me a copy of that letter Ivan L. Miller wrote to you.

When I was in Cleveland for the library dinner, his organization was well represented at our meeting. I was asked by half a dozen people to urge you to be the speaker at their meeting in December.

As you know, I only want you to use your own judgment, but I believe you could do the country and the Democratic Party a lot of good if you found it possible to accept the invitation. As the fellow on radio says, "That's one man's opinion."

Sincerely yours,

Harry S. Truman

Acheson sent Truman a copy of his new book, with an inscription on the inside front cover which read, "To Harry S. Truman, The first of living Democrats who will rank with the greatest of them all."

November 9, 1955

Dear Mr. President:

I was delighted to be able to pass along to the Canadian Ambassador the information contained in your last letter that the error about lend-lease to Canada was found and corrected in the book galleys, although it was missed in the *New York Times* prints. He is most understanding and most happy that this is the case. He would appreciate a line from you so that he can officially report to Canada that you yourself told him that you had already found the error and were quick to correct it. It will make a good impression in Canada all around.

You ask me about *A Democrat Looks at His Party*. You remember that some time ago I told you that I was working on a book and this is it. The week before last I sent off to you a copy of it with a word from me to you in the front. When you find a few hours in your busy life to relax, I think you will find some amusement, some interest, and perhaps some subjects for future talks in the book.

A chapter from it was published in this month's *Harper's* and seems to have stirred the Republican press into ecstasies of rage. I have editorials from the two Richmond papers which quite lost the power of coherent statement in their fury. If one chapter raises the Republican blood pressure to this extent, we may win the next election through the collapse of our opponents.

I believe that Dave Lloyd is working out a chance for me to see you next month, to which I am looking forward.

With warmest greetings to Mrs. Truman and yourself from Alice and me.

As ever,

Dean

Truman has some harsh words for "intellectual prostitutes," including conservative journalists Raymond Moley, Frank R. Kent, David Lawrence, George E. Sokolsky, and Westbrook Pegler. Speaking in New Orleans in early November, Truman said he thought Southern Democrats who voted Republican in 1952 would return to their party in 1956, and he praised both Adlai Stevenson and Averell Harriman, saying he would not run himself. "Our old Snollygoster" is John Foster Dulles.

November 10, 1955

Dear Dean:

I have just finished reading your book on why you are a Democrat. It is the best treatise on politics, the why and wherefore of parties, and what a man ought to do when he comes to select his party, that I have ever read. And Dean, I've read a lot of them. The review of Elmer Davis in the *Saturday Review* says what I would say if I had the words and ability to put them together. I'm so glad you wrote the book that I can't really express my feeling adequately on it.

My spasm seems to have stirred up the animals to some extent. Between us I'm sure we'll leave a record that the so called analytical boys will have a hell of a time doing their analytical sob sister stuff. You've no idea what a kick I've had from the intellectual prostitutes, Moley, Kent, Dave Lawrence, Sokolsky, Pegler and the rest. I've always been of the opinion that a street whore who sold her body to make a living is far and away above an intellectual who sells his brain and ability to put words together logically for the same sort of a fee.

The Boss and I took a ride to New Orleans last week and what a grand time we had. Our train arrived at Alexandria, La. at 6:30 A.M. and there on the platform was Mrs. John Overton, her two daughters, a nephew and several other members of her family. We had a grand visit and Mrs. O. gave us a lot of homemade pralines. How good they were!

When we landed in New Orleans they mobbed us — with kindness of course. It was like wading in the Gulf at Key West only it was people to wade through.

I preached a sermon that night to 2000 Jews from all parts of the country, went to Biloxi on Sunday to see a couple of old people who took care of Margie in 1933, 35 and 38 when she was having throat and heart trouble. It was a grand visit.

But Dean what do you think of our old Snollygoster now "Mr. Dull, Duller, Dulles"? He's lost us our friends in South America by trying to put Sullivan & Cromwell again in control of tin in Bolivia and copper in Chile. He fixed the eastern Mediterranean so that his friend Dewey can bleed Turkey for what the Turkish Ambassador should do and he has given Egypt and East Germany to Molotov. I don't know what he's doing in Spain but there's some fee for somebody when he deals with that lousy totalitarian Franco.

An old lady in the Edgewater Gulf Hotel where Bess & I had lunch came up for an autograph and said she didn't like to quarrel with God but he'd been a little slow in giving Ike a heart attack but it might yet save the country! Looks from yesterday's elections that a lot of people are worried.

My best to Alice.

Sincerely,

Harry

That inscription you wrote in the copy of your book is too good to be true!

Dear Dean: November 21, 1955

I wrote you a longhand letter commenting on your good book and this is in answer to yours of the ninth. I am sending a letter to the Canadian Ambassador along the line you suggest.

I don't know when I have read a book I appreciated more and got more of a kick out of than *A Democrat Looks at His Party*. I read the *Harper's* chapter after I had read the book and it really did impress me. *Harper's* also had a good review on my spasm.

Dave [Lloyd] tells me that he is working out a program so we will get together in the not too distant future.

I am enclosing for you a copy of the letter I have written to the Canadian Ambassador.

Sincerely yours,

Harry S. Truman

The "new publication" mentioned here is William F. Buckley's National Review. *Acheson makes an early observation of what would become a remarkable rise in esteem for Truman among the American people in the years following the difficult last period of his presidency. President Eisenhower had suffered a massive heart attack on September 24, 1955, and Acheson assumes here that he will not run for re-election in 1956. (However, the President not only ran for re-election, but won, and therefore Acheson's predictions were moot, and their hopes for a Democratic victory were dashed.)*

Dear Mr. President: November 23, 1955

You were very good to write me so warmly about *A Democrat Looks at His Party*. If you, with all your knowledge of and experience in politics, think what I have written about the political scene is good, I am very happy indeed.

I am pleased and excited at the reception which it has had. The reviews have been for the most part enthusiastic, though I, of course, expected and have received sarcastic criticism from such reviewers as John Chamberlain in the *Wall Street Journal.* I am told that our friend Senator McCarthy is going to review it for a new publication put out by Buckley. When asked what he thought about the book, he is said to have replied, "Hell! Of course, I wouldn't read it."

The article taken from the book, which appeared in the November *Harper's* produced quite a barrage of criticism. In a way I think it was a mistake to publish one small part of it without the argument which built up to that part and the discussion that followed it. However, the publisher does not think so. He tells me that it is selling well.

The reception of your own book must have pleased you. It certainly did me. One of the nicest and most thoughtful reviews is the one in the November *Harper's* in which they deal with Oppie Oppenheimer's book [*The Open Mind*] and your book together, using his to discuss the conception of style in science and yours to illustrate style in politics. It seems to me far more thoughtful than any I have seen. I am looking forward to the second volume, which I, of course, read in manuscript, before you put the finishing touches on it.

In connection with the publication of my book there was the inevitable barrage of requests for appearances on television and radio. I insisted that these be cut down to two—one on the Dave Garroway show on NBC; the other on the Bill Leonard show on CBS. I thought that I had an understanding with both men that I would not go into personalities and discuss candidates for the Democratic nomination in '56. However, Bill Leonard departed from this and asked me what I thought of Adlai's announcement of his candidacy. I thought of—who was it?—Mark Twain's? admonition that it was better to tell the truth because it was then easier to remember what you said. So I said that I had been for Adlai in '52, had reiterated the view that he was the best candidate when asked in '53, '54, and so far in '55, and I saw no reason for doubting that view now. I was sorry to be asked this, not because I have the slightest reluctance in saying what I think, but because, under the present circumstances, I thought it might unnecessarily wound Averell, to whom I am devoted. However, I am sure that he is broad enough and experienced enough to know that he cannot be involved in politics and harbor resentment for those who honestly believe that somebody else is a better candidate.

You know far more about these things than I do, but it would seem to me that Averell's greatest usefulness now lies, not in the possibility that he will be nominated and elected, but in the effect that he can have on Adlai, keeping him pointed up close to the wind and not letting him fall off with phrases like "the relentless pursuit of peace." With Eisenhower out of the picture, as I suppose he is, I should look with undisguised horror at any of the present Republican candidates being in the White House. ([Earl] Warren, I exclude, because he is a man of honor and of his word, and I believe would not accept the nomination whether drafted or not.) In that case a Democratic victory seems to me of the greatest importance to the welfare of the country, and Adlai seems to me the best person to achieve it. How do you feel about all of this?

The visit which you and Mrs. Truman paid to New Orleans sounds delightful, and I know that your hearts were touched by the reception you describe. I think that every day and every year the affection of the American people for you rises. You typify for them—and rightly—the healthy-minded, direct, generous, courageous, friendly person, who is Mr. American for them.

Dave Lloyd seems to be having a terrible time in getting the Library meeting set up in Kansas City. As I understand it, various meetings are now to take place over the 19th, 20th, and 21st of December. I have, unfortunately, been deeply committed here for the evening of the 19th, and so cannot arrive until the 20th, but Dave says that this is quite all right. I had hoped that I was going to be able to see you and talk with you in the week of December 6. Let's now hope that it is only postponed for a couple of weeks.

Let me end up this rambling letter with an episode which illustrates my cold and frigid manner, which has been so often described in the press. Last Thursday morning I was walking east on 38th Street in New York from a friend's house to the air terminal and was not quite sure that the terminal was on 38th Street. On Third Avenue there were four or five men with picks and shovels digging up a broken place in the pavement, surrounded by the yellow barricades with "Men Working" which give them a little island of safety. I stopped there and asked one of them whether I was on the right street for the air terminal. One of them looked up from his work, beamed broadly, and said, "For the love of God, if it ain't Dean Acheson. I seen you on the Dave Garroway show on television yesterday morning." At that point they all threw down their tools, shook hands with me, and we discussed for five minutes the prospects of a Democratic victory in 1956. None of them seemed to be dismayed by the cold exterior.

Alice sends her most affectionate greetings to you and Mrs. Truman, as do I.

Sincerely,

Dean

Truman was ill for a few days and unable to attend the memorial service of one of his best friends, his old haberdashery partner Eddie Jacobson. Truman's doctor called his ailment an "intestinal illness." Acheson once again asks Truman to allow historians from the State Department to see his documents relating to the Potsdam Conference for use in preparing a volume in the series Foreign Relations of the United States. *Truman did eventually permit the historians to see the documents, but he remained very reluctant to permit access to his White House office file and some related papers, and kept them in his personal custody until he died.*

December 8, 1955

Dear Mr. President,

Alice and I were distressed to read of your illness after the Pacific coast trip. Your malady was one on which I am the world's greatest expert, having learned the hard way. And so Dr. Acheson says that you have been doing too much, what with politics and the library, and that you ought to cut down on this travel of yours. Of course, you will agree with this advice, and then go right on doing the same thing. The only hope is Mrs. Truman. Shall I bring her a baseball bat when I come out.

A few days ago I had a call from a man suffering badly from frustration—Dr. [G. Bernard] Noble of the Historical Division of the State Department, a good man. You were the cause of his frustration. He showed me a letter from you last spring saying that you would take up his request to look at some of the Potsdam papers when the book was out of the way; then a recent one saying that you would get to it when the library was finished and the papers installed. Poor Dr. Noble! He said sadly that he wasn't even staying in the same place. He was going backwards. We had a long talk in which I said that I would intercede for him when I saw you in late December to the extent of urging you to let him, with Grover's men [one of the archivists who were working on Truman's papers] and anyone else—say Hiller [*sic*; probably William Hillman]—you wanted to supervise, look at certain specified papers which were not personal and private but governmental in nature—communications with foreign governments, etc. Some of the ones he once listed have since appeared in your book, others he has had available in Adm. Leahy's papers. I think this is fair and right. He doubts whether the Potsdam volume will be out for years as the British do not propose to be treated again as they were in the Yalta papers—a trick of our friend Foster's which bounced back on him. Noble will give me a new list of documents before I come out and I hope you can find a few minutes to talk with me about it.

I was honored and pleased beyond words to join you last Sunday on the *N.Y. Times* best seller list.

Most affectionately and sincerely,

Dean

Responding to Acheson's letter of November 23, Truman mentions the passing of his close friend John Caskie Collet and the pleasures of being a "lightfoot" Baptist. He also writes about some generous gifts in kind to his library, now under construction. Wilmer Waller was the treasurer and Basil O'Connor the president of Harry S. Truman Library, Inc., which raised the money that built the Truman Library.

December 9, 1955

Dear Dean:

I more than appreciated your good letter. The last paragraph was out of this world. I knew very well that it was all there, just as the workmen in the street found it. I pride myself on being a judge of the hearts of men, and I know I had yours in the right category.

Your book is really the best essay on the Democratic Party that has ever been written. I keep one copy on my office desk and another on the table where I work at home. When I get to thinking about some of the things our fellow Democrats are doing, I open up your book and read a paragraph or two. It puts me back in the right groove.

I had a very sad duty to perform yesterday. Judge Collet died, and his family asked me to say a few words about him from the pulpit of the church to which he belonged. He and I are members of the "lightfoot" Baptist fraternity. We do not like to have a harness around us to prevent our doing what we want to do. I think you are somewhat familiar with that facet of my character. As you know, Roger Williams organized the Baptists in Providence, Rhode Island, because he could not get along with the Puritans. He later found that he could not get along with his new group either and had to try something else. Caskie and I are in that same class.

I received a copy of Clement Attlee's review of my book which appeared in the *London Times*. It is simply out of this world. In fact, the reviews in England are even better than those in this country, and your treatise on the Democratic Party has received the same sort of treatment. It is a great satisfaction when these birds have to eat crow because of the both of us, although I never gave a crow dinner to anyone and don't expect to.

I am looking forward to a most pleasant visit here on the 19th and 20th of this month. I believe everything is in order, and I hope that you will find it that way. I am very anxious for you and Waller and Doc O'Connor to become acquainted with the contractor and builder. He is one of the finest men I have ever known, and he refused any compensation for the operation. The same thing is true of the contracting plumber. He is Eddie Jacobson's brother and the biggest operator in the business in this part of the country. Besides the fact that there will be no compensation whatever to his company, he has also made five or six contributions to the library fund. The electrical work is also being done on the same basis.

It seems that we will receive something over two hundred thousand dollars from the West Coast trip to put us within a very short distance of our goal.

Please give my best to Alice and tell her I hope she will come to Kansas City with you. We'll put you up, as before, in the second hand accommodations we have to offer.

Sincerely yours,

Harry

December 10, 1955

Dear Dean:

Just as I'd put an air mail letter down the chute in answer to yours, here comes this handwritten letter telling me you are an expert on upset insides! Well, you are an expert on many things including politics, foreign affairs and shoes and sealing wax and whether the sea is boiling hot and pigs have wings—but I didn't know that you are familiar with the ramifications of 5000 feet of—should I say guts or intestines?

If I show your letter to the Boss she'll say, "Of course, tell him to bring the baseball bat with spikes in the business end." Maybe I won't tell her but of course I will.

It's too good to keep. I'm looking forward to a most pleasant session with you—bring Alice.

Sincerely,

Harry

Acheson is still anxious to ensure that the historical records of the State Department are complete. Here he sends Truman a list of documents relating to the Potsdam Conference requested by the State Department historians. Acheson also writes about the problems caused by the Eisenhower administration's consulting with only one Democratic senator on foreign-policy matters—Walter F. George of Georgia, chair of the Committee on Foreign Relations. Senator Arthur Vandenberg of Michigan led Senate Republicans in bipartisan support of many of Truman's most important foreign-policy initiatives. Wayne Grover, archivist of the United States, was very involved in establishing the Truman Library.

Dear Mr. President: December 14, 1955

Your two letters arriving so close together whetted my appetite for the meeting which we were to have had next week and then only yesterday Dave Lloyd told me that the figures would not be ready and that we would have to postpone our meeting together until January.

I had intended, while in Kansas City, to go over with you Dr. Noble's list of papers which he would like to see and photostat. Since this is being put off, I thought that we might get on with the matter by my sending them to you in this letter with a suggestion.

You will see that all of these papers are entirely official in their nature; so much so, that I am greatly surprised that copies of them do not exist in the files of our government. I think that it is quite understandable, natural, and proper that Dr. Noble should want to keep the official files complete by asking the opportunity to photostat these.

I do not want to cause you inconvenience at all, and most certainly I do not want to have him do that. Also you will want to be sure that these papers are properly handled and returned unharmed to their

proper places in your files, and you do not want to give the time necessary or have Rose bothered with this task. It seems to me wholly possible that, if you will approve Dr. Noble's photostating these papers, Dave
Lloyd can then arrange through Dr. Grover that Grover's men will find
the papers, show them to Dr. Noble in their quarters in Kansas City,
supervise the photostating, and return them to their proper place.
Since all of these documents have to do with the period already covered by Volume I of the Memoirs, it would seem clear that no problems
would arise in connection with your contract with *Life*.

Does this seem sensible to you, and if so, will you let Dave and me try
to work it out?

On Monday afternoon I had a very fine call from Averell who spent
an hour and a half with me prior to having dinner with Lyndon Johnson and some of his colleagues. I was impressing on Averell the need
for Lyndon's requiring real consultation with the Democrats instead of
merely personal consultation with Walter George, as the result of
which the Democrats in the Senate and House find themselves committed to courses of which they never heard anything. Averell called
me this morning from Albany to say that he thought he had made some
progress with this idea. I pointed out that Vandenberg never made any
blind commitments for the Republican Party and, since Lyndon prides
himself on being a shrewd Texas trader, he ought to do at least as well
as Van. One of the great difficulties in the way of Democrats on the Hill
at present is that they know nothing except what Dulles tells them, and
this leaves them in pretty profound ignorance of the real issues.

I shall now look forward to January instead of December and store
up matters to talk over with you. In the meantime I am preparing the
baseball bat with spikes.

Faithfully yours,
Dean

The book Truman sent was the first volume of his memoirs, Year of
Decisions.

December 20, 1955

Dear Dean:

I was completely and thoroughly disappointed when our visit was
called off, but I am looking forward to the time when that architect gets
things in shape.

I will be glad to do what I can with regard to the photostatic copies you mentioned. One problem is that these papers are going to be very difficult to work with, because they are scattered—some of them in the vault of the Federal Building at 9th [and] Walnut Streets in Kansas City, a few in the office, and the vast majority of them are in the archives file in the basement of the Memorial Building in Independence.

If Dr. Noble will come out here the first part of January some time, I will be happy to cooperate with him the best I can along the lines you suggest.

Again, I am just as sorry as I can be that you are not here.

Sincerely yours,

Harry S. Truman

[Handwritten postscript:] My best to Alice. Sent you a book today.

December 27, 1955

Dear Dean:

The "Boss" and I certainly did appreciate those beautiful gladioli which you and Alice sent us for Christmas. We placed them right under Winston Churchill's picture of Marrakech, so that everyone who came in could see them. I hope you and Alice had a wonderful Christmas.

Sincerely yours,

Harry S. Truman

At the end of December 1955, Truman sent Acheson another "spasm" as a kind of New Year's present. This spasm was directed at the "prostitutes of the mind" who filled the press with lies and menaced free government.

December 29, 1955

Dear Dean:

Well, I have the urge to give some of these lying, paid prostitutes of the mind a little hell, and rather than speak out publicly, you are the victim. Old man Webster, who is purported to have written a collection of words with derivations and definitions, says that: Prostitute: 1. To submit to promiscuous lewdness for hire. 2. To denote to base or unworthy purposes; as *to prostitute one's talents*. Prostituted; now, chiefly denoted to base purposes or ends; corrupt.

The same source (from old man Webster) gives this definition of prostitution: 1. Act or practice of prostituting; as, the prostitution of one's abilities. Dean, that's the end of Mr. Webster's dissertation on the oldest profession in the world, and as you see it is not confined to the occupant of a bawdy house.

We have men, in this day and age, who are prostitutes of the mind. They sell their ability to write articles for sale, which will be so worded as to mislead people who read them as news. These articles or columns are most astute and plausible and unless the reader knows the facts are most misleading.

These men are prostitutes of the mind—they write what they do not believe for sale. Mr. Webster has clearly defined them for what they are. In my opinion they are much worse and much more dangerous than the street walking whore who sells her body for the relief of a man whose penis is troubling him.

Prostitutes of the mind have been the great menace to free government since freedom of speech and freedom of the press was first inaugurated.

Presidents and the members of their Cabinets and their staff members have been slandered and misrepresented since George Washington. When the press is friendly to an administration the opposition has been lied about and treated to the excrescence of paid prostitutes of the mind.

A prostitute of the mind is a much worse criminal in my opinion than a thief or a robber. You know old man Shakespeare said:

> "Good name in man and woman, dear my lord,
> Is the immediate jewel of their souls.
> Who steals my purse steals trash,
> 'tis something, nothing; . . .
> But he that filches from me my good name
> Robs me of that which not enriches him
> And makes me poor indeed."

Prostitutes of the mind are skillful purveyors of character assassination and the theft of good names of public men and private citizens too. They are the lowest form of thief & criminal.

Well, I don't have to name them. You know 'em too.

Hope you and Alice had a grand Christmas. We were sorely disappointed when you didn't come out.

Sincerely,

Harry Truman

Acheson is delighted with Truman's December 29 "spasm." Herblock is political cartoonist Herbert Lawrence Block. Acheson uses "HP2x" to characterize misleading statements to the public from President Eisenhower and Secretary Dulles.

Dear Mr. President,   January 3, 1956

It was a great idea you had to make that speech—the one in your letter of December 29th—in a letter to me and not to the great American public, about to go into a New Year's binge full of what Herblock calls the new secret ingredient HP2x (Hocus Pocus twice multiplied). The new Truman doctrine of intellectual prostitution is great stuff, but it is best to start with a few of the faithful first and let the word spread. The man in the street is so conditioned to intellectual prostitution that an old fashioned fellow who tells the truth every once in a while is sure to be charged with unnatural practices. We are so used to—in another of Herb's prize expressions—"genuine simulated prosperity" that just an ordinary fair break looks like poverty now. So I win by all this, and get one of the best H.S.T. letters yet produced. The only trouble is I can only pass on the doctrine in a highly expurgated edition which loses a good deal of the pungent outrage flowing off your pen.

What, I wonder, was it that caused that incandescent moment? There are a lot of candidates for the crown of Queen of the intellectual prostitutes, but most of them are too much fat old madams to arouse passion—Walter Lippmann, Arthur Krock, even Pegler and Sokolsky. Who in the world was it who set you off into such a fine rage that it glowed even through old man Webster's definition? Whoever it was I am grateful to him. Whenever he gets your "Missouri" really boiling again, reach for a pen and begin "Dear Dean." Your letters are at the top of my best seller list.

And your own best seller, the Memoirs in that superb edition and with the most moving and generous inscription, delighted us both beyond words. That was a real present for the archives. Alice and I are immensely grateful to you. Thinking about all that those years meant, seeing your writing, and reading your letter, made me wish that you would forget these things called years and run the show once again before it all goes completely to hell in a hack. The Presidency today is not even visible. It is as intangible as an odor which some call a perfume; and others, a smell. The best 1956 imaginable to you and Mrs. Truman.

As ever,

Dean

Acheson had participated in officially inviting Truman to attend a dinner given each year in Washington by the Alfalfa Club, a select organization whose only purpose was to hold an annual dinner in late January. The club allegedly got its name because the alfalfa plant is perpetually thirsty and will do anything for a drink. Truman's "doldrums" stemmed from his ongoing dislike for Eisenhower and Dulles.

January 19, 1956

Dear Dean:

What a wonderful letter you sent me in reply to my letter on mental prostitutes!

You'll come to a conclusion some day that I'm only fishing for those grand communications—and you'll be more than half right too. You've no idea how much you contribute to keeping [me] out of the doldrums and keeping me from literally exploding when I read the sugar on Ike and about the decisiveness of the Snollygoster who is now Secretary of State, author of Foreign Policy since U.S. Grant and the Savior of you and me. Well, to hell with all that—I wonder if Bobby Burns had John Foster in mind when he said a "man's a man for a' that." Reckon he did?

But what caused this effusion[?] I have a card inviting me to cocktails at 6 o'clock prior to the Alfalfa Club Dinner at the Statler on Saturday evening Jan. 21, 1956! That card is in the name of a personal friend of mine, one Dean G. Acheson, Edward Burling, Jr., with whom I'm not well acquainted, and John Lord O'Brian of whom I think most highly.

Now what stumps me is that I'd be willing to risk my front seat in Beelzebub's domain against a jet flying machine that not one of those gentlemen knows where Alfalfa came from, what it is used for, how deep the roots go and what they do for the soil: nor do they know the principal use of the seed, nor do they know how many crops per year are harvested and which one is the seed crop.

I'm of the opinion that these three excellent gentlemen think that Alfalfa is the basic commodity in either Scotch or Bourbon Whiskey! Anyway I wish I could be there.

My best to Alice.

Sincerely,

Harry Truman

Acheson refers to an upcoming trip to Kansas City, where he will visit Truman and meet, in his capacity as vice president of the Harry S. Truman Library, with the members of the building committee, to discuss progress

building the library. Mr. Rabinowitch's letter discussed leaks from the so-
called Acheson-Lilienthal Report of 1946, which had made recommenda-
tions to Truman about the international control of atomic energy.

February 9, 1956
Dear Mr. President:

I am looking forward to Monday and seeing you. I hope the meeting
will take place as planned.

In the meantime I am sending you, in the thought that you might be
interested in seeing it, a letter from the editor of *The Bulletin of the
Atomic Scientists,* Mr. Rabinowitch, and of my reply to him.

Alice joins me in the most affectionate greetings to you and Mrs.
Truman.

Most sincerely,

Dean

*Acheson wasn't able to stay at Truman's home while he was in Kansas
City, and stayed instead in the Presidential Suite on the eleventh floor of
the Muehlebach Hotel, which Truman and his staff had apparently called
the "penthouse" when they stayed there during Truman's presidency. The
three people Truman fired during his presidency were Douglas MacArthur,
James F. Byrnes, and Harold L. Ickes, and in a famous meeting shortly
after he became President he spoke very bluntly to Soviet Foreign Minister
Vyacheslav Molotov.*

February 21, 1956
Dear Dean:

Well, you are sunk again! I don't know when I've been so down in the
mouth as I was when you were here. Vietta, the old cook and general
factotum who has been with us since 1922 and who tried to show the
White House cooks how to make pies, biscuits and other things good to
eat, was down with a flu bug and the "Boss" had been having arthritis
pains in hands and knees—so you were treated like a stepchild coming
home to see his family.

I hope you'll forgive me. That's what I was thinking when I came up
to the Muehlebach penthouse. So if I appeared absent minded you'll
know why. Things seem to be in the groove since you were here and the
Library is an assured fact now. I'm glad we did it.

The present occupant of the White House seems really to have re-
pented—Homburg Hats, Formosa Straits, Korea visit, Egyptian Arms,

Saudi Arabia, etc., etc., ad lib. But Dean I'm not sure that election year repentance will get him into Heaven or Hell which ever title you think is the correct one for the great white jail at 1600 Connecticut Ave.

The National Committee of the Democratic Party I'm sure is of the opinion that "moderation" is the word. Maybe I'd [have] been much better off if I hadn't told Molotov, MacArthur, Byrnes, Ickes and Ike where the track ended and it was time to get off.

Maybe I'd better go to Europe and speak softly and bow and scrape in tails, tux and preacher coats. What about it.

My best to Alice and to you and yours.

Sincerely,

Harry Truman

"Stanley and Shirley" are Mrs. and Mrs. Stanley Woodward, who would accompany Truman on a two-month trip to Europe that began on his birthday, May 8. Woodward had been State Department chief of protocol and ambassador to Canada during the Truman administration. Acheson still thinks Eisenhower may not run for re-election. Christian Herter was at this time governor of Massachusetts. He would succeed John Foster Dulles as Secretary of State in 1959. Herter and Nixon were thought to be Republican moderates, compared with the right-wing isolationists of that time.

February 23, 1956

Dear Mr. President,

As I told you in Kansas City, I had a delightful time on my visit. And our talk on Tuesday afternoon will remain with me for a long time. We have seldom had such a quiet, private and uninterrupted chance to "jaw"—as old Judge Holmes used to say. It was great fun and you must not feel that I expect or want to be entertained when I come out. It is joy enough to see you and put all our thoughts on the table. And as for the missed dinner by reason of Vietta's excessive social life while you were East, I understood and sympathized with her and you.

Last Saturday we had a good evening with Margaret. She was very pretty and full of ginger. Her radio program, she told us, she is going to stop because it is so dull. This is a sure sign that she is getting too successful for words. I prescribe a few weeks in a law office to get her in the mood where even the commercials sound exciting. Stanley and Shirley were there full of eagerness for their trip with you this May and

June. I don't believe for a minute that this is going to turn you into a socialite, as you suggest, and know that when you get back we shall have the devil's own time getting a halter on you.

Adlai called me Sunday evening saying that he was being pressed to make some more statements on Israel and segregation. I urged him not to do so. Here are two matters which extreme talk can only make even more insoluble. The sensible people, and there are some, connected with Israel, the Arabs, the Southern Whites and the negroes are made to appear traitors when the field is left to the extremists. The press people here are all convinced that Ike's decision to run has already been made and is only delayed in coming out by (1) his wish to appear to be forced to run and (2) by the battle between the anti-Nixon forces who are pushing Herter, and Nixon and the right wing. However, I am not ready yet to hedge my bet that he won't run.

In all the exchanges over the memoirs no one has put you second best yet. That's pretty good going. I wish you had hit MacArthur harder. He never was a great soldier!

Faithfully yours,

Dean

Truman reports that his daughter, Margaret, is going to be married. Her fiancé was E. Clifton Daniel, a New York Times *journalist. Jonathan Daniels was a newsman and White House Press Secretary.*

March 26, 1956

Dear Dean:

Well, here you are a victim again. Margie has put one over on me and got herself engaged to a news man! He strikes me as a very nice fellow and if Margaret wants him I'll be satisfied. He seems to be very highly thought of in newspaper circles and particularly the *N.Y. Times* people.

The young lady told us about it just a week or two before the announcement and swore us to secrecy. In fact, she made me hang up while she told her mother. Did your daughter do you that way? I was forbidden to tell my brother and sister. Like a couple of amateurs they went to North Carolina to see his mother and father (nice people by the way) and then had dinner with Jonathan Daniels, of all people, hoping to keep a secret! The next day they called Daddy and wanted to know what to do. Well, Dad announced the engagement the next morning without a chance to tell his friends. Again, did your daughter do that?

Well, we've had at least two thousand letters and telegrams and she's had twice as many—serves her right. As every old man who has a daughter feels, I'm worried and hope things will work out all right. Can't you give me some consolation?

Sincerely,

Harry

Mary and Dave are Acheson's daughter and son.

March 27, 1956

Dear Mr. President,

Consolation is just what I can give. In the first place about Margaret's choice. She has always had good judgment and has shown it again here. Alice and I had dinner with them here on her birthday—just a year before we [had] celebrated it in Independence with you—I was completely captivated by Clifton Daniel. He has charm and sense and lots of ability. On the way home I told Alice that there was romance in the wind and that I was all for it. She somewhat acidly remarked that I had so monopolized Mr. Daniel that she hadn't been able to get any idea of Margaret's view of him, and that I was getting to be an old matchmaker. This only made my triumph all the sweeter when the announcement came. I stick by my guns and am sure that the man Margaret has chosen is first class and just the one for her. Marriage is the greatest of all gambles. But character helps and my bets are all on the success of this venture.

Now as to the behavior of daughters and the position of the father of the bride. Daughters, I have found, take this business of marriage into their own hands and do as they please. So do sons—or perhaps some one else's daughter decides for them. I explained most lucidly to Mary and Dave that they should wait until the end of the war to get married. So they got married at once. All in all, the father of the bride is a pitiable creature. No one bothers with him at all. He is always in the way—a sort of backward child—humored but not participating in the big decisions. His only comforter is a bottle of good bourbon. Have you plenty on hand?

At any rate all this will take your mind off politics which seem to me royally mixed up—at least on our side. One thing I don't understand. Some of the wise men say—and I hear you quoted to this effect—that the desirable thing is to have an open convention where the nomination can be worked out. But why isn't this a pretty sure road to getting some one whom nobody trusts? The only real possibilities—good possibilities—seem to be Adlai and Averell. Adlai, if nominated, would seem to have the better chance to win—though not a very good chance. Averell, if nominated and defeated, might, as the Governor of the most important Democratic state, be able to maintain a vigorous party committed to liberal principles through the difficult years until 1960. But by then he might be rather old for another try—and not realize it. At any rate, isn't that about the choice? And wouldn't it be rather good to have it made before rather than attempt it in the confusion of the convention? If you ask me, made by whom? I don't know. What I need from you is some political education. This is a fair exchange for consolation.

Alice sends her love to Mrs. Truman and to you. Her exhibition in New York has been—at the half-way mark—a great success. She has sold nine pictures. The latest purchaser, Mrs. Herbert Lehman.

Affectionately and sincerely,

Dean

On April 21, 1956, Margaret Truman and E. Clifton Daniel were married at Trinity Episcopal Church in Independence, Missouri—the same church where Harry and Bess Truman had been married thirty-seven years before. It does not appear that the Achesons attended the wedding.

Stanley Woodward urged Acheson to provide material for Truman's speech to the Pilgrims Society in London on June 21.

May 3, 1956

Dear Mr. President,

Stanley asked me, as your agent, to make some suggestions for your speech to the Pilgrims in London. It has been done and is enclosed. I talked over the general nature of the speech with David and Charles. We agreed on the general approach here used. I am alone responsible for the execution.

I am rushing to get this off so that you and David can look at it together.

As ever,

Dean

Acheson writes to Truman in New York City, where the Trumans would soon board ship for Europe. The two books were Harold Sinclair's The Horse Soldiers, *a Civil War story about a Union raid behind Confederate lines during the Battle of Vicksburg, and L. E. Jones's* A Victorian Boyhood, *a reminiscence of Victorian England. May 8 was Truman's birthday.*

May 9, 1956

Dear Mr. President,

The 8th eluded me. So birthday greetings go off to you today a little late but no less warm for all that. We send, also,—Alice and I—every wish for a wonderful trip. Do not let people impose on your good nature to go to dreary functions and make speeches to every kind of group. Mrs. Truman is the perfect answer to all these requests. This is her trip and you just can't do any of these unwanted things as you have a date with her. And a mighty good one it is, too—both answer and date.

Our affection goes with you, as do a couple of books we are sending to the ship. They are good ship-board reading and won't immerse you in problems. Please give our warmest greetings to Margaret and her nice husband.

Most sincerely,

Dean

Harry and Bess Truman, accompanied by Mr. and Mrs. Woodward, departed for Europe on the liner United States *on Truman's seventy-second birthday, May 8. Their seven-week grand tour took them to France, Italy, Austria, West Germany, Belgium, the Netherlands, and England. Crowds of admiring and curious people greeted Truman everywhere; reporters followed him; he had an audience with the Pope; he visited all the great monuments, historical sites, and museums along the way; in England, he received from Oxford University an honorary doctorate, met with Winston Churchill at his country home, had lunch with Queen Elizabeth, and delivered the speech Acheson wrote for him for the Pilgrims Society meeting. The Trumans sailed for home on June 28. Their grand tour of Europe was the best vacation of their lives.*

Acheson had plunged into presidential politics. The Democratic National Convention was only about a month away. In this letter he comments on Stevenson's and Harriman's candidacies.

July 15, 1956

Dear Mr. President,

The trip was clearly a great success. One could see that you were having the time of your life and it was a fair inference from this that Mrs. Truman was, too. We have not seen the Woodwards but, when they get back, shall look forward to all the details. Oxford and the Pilgrims dinner seem to have been a great success. In fact, even *The Washington Star,* under the delightful alliteration "Harricum Heads Home," said that you both were the best ambassadors we have. I hope you have not been tired out by all your experiences.

We are spending a quiet summer. In fact for the next two days it will be excessively quiet for me since I am having a check up to see why some of my machinery doesn't work better than it does. But some work goes on, too. I have been working with a group here to get up some suggestions on a foreign policy plank for the platform committee. In a day or two I shall send you the latest draft for your comments.

Averell was here last Friday and seemed in good health and spirits, though inclined to believe that during his time in the hospital Adlai had gotten a bandwagon started. I like Averell's fighting attitude and his good knowledge and judgment about foreign affairs. It seems to me that he is deceived about his chances by the talk of some of the politicos. He wants you to come out for him privately now on the theory that this would stop a pure bandwagon performance and allow a more deliberate consideration and choice. I told him that I thought you were wise in remaining neutral at this time in order to be effective later if the necessity arose in a deadlock. I recognize that this at the moment helped Adlai more then Averell, but I thought one who produced a deadlock, rather than resolved one, was assuming quite a responsibility.

Alice and the children and grandchildren are all fortunately well. We send you and Mrs. Truman affectionate greetings and a warm welcome home

Most sincerely,

Dean

P.S. One of my principal purposes in starting this letter was to send you my thanks for the handsome and inscribed copy of Volume Two of your memoirs. I am most grateful and appreciative. It will be preserved and treasured in its place of Honor.

Sherman Adams was Eisenhower's chief executive assistant.

July 20, 1956

Dear Dean:

Your letter of the 17th [sic] was as highly appreciated as your letters always are. I was afraid I'd let you down at Oxford but apparently I didn't.

Our trip was fantastic. At the ship going and coming we were treated as if we still lived at 1600 Penna. Ave! At LaHarve [Le Havre], Paris, Rome, Naples, Assisi, Venice, Vicenza, Salzburg, Munich, Bonn, the Loire Valley, Brussels, The Hague, Amsterdam, Harlem, London, Oxford, Chartwell, 10 Downing Street, Buckingham Palace, Southampton we were overwhelmed with kindness.

Paris, on our arrival from the ship on the way to Rome, they mobbed us. There were 2000 people at the station and only four police, two gendarmes, and one security officer. The Boss and Mrs. Woodward were squeezed out and almost mashed. I had to send a policeman for them. Rome same way, same experience.

We went to the Greek temple area at Paestum and the ladies' hair dos were as now and so were they in Pompeii. My sympathies were with the slaves of the time, most of whom knew more than did their owners.

Back in Rome we looked over some of the art of Michelangelo. His David, about which there are ravings, is not a Jew at all. He is not circumcised!

At Assisi the old priest who ran me upstairs and down, with a sprained ankle, kept asking me what St. Francis had done for me and I told him nothing but give me a sore throat and a stomach ache in his town of San Francisco. Questions stopped after that.

In Venice, we had a very highly educated young lady who took us through St. Mark's Cathedral [Basilica] and when I asked her where the Venetian Doges had stolen this article and that she was very much embarrassed. When I'd ask her which Doge authorized the great painting in the palace she could not tell me. She knew all about the artists and I was somewhat familiar with the men who made the artists possible— She wasn't but I didn't tell her!

At Vicenza we saw the first covered theater and an old bird put on a show for us by conversation. Margie had been there and signed the book and a program that I signed under her name and explained that I am Margaret's pop. It surprised the caretaker! It was the same all around the trip but it was a happy experience!

With the heads of State, Kings, Generals, Presidents, Princes and Foreign Ministers, I had some most interesting conversations, as I did with cooks, waiters, taxi drivers, little merchants and farmers. Dean, I'm sure they like us and if we had a Secretary of State and a President they'd love us as they did in the past.

In New York some fellow made the remark that it would be a terrible thing if Ike died and Nixon became President. The man he was talking to said he thought it would be worse if Sherman Adams died and Ike became President. I heard some more like that I'll have to hold and tell you later.

My best to Alice and all the family. Glad they are well. Hope that internal machine of yours becomes O.K. Hope to see you soon.

Sincerely,

Harry

Acheson congratulates Truman on his August 17 speech at the Democratic National Convention in Chicago, in which Truman expressed support for his former adviser Averell Harriman for the presidential nomination and publicly criticized Adlai Stevenson, saying, "He lacks the kind of fighting spirit that we need to win. . . ." When the convention gave the nomination to Stevenson on the first ballot, Truman quickly and effusively supported him, saying, "Governor Stevenson is a real fighter, and I ought to know. . . . He's given some of us here a pretty good licking."

August 21, 1956

Dear Mr. President,

We were proud of you Friday evening. You ate your crow graciously and with high good humor. It did a lot to restore an atmosphere of unity and confidence. The reality of unity is, I fear, a little further away. It depends on a real change in Averell's attitude. Publicly he, too, was gracious and good tempered, but that is not his state of mind, as you know better than I. For quite a while now he has been engaged in operation self-deception. It is going to be hard to wake up to the realities of life and the necessity of forcing on himself an attitude which will not be self-destructive. The most pathetic figure of the new deal was Al Smith, a magnificent figure eaten away by the leprosy of resentment and bitterness. I remember so well my father, after Mr. Roosevelt fired me in 1933, quoting St. Paul—"Think not on those things which are past, but on those which lie before us." You more than anyone, in view of what you have done for him and suffered because of it, can point this out to him. I hope you will.

Averell said to me not long ago that Adlai could not carry New York. Nothing will contribute more to this result than Averell's belief in it. Nothing will refresh and revive his own spirit more than to put all he has into proving his prediction wrong. I shall do my best to persuade him of all this; but you are the man who can do it.

If you want to read a delightful and most informative book get George Kennan's volume just out, *Russia Leaves the War.* It shows the confusion in conducting foreign policy in World War II as almost a carbon copy of that in World War I. It also throws a flood of light on the causes of the bewildering contradictions in United States–Soviet relations.

Alice is delighted that she spotted the new necklace and gives Mrs. Truman a big hand on it. Stanley Woodward and I are lunching together next week when I shall hear all about the trip.

Our most affectionate greetings.

Most sincerely,

Dean

August 29, 1956

Dear Dean:

As usual you "set me up" if you understand a Missouri bowling term. I talked to Averell for a half hour—at his expense!—wrote Sam Rosenman and it looks as if things are moving in the right direction.

When I arrived in Chicago things were dead, no life, no nothing. I decided to wake them up. It worked. We obtained a platform that is the best we've had, forced the candidate to endorse the New Deal and I'm sure he'll get around to the Fair Deal and you and me before he's finished on November 5th, Monday before [the] election.

You are right as can be about Al Smith. If he'd known some history and some results of what happens to bad losers he'd have been in a better position to help Franklin.

I am going to do all I can to help win this election. How I wish I were ten years younger! But I *ain't,* so there.

The professors of political science want me to talk to them in Washington on Sept. 7th and I may do it if you think I can do any good toward teaching the next generation what they have and what to do to keep it.

I've been reading a book about the ten years from '45 to '55. It builds up the small things and overlooks the big ones. Maybe that's history. If it is we must do what we can to leave facts to off set it.

Just got stuck with a speech to the Political Science Association in Washington September 7, 1956. You know I can't say "No" so it is understood. We'll see you then.

My best to Alice—the Boss joins me—and to you.

Sincerely,

Harry

Sam is Sam Rosenman, the highly respected assistant and speechwriter for President Roosevelt.

Dear Mr. President,   September 1, 1956

What good news about your talk with Averell and letter to Sam. I am sure both will do a lot of good.

Alice and I are very sad that we are going to be away just when you will be in Washington. We leave on Tuesday, Sept. 4, for a visit with our daughter, Jane, in Martha's Vineyard and friends on the way to and from. What bad luck! I am glad you will speak to the professors. They were kind enough to ask me, also, but I have been working on briefs all summer and just had to get away. This note is merely to bring you and Mrs. Truman our regret and affection. I shall write a proper one later on.

Sincerely,

Dean

Harry and Bess Truman with Margaret Truman on November 18, 1953.
Event is unknown.

5

November 1956 to December 1957

*Foreign-Policy and Civil-Rights Crises – A Meeting
in Washington – More Politics – The "S"*

*T*ruman and Acheson did not write each other for almost three months, September through November 1956. Truman was busy campaigning coast to coast for Adlai Stevenson and other Democrats, and stopping for a time to see his daughter and grandson (born in 1957) whenever his itinerary took him to New York City. Acheson got pneumonia at the time of the presidential election. His wife wrote Mrs. Truman that she thought the election was responsible for the pneumonia. "He refuses to see any ray of light ahead anywhere," Mrs. Acheson wrote.

When Truman and Acheson began writing again, their attention was fixed on a foreign-policy crisis in the Middle East regarding control of the Suez Canal and involving three American allies—the United Kingdom, France, and Israel, two of which were members of NATO. Acheson was highly critical of President Eisenhower's response to the crisis, which put the United States in agreement with the Soviet Union. He was also displeased with Truman's support for the President's so-called Eisenhower Doctrine proposal to offer U.S. military assistance to countries in the Middle East facing armed communist aggression. Acheson wrote some harsh words to Truman, but, as always, the friendship withstood the momentary disagreement, even over an important matter.

A civil-rights crisis in Little Rock, Arkansas, renewed Truman's and

Acheson's conviction that what they saw as President Eisenhower's weak leadership was damaging the U.S. position in the world. The two friends also wrote about the dedication of the Truman Library on July 6, 1957, and the cool message Eisenhower sent for the occasion. Their travels, lecture commitments, and too-infrequent meetings with each other always required some attention in their letters. They also wrote about the importance of combining their efforts to fight against a soft, pacific, trusting approach to foreign policy, as advocated by well-meaning but wrongheaded people such as Adlai Stevenson and George Kennan, and to fight for a foreign policy grounded in incisive understanding of national interests and power balances, and executed through a well-maintained alliance of free nations.

.   .   .

The speech Truman sends Acheson is actually drawn from Truman's Inaugural Address, not the State of the Union Message of 1949. The speech puts forward, like the Inaugural Address, a "program for peace and freedom" and calls on the leaders of the new Democratic Congress to "come up with what it takes to assure peace, liberty and the welfare of all nations." In this letter Truman also expresses worry about, among other things, the crisis in Egypt over the Suez Canal.

November 30, 1956

Dear Dean:

I sincerely hope that virus infection has left you and that you are well on the road to recovery.

I sent you a copy of the speech I made in St. Joseph night before last which undoubtedly went to your office. I am sending you another copy so you can contemplate it at home. Maybe it will contribute to your recovery—it is a paraphrase of the State of the Union Message of 1949 and it seems to me it is just as good now as it was then.

I have been terribly worried about the foreign situation as well as the domestic one and I am urging all the members of Congress, with whom I can get in touch, to come up with something because I don't think there will be any leadership from the other end of Pennsylvania Avenue.

Tell Alice that Mrs. Truman joins me in best wishes to both of you.

Sincerely yours,

Harry S. Truman

Truman writes a somber letter about U.S. foreign policy in the eastern-Mediterranean area. "This ignorant top notch man and Sullivan and Cromwell" refer to Secretary of State John Foster Dulles and the New York City law firm for which Dulles had worked before becoming Secretary of State.

November 30, 1956

Dear Dean:

I dictated a political letter to you this morning about the national and international situation. You know I'm worried as you are about it. Never do I like to talk about what might have been. You know that old abolitionist John G. Whittier said in his Maud Muller poem "Of all sad words of tongue or pen / The saddest are these: 'it might have been.' "

In my opinion the meanest of all words are "I told you so." In 1948 I had the Secret Service take down the crow eating invitation on the *Washington Post* Building.

But had the man with power said No emphatically and then have stood by our friends and allies no eastern Mediterranean crisis would have arisen. [About three words are indecipherable] be a mentally and physically tired man and we'd have had a peaceful settlement of Greece, Israel, Egypt, and *"Oil."* Well, here we are telling behind the Iron Curtain countries to rebel and then letting them be slaughtered!

What the hell can we do?

Tell me something to make me feel better. You and I did the right thing and this ignorant top notch man and Sullivan and Cromwell threw it out the window.

Get well and maybe something can be done.

My best to Alice and all the family.

Harry

Acheson writes a Trumanesque "spasm" on the "negation of leadership" in American foreign policy. Acheson was concerned that Eisenhower's administration was not addressing the realities and challenges of U.S.-U.S.S.R. hostility, particularly regarding the future of Germany.

December 4, 1956

Dear Mr. President,

Alice had such a nice note from Mrs. Truman giving me her sympathy and cheer. Now I have two from you. I am already on the way out of this horrid imprisonment. The doctor says about a week more. It has been an awful bore.

One of my friends believes that his ills of the flesh are inflicted on him by a just and implacable old testament God in punishment for evil thoughts or words which he has entertained or expressed. I am afraid that even a month of pneumonia would not atone for the flood of invective which the events of the past month have evoked from me. They have encompassed not merely our sanctimonious and unutterably stupid rulers, but the press which misinforms us, and our complacent, ignorant and fat-headed, fat bellied fellow citizens who create the environment for this negation of leadership.

We cannot seem to understand that we are playing for keeps in a deadly serious operation in which there are no rules, no umpire, no prizes for good boys, no dunce caps for bad boys. In this game good intentions are not worth a damn; moral principles are traps; weakness and indecision are fatal. This is what Americans have been taught since they went to Christian Endeavor meetings cannot and must not happen—"the law of the jungle," where the judgment of nature upon error is death.

And so we commit every error of every sort against nature. We make ourselves unworthy of the trust of our allies, we disregard their interests, we join with their and our enemies to weaken, humiliate and destroy them and our alliance with them. We believe for some incomprehensible reason that the U.N. is some disembodied moral force apart from ourselves. We are elated when it serves as the front for the combination of Russian and American power which crushes our allies. This is principle. We turn away when American desires running counter to Russian have no more effect than a peashooter on a tank.

I do not agree that your 1949 speech is appropriate today. Surely it is true and all that. But the truly false philosophy of 1956 is the American philosophy—by General Motors out of Eisenhower—two televisions in every pot, not a worry in a carload, live now and pay later—or leave to one's children. The finest flower of democracy—thirty-five million Americans can't be wrong— Or can they be.

As ever,

Dean

Truman continues the "spasm" against Eisenhower and Dulles. It's not clear whom he means by "Kenetsy, Bully et al.," but he is referring to the Suez crisis, when the United States took effective measures, some in the

United Nations, to force Britain, France, and Israel to stop their invasion and withdraw their forces from Egypt. It was generally thought that Eisenhower's position was the right one, but there was suspicion at the time that Dulles had encouraged the British-French move against Suez and only backed off when Khrushchev threatened to intervene, a suspicion that was strengthened by Harold Macmillan's memoirs, in which he said as much.

December 7, 1956

Dear Dean,

You've no idea how very much I appreciated yours of the 4th. Never was anyone gifted with expression of the facts in clear and understandable English as are you.

Since Jan. 20, 1953, I have had mental spasms over what has and has not come from 1600 Pennsylvania Avenue, Washington, D.C. Apparently nothing can be done about it. Public communications, printed word, radio, television have all been joined in a cover up and distortion program to help a do nothing attitude from the head of the greatest free government in the world.

What can we do to meet a situation such as that? How can we meet a fake sanctimonious and counterfeit prayer approach to a situation of "force makes right"? As you say we are playing for keeps and there are no rules and no umpires, no dunce caps for Stalinists, no rewards for good relations. Only the iron fist with a hundred yard saber in it will be understood by Stalin's successors.

Wonder what Nehru thinks now. What in hell was Ike thinking when he joined Kenetsy, Bully et al. in the U.N.[?] There can be no U.N. without guts and guns from us. Look, as if we have neither.

Get well and you and I can have a real get together and cuss everybody and settle everything—on paper and by words only.

Sincerely,

Harry

Truman praises Acheson for his statement a few days earlier before the House Committee on Foreign Affairs opposing Eisenhower's request for congressional authority to offer U.S. military assistance to any country in the Middle East facing armed aggression by a communist power. "The more one studies this proposal," Acheson had said, "the more vague, uncertain, and inadequate it appears as a statement of policy; and the more undesirable as an exercise of the legislative power of Congress."

January 14, 1957

Dear Dean:

Dave Lloyd sent me a copy of your statement of Friday to the House Committee on Foreign Affairs.

In Missouri language, *it is a humdinger.* Wish I'd been present to hear it. They asked me to appear and I told them that the Boss had been unfortunate and had broken two bones in her left foot besides pulling a ligament loose, that our old black cook had a heart attack and that I am chief cook and bottle washer at 219 North Delaware—would the Committee let me send a statement.

Had a most courteous telegram from them saying they'd be delighted to have the statement. Now—I don't know what to say. You've said it all.

But you know what, I'll crib some of your stuff, some of Paul-Henri Spaak's in the last quarterly of *Foreign Affairs* and some of my Greece and Turkey message of March 12, 1947, and a few other things, some of which I can't use, and there it will be.

Damn it, I wish I could see you oftener. You always give me a lift.

Bess is in a cast and has to behave. You should try it on Alice. I have a couple of black women who come in all day about to be sure the Boss doesn't fall again and I've cancelled my trip to Jefferson City, St. Louis and one or two other places so I can stay home nights. I wanted to see our Governor inaugurated today but can't do it. It would be my first since 1932. My best to Alice and tell her to stay away from that cast.

Sincerely,

Harry

Acheson writes an unusually strong criticism of Truman's North American Newspaper Alliance (NANA) article. Acheson was exasperated with Truman for undoing the considerable work Acheson had invested in a foreign-policy formulation that he had recently outlined while testifying before Congress. "If I were now a member of the United States Senate," Truman's article began, "I would support the request of the President for Congressional authorization to use the armed forces of the United States against any communist or communist-dominated aggressor in the Middle East. . . . Congress has no alternative but to go along with the President in this program to prevent the Russians from taking over the whole strategic Middle East. . . ."

January 15, 1957

Dear Mr. President:

I wish it were possible for us to coordinate our efforts a little better on foreign policy matters. Your article in last Sunday's *New York Times,* the first of your North American Newspaper Alliance articles, has, I am afraid, cut a good deal of ground out from under an effort to put some sense into the Administration's foreign policy and to put some fighting spirit into the Democrats.

Your article says that "Congress has no alternative but to go along with the President in this program." If this is so, then I spent four useless hours before the Foreign Affairs Committee and a good many useless days of work in devising what I thought an excellent alternative, and one which was thoroughly in accord with steps which had been taken during your Administration.

The article says later on, "Now that the President proposes to adopt a clear-cut policy of action, we should do everything to back him up." I do not think that, upon reflection, you will really regard this as a clear-cut policy. In fact, there is no policy about it at all, as I tried to show in the statement before the Committee, which David Lloyd sent to you.

Again, the article says that "We must at this stage accept the President's assessment of what the situation is, for only the President is in possession of all the facts." This seems to me a wholly artificial view to take. I don't think we have to accept the President's assessment; and I doubt very much that he is in possession of more facts than the rest of us here. Certainly he is not in possession of any more than Dulles told him about, and I would hesitate to rely on that source of information.

Finally, the article says, "The proposals made by the President, when approved by the Congress, will strengthen the position of the free world." Again, I don't think they will strengthen it at all. There are alternative courses of action which would strengthen it far more.

However, the main purpose of this note is not to stick on what has been done, but to urge that in the future we try to get together and not be at cross purposes. I had thought that we were in agreement when you were in Washington. Of course, I did not know that you were about to publish an article saying that you would, if you were a Senator, vote for a proposal which I was about to urge Congress to supplant with a better one.

I hope that Mrs. Truman is completely over all the pain and discomfort of her accident. Alice and I send our love to her and to you.

As ever,

Dean

Acheson likes the statement Truman sent to the House Committee on Foreign Affairs much better than the NANA article. The statement, while still saying that the Congress had no choice but to act in response to the President's request, placed some of the blame for the Middle East problems on the Eisenhower administration and criticized the vague plan the President put before Congress. Truman advised Congress to provide some guidance to administration actions in the Middle East and watch the developing situation carefully. Archibald MacLeish served for a brief time with the State Department; he had also served as Librarian of Congress and was a noted poet and dramatist.

January 26, 1957

Dear Mr. President,

The *New York Times* brings me your statement given to the House Committee. Since I criticized the statements in your article, may I praise those before the Committee. You still go further than I would, but that is all a matter of judgment on which I could well be wrong. But the new statement helps in placing the blame where it should be and, in this way, destroying the new myth of Eisenhower's infallibility. I thought Bill Fulbright's statement was excellent from this point of view.

Alice and I have had a week of lovely sun here in Bob Lovett's house. We have another week and then go on to Archie MacLeish in Antigua, B.W.I. I can get along very well without work.

Alice, who is painting, joins me in sending our affectionate greetings to Mrs. Truman and to you.

Sincerely,

Dean

Truman responds to Acheson's highly critical January 15 letter as well as to the more positive January 26 letter. The "proper reaction" mentioned would be that the House committee, or at least the Democratic members, would endorse Acheson's suggestions. "Mon Wallgren" is Senator Monrad Wallgren of Washington.

January 28, 1957

Dear Dean:

You certainly "took a load off my mind" with your good letter of Jan. 26th. Of course I want your views frankly on any subject at any time.

But I was somewhat flabbergasted when your formal letter, all beautifully typed, came on January 17th. I felt the same way I do when Miss Lizzie gives me hell for something I know nothing about. She's still in plaster of paris half way to her knee and I have the advantage. I can run and she can't catch me.

The final result of your statement to the Committee and mine has been a proper reaction that both of us are hoping may create a foreign policy. I am going to send you a copy of all the statements I've made in the last week or so and then if you want to give me further hell—do it—and I'll continue to like it.

Mon Wallgren told me a story about a Swede in North Dakota who had been forced to leave Minnesota because of a mix-up with a lady. After he was established in N.D. he began going with Gina Olsen. One day she came to see him and told him she thought she was pregnant, that she would go see the doctor and let him know. Well, Olie walked the floor of his store, kicked himself and felt very badly. Gina came back and reported the doctor out. So they took a walk to discuss things. Going by the town water reservoir Gina said to Olie, "If dot Doctor tell me the worst tomorrow, I coming up here and jump in that pond." Olie grabbed her in his arms and said, "Oh Gina you take a load off my mind." Well you did it too.

My best to Alice and you in which Bess would join if I'd ask her.

Harry

Truman had recently suffered a bad fall on an icy walkway. Acheson's reference to Senator Mike Mansfield of Montana may refer to the attachment of a so-called Mansfield Amendment to the Eisenhower Doctrine. This amendment, which was viewed as an indirect security guarantee to Israel, stated that preserving the independence and sovereignty of the Middle East nations was in the national interest of the United States.

February 12, 1957

Dear Mr. President,

Please stay right side up. We want your head unbowed but not bloody.

Your letter about Gina Olsen was a joy. I'm glad that I took a load off your mind. What a fine job Mike Mansfield did in his Senate speech.

This is only a line to send you and Mrs. Truman our love and to urge you both to keep your feet on the ground.

Sincerely,

Dean

We go home on Saturday.

Truman did not send this letter about the Potsdam Conference to Acheson. Instead, he incorporated its content into a longer letter dated April 8.

March 15, 1957

Dear Dean:

It was certainly a pleasure to talk with you about Potsdam and the Doctor who is interested in that phase of our foreign policy.

I hardly ever look back for the purpose of contemplating "what might have been." Potsdam brings to mind "what might have been" had you been there instead of the Congressman, Senator, Supreme Court Justice, Presidential Assistant, Secretary of State, Governor of Secessionist South Carolina the Honorable James F. Byrnes!

At that time I trusted him implicitly—and he was then conniving [to] run the Presidency over my head! I had Joe Davies, at that time a Russophile as most of us were, Ed Pauley, the only hard boiled, hard hitting anti-Russian around except the tough old Admiral, Bill Leahy. Certainly things were presented because Russia had no program except to take over the free part of Europe, kill as many Germans as possible and fool the Western Alliance. Britain only wanted to control the Eastern Mediterranean, keep India, oil in Persia, the Suez Canal and whatever else was floating loose.

There was an innocent idealist at one corner of that Round Table who wanted free waterways, Danube-Rhine, Kiel Canal, Suez, Black Sea Straits, Panama all free, a restoration of Germany, France, Italy, Poland, Czechoslovakia, Romania and the Balkans, and a proper treatment of Latvia, Lithuania, Finland, free Philippines, Indonesia, Indo China, a Chinese Republic and a free Japan.

What a show that was! But a large number of agreements were reached in spite of the setup—only to be broken as soon as the unconscionable Russian Dictator returned to Moscow! And I liked the little son of a bitch. He was a good six inches shorter than I am and even Churchill was only three inches taller than Joe! Yet I was the little man in stature and intellect! So the Press said. Well, we'll see.

Wish you'd been there. Tell your friend I'll help him all I can. My best to Alice.

Sincerely,

H.S.T.

The article by Max Freedman (Manchester Guardian) *titled "Lessons in How to Master a Crisis," which Acheson encloses, contrasts the Truman Doctrine and the Eisenhower Doctrine. Eisenhower's response to crisis compared with Truman's is "shabby," wrote Freedman. Truman was about two months away from becoming a grandfather when Acheson wrote this letter. Truman was, with very few exceptions, opposed to having anything named for him, and this applied to grandchildren too. Many things have been named for him anyway, especially in the Kansas City area. But not one of his four grandsons was given his name, with the exception that his first grandson's name is* Clifton Truman *Daniel.*

April 5, 1957

Dear Mr. President,

It was a sad disappointment to miss lunching with you last Tuesday but, as David told you, my brother-in-law's funeral was that morning. Perhaps I shall see you in May. For my sins I am to be chairman of the Democratic dinner on May 4. The whole outlook would change if there should be the possibility of introducing you.

The enclosed piece by Max Freedman in the *Manchester Guardian* draws a contrast which you will be glad to see noted. You might want to put it with your Greek Turkish papers.

I hope all goes well with Margaret. What is this about your being adamant against having a grandchild named for you? Have you had an offer? I never had one, perhaps for the reasons you gave.

Warmest regards to Mrs. Truman and to you.

As ever,

Dean

This letter incorporates the one Truman wrote on March 15. Something may have still worried him about this letter, and he probably didn't mail it for several days. Dick Stone is Richard Stone, Democratic senator from Florida; Donald Dawson had been a presidential aide; and Scott Lucas was a former Democratic senator from Illinois.

April 8, 1957

Dear Dean:

On March 15 I wrote you one of my long hand spasms after I'd talked to you about Potsdam and the Doctor who is interested in that phase of your foreign policy.

This morning your long hand letter came with the photostat of the piece from the *Manchester Guardian*. I immediately dictated a note to you telling you how I appreciated the enclosure and how much I regretted missing you in D.C. the day I was there.

Mrs. Truman's youngest brother was taken to the hospital yesterday and, I'm told, may not go back home. So—I can understand exactly why we did not have that meeting at the noon day lunch with Charlie Murphy, Dave Lloyd, Senator Dick Stone and Don Dawson. Of course it was a disappointment—but we'll try to alleviate that between us when the Boss and I come to the capital on May 3rd.

On May 2nd I'm lecturing the Student Body of N.Y. University on the President's duties and prerogatives, as was done at M.I.T., Harvard Law School and Oklahoma A and M recently. What a lot of fun I had at those places. Been reading your book on the Congress. Between you and Woodrow Wilson I'm learning a lot—and hope to learn a lot more!

I hardly ever look back for the purpose of contemplating "what might have been." Potsdam brings to mind "what might have been" had you been there instead of the Congressman, Senator, Supreme Court Justice, Presidential Assistant, Secretary of State, Governor of Secessionist South Carolina, the Honorable James F. Byrnes.

Makes me think of a [former Senator] Scott Lucas [D., Illinois] story about a trial in Illinois when Scott was on one side and an astute cross examiner was on the other. One of Scott's witnesses was an old electioneer, who, of course, was addressed as Colonel. The astute cross examiner took him over and asked, "Mr. Jones just what does that Colonel in front of your name stand for?" The old Colonel said, "My friend, it is just like that Honorable in front of yours it don't mean a damn thing." Cross examination ended there.

Well, at Potsdam I trusted the "Honorable" Jimmy implicitly. He was then conniving to run the Presidency over my head just as old Seward tried it on Lincoln. Seward learned his lesson. "Hon." Jimmy did not.

I had Joe Davies at that time, a Russophile as most of us were, Ed Pauley, the only hard boiled, hard hitting anti-Russian around except the tough old Admiral, Bill Leahy. Certain things were presented because Russia had no program but to take over free Europe, China and Korea, kill as many Germans, Poles and Lithuanians as possible and break up the Western Alliance. Britain only wanted to control the Eastern Mediterranean, keep India, oil in Persia, the Suez Canal and whatever else was floating loose, including control of the seas of the world!

There was a nice, innocent idealist (good definition for a diplomatic damn fool) in one corner of that Round Table who wanted free waterways, Rhine-Danube, Kiel Canal, Suez, Black Sea Straits, Panama, all free, a restoration of Germany, France, Italy, Poland, the Czechs, Romania, the Balkans, Estonia, Latvia, Lithuania, Finland, Indonesia, Indo-China, a Chinese Republic, a Philippine Republic, and a free Japan. That damn fool wanted a free trade agreement between all the countries in the world and a full development of their resources for the benefit of the people in their various locations.

Well, what a show that was! In spite of the set up a great number of agreements were accomplished — only to be broken when the Dictator of all the Russians without a conscience returned to his home dunghill. And I liked the little son of a bitch — self made of course, no reflection on his mother. He was a good six inches shorter than I am and even the great Churchill was only three inches taller than that Russian.

But I was the little man there present in stature and intellect! At least that's what our "free press" said.

Wish you'd been there. Tell your friend I'll help him all I can. I'm looking forward to a grand visit with you on May 3rd, 4th and 5th.

My best to Alice. Wish I could have seen her picture exhibition.

Most sincerely,

Harry S. Truman

April 11, 1957

HONORABLE DEAN ACHESON
CONGRATULATIONS ON ANOTHER MILESTONE. I HOPE YOU HAVE MANY MORE OF THEM AND THAT ALICE DOESN'T THINK YOU ARE BECOMING CRANKY ON ACCOUNT OF AGE.
HARRY S. TRUMAN

Truman is responding to Acheson's letter of April 5. He did eventually send the longhand letter he mentions (dated April 8; see above).

April 12, 1957

Dear Dean:

You don't know how much I appreciated your note enclosing the photostat from *The Manchester Guardian,* which will be placed where you suggest.

The reason I couldn't stay over in Washington was that I had to be back here to prepare a speech for Topeka, Kansas, for the celebration of the election of a Democratic Governor in Kansas. We had a most successful meeting and a lot of fun.

I wrote a longhand letter after I had talked to you about the Potsdam papers but I haven't made up my mind to send it.

For your information, you are going to have an opportunity to introduce me at that May 4th meeting and Mrs. Truman will also be there. Even if I had decided not to come, when I found out you were going to preside nothing could keep me away.

Sincerely yours,

Harry S. Truman

Acheson looks forward to seeing Truman during his upcoming trip to New York and Washington.

April 17, 1957

Dear Mr. President:

The last few days have delighted me by bringing your two letters and a telegram. Why should you have hesitated to send me the longhand one? It is one of the most delightful letters I have had from you and gives your reflections on most important events in an incomparable way.

I am looking forward to seeing you and Mrs. Truman and introducing you to the assembled Democrats.

We want very much to introduce you to another and much smaller assembly. My daughter Mary, in conjunction with her sister from New York and her brother from Washington are putting on a small party at Mary's house on Sunday night, May 5, to celebrate Alice's and my Fortieth Wedding Anniversary. It would give all of us the greatest joy if Mrs. Truman and yourself could come, even if only for a short time.

She will have dinner and supper and people will stay on after. If you are not going back on Sunday, let me put in our claim on both of you now.

With warmest regards.

Sincerely,

Dean

Your birthday telegram gave us both a glow of pleasure. D.

Dear Dean: April 23, 1957

I appreciated your letter of the 17th as I always appreciate any communication from you.

Our schedule calls for our arrival in Washington on May 3rd. We will be there the 4th and 5th but will have to leave on the B and O Diplomat at 9:30 on the evening of the 5th. You may count on our coming Sunday, but we will not be able to stay as long as we would like.

You are ahead of us in anniversaries by two years. The "Boss" and I will celebrate our 38th in June. Both you and I are very lucky in the partners we took for life.

Please give our best to Alice and all the rest of the family, and as soon as we get to Washington, we will work out a plan so that we can put in an appearance at Mary's.

Sincerely yours,

Harry

Truman spoke to student groups at Columbia University and New York University on May 1 and 2, to a Democratic Party dinner in Washington on May 4. On May 5 he attended the party celebrating Dean and Alice Acheson's fortieth wedding anniversary.

Michael is a son of Mary Acheson Bundy, Acheson's younger daughter. Michael attended the Sunday-evening anniversary dinner.

Dear Mr. Truman,   May 7, 1957

Our warmest greetings on your birthday. I wish that I could be at the dinner your friends and neighbors are giving you and to which they kindly invited me. But we shall be thinking of you and Alice and I drink a toast.

You both gave everyone a great thrill on Sunday evening. Michael has not calmed down yet. Yesterday when Mary picked him up at school his first words were, "Boy, what a party that was!" He then went on to say that he was going to write a book about you. "And I have a title, too," he added. Mary asked what it was. "The Best Natured American," he said. So there is an endorsement for you to use with the boss when she gives you hell for wondering who lives in the White House now.

We all feel better for your visit and because you both looked so well.

As ever,

Dean

A few weeks after the 1956 presidential election, the Democratic National Committee (DNC) formed the Democratic Advisory Council (DAC), which was charged with formulating policy positions for the Democratic Party. DNC Chair Paul Butler asked Truman to ask Acheson to chair the DAC's foreign-policy committee. Truman sends Acheson a telegram, and Acheson subsequently accepts the position.

May 27, 1957

HONORABLE DEAN ACHESON
THE NATIONAL CHAIRMAN CALLED ME ABOUT A FOREIGN POLICY PROGRAM FOR THE NATIONAL COMMITTEE. HE WANTS YOU TO HEAD THE ORGANIZATION. I HOPE YOU CAN DO IT. I WILL WRITE YOU AS SOON AS I HAVE AN OPPORTUNITY TO SIT DOWN.
HARRY S. TRUMAN

The Harry S. Truman Library was to be dedicated on July 6. Truman wants Acheson to be with him that day.

June 1, 1957

Dear Dean:

I am starting the first month of summer with a letter to you. I sent you a telegram on May 27th at the behest of Paul Butler. Maybe it isn't worthy of any consideration. As you know from long experience some—maybe all—my aberrations need looking at very carefully.

That anniversary party your children gave you was quite the nicest one I've been to in all my checkered career. That young grandson of yours has a real political future. He has the public relations touch to start with. It is hard to cultivate if it isn't a natural asset to begin with.

I've been doing more things I shouldn't than ever before. A local keynote speech for local Democrats, a series of invitations to public officials and has been public officialites, an agreement to address the Police Chiefs of Missouri on the Bill of Rights, appearances here and there for no reason whatever but some friend and former supporter in hard times past asked me.

The "Boss" has about made up her mind to go in with some Independence people and run me for Mayor! And then charge admission to the City Hall to see the striped mule from Missouri. I think she's ridiculing me, don't you?

Anyway I'm having a hell of a time and a lot of fun. I expect to be knee deep in "Big Shots" July 6th and I want you and Alice to be here to help me out of what Huey Long would call a deep "More Ass." It's in the Congressional Record.

Be sure and come. I may tell some Ambassador or Senator "to go to hell" and you'll have to keep him from going. As you know Stanley's gone to the other side of the pond. I rather think he went because there'll be too much protocol here on July 6th—or none at all!

Be sure and come. I won't mix you in my difficulties, but I want you and Alice here.

You helped more than anyone to make things come out right.

Sincerely,

Harry S Truman

Acheson has in effect become the Democratic Party spokesman on foreign-policy issues. Paul Nitze was associated with the School of Advanced International Studies at Johns Hopkins University, and Milton Eisenhower, President Eisenhower's brother, was president of Johns Hopkins University. An interview with Soviet Premier Nikita Khrushchev was broadcast on the CBS news program Face the Nation *on June 2. Acheson portrays the interview as free propaganda for Khrushchev. The Soviet premier had bragged that the Soviet Union would soon outpace the United States in agricultural production and predicted, "Your grandchildren in America will live under socialism." Most important, and potentially most damaging to American interests, he portrayed the Soviet Union as a peaceful nation that wished to end nuclear testing, end all trade restrictions throughout the world, and bring about the withdrawal of all Soviet and American troops from Europe. About ten million Americans saw or heard Khrushchev's interview. In the P.S., he refers to the birth of Truman's first grandson, Clifton Truman Daniel, on June 5.*

June 5, 1957

Dear Mr. President:

There is no better way for me to start the summer than for you to start it by writing me—and you pleased us both mightily by what you said about the children's party for us and about Michael. He is the only source of energy I know of which equals the atom. After he had spent a month with us while his parents went around the world Alice reports saying to me "Don't you miss Michael?" and my exhausted reply, "Not yet." I feel sure that if he ever landed in the White House no puzzled countryman would have to ask, "I wonder who lives there now?"

The boys finally twisted my arm until I agreed to be Chairman of the Foreign Affairs Committee appointed by your Advisory Committee, about which you telegraphed me. Charlie Murphy was eager to have me do it because, he said, the party was getting over the foolish attitude of backing away from the Truman administration and that I would help the reform by joining the Committee. What the Committee can do still puzzles me, but then if it doesn't do anything it won't do any harm, which for some Democrats these days is a big achievement. Paul Nitze has agreed to be Vice Chairman, which is fine and hard for him in view of the necessity of his School's access to the State Dept. and the fact that the President of the University to which it belongs is Milton Eisenhower. So we shall see what can be done.

This recent flap about the Khrushchev interview is a good example of what I talked about once as "total diplomacy"—that the diplomacy of a democracy was not at all restricted to what the government did, including the disorderly performances of the Congress, but included the press, radio and television, the movies, churches, labor unions, business, women's clubs, etc. Here comes C.B.S. blundering into the picture with three interviewers who act as though they had never finished the sixth grade and give Khrushchev more free propaganda—which he used admirably—than he could have obtained in a year. As I see it, he had only one point to make—which happened to be untrue but which he put over to the Queen's taste—that the Russians were willing to "ban the bomb", move out of Europe, get on with mutual travel and cultural exchanges, trade, etc., etc. but that the Americans seemed to be afraid to do so. Communism was, he said, bound to win and we knew it. So we remained frozen like frightened rabbits. All the early part of the interview where he flubbed around with the agricultural situation, about which he clearly knew little, gave the impression—and was intended to—of a simple, honest fellow doing the best he could with great problems. He gets the prize for 1957 and CBS gets the dunce cap—and probably a big boost in income.

I shall, of course, be with you on the sixth of July. Alice says she has "every hope of being with me." I ask what that means to which she replies with exasperating calm that it is too early for her to say absolutely that she can come. So I shall make a plane reservation for her anyway and, if the temperature is under a hundred I think she'll go.

I am doing a piece for a European magazine on NATO which I think you will like and will send along soon. Our most affectionate greetings to Mrs. Truman and to you.

As ever,

Dean

P.S. Since writing this the radio has told us that Margaret has given you the only gift remaining to make your happiness complete. Our warmest congratulations and every good wish to Margaret and the grandson. The poor father is always neglected on these occasions, so we include him, too. D.

Truman is upset about the impersonal message from Eisenhower which the Administrator of General Services had read during the Truman Library dedication ceremony. It was clear to Truman and others that Eisenhower still bore grudges against Truman, largely because of things said and done during the 1952 campaign. Frank McKinney is a former DNC Chair.

July 10, 1957

Dear Dean:

I'm very much perturbed because I think I treated you and Alice like step children last Saturday. I hope you know that would not happen intentionally. The sun, the day and everything went off much more happily than I hoped it would go.

I hope you were impressed with Ike's telegram to the peepul! What in hell makes some of us tick? Maybe you and I could find out if they'd let us.

It has rained every day since the dedication. I am as happy as I can be that the sun did shine.

Frank McKinney was here. Dean, he has a boy, named for him, who wants to go to Yale. He's late starting for entrance. Wish you'd get him in. He has a remarkable scholastic background as well as an acrobatic one— He won some world championships in Australia.

My effort for the study of Presidential papers seems to be working.

My best to Alice and to you.

Harry

Acheson is puzzled why a copy of the Milwaukee Journal *for May 3, 1957, carrying an account of the Senate funeral services for Senator Joseph McCarthy, was put in the sealed container that would go in the Truman Library's cornerstone. "That paper won't go in the box . . . ," Truman told the press the day the outrage was discovered. "Someone just didn't know what he was doing when he put that in there." Actually, Truman had intended to include a copy of the* Journal, *a newspaper he admired. The copy the* Journal *staff sent to Truman for the cornerstone was dated May 3 and happened to carry a headline about Joseph McCarthy, who had died the day before. Truman, meanwhile, had changed his mind at the last minute, deciding to include only local newspapers, but this decision was not conveyed to his assistant, so the* Journal *stayed on the list of items for the cornerstone. The big problem was not the McCarthy headline, but the fact that the list of items was read aloud to the crowd in front of the library on dedication day, and the* Journal *was identified as the newspaper "with the headline 'Senate Prepares Rites for McCarthy.' "*

July 10, 1957

Dear Mr. President:

My curiosity cannot stand the strain another day. What is the true story of the *Milwaukee Sentinel's* [sic] edition on McCarthy appearing on the list of contents for the cornerstone? I felt as I have at some weddings when the minister invites anyone so inclined to louse up the proceedings.

The dedication was a great occasion. I hope it gave you and Mrs. Truman some sense of the respect and affection which is felt for you both.

As ever,

Dean

P.S. Is the Fed. Res. Bank Bldg. address still official? D.

P.P.S. Your note has come since I finished this. Put all those worries about us out of your mind. We wouldn't have missed the party. It never occurred to us that we were step-children. We are honest-to-God family and don't have to be fussed over. What luck it was that the rain held off and what further luck to have some now. We are having a bad drought. For gardeners like Alice and me that is real trouble.

Frank spoke to me about his boy who certainly has all the qualifications. He said that he would give me further details. The trouble is that the boy waited until we have accepted a good many more than we can take—some always drop out. But the entrance authorities can't tell until the returns are in. I shall do what I can. D.

Truman is pleased that legislation authorizing the Library of Congress to arrange and microfilm its large collection of presidential papers has passed in the House of Representatives. He had testified in its favor on June 21. The bill was signed into law on August 16. Truman loved history, studied it all his life, and was grateful for all it had given him. He wrote in his memoirs, "My debt to history is one which cannot be calculated." He wanted historians to write objective accounts based on careful research in documentary resources, not on political bias. He believed some nineteenth-century historians, especially those from Whig New England, had presented unfairly negative accounts of such Presidents as Jefferson and Jackson.

July 16, 1957

Dear Dean:

You'll never know how happy you made me feel when you wrote me that you and Alice had not been treated as "step children."

It was a hell-of-a-day, and the reason for it was that there was an objective. Just had a letter from John McCormack informing me that the legislation authorizing the indexing and microfilming of Presidential papers has past! [*sic*]

If Hoover, those Republican Congressmen, Knowland and our Democrats had not been asked, it wouldn't have happened. We've accomplished something that should have been done two generations ago.

I'll send the telegram you suggest. Wish I could tell you all the maneuvers I've been making to place the history of the Legislative, Executive and Judicial Departments in a position that young students can understand.

You know I'm no scholar in any line—but I do know that our history and the men who made it have been left in the lurch. The New England historians saw to that. Why so called Puritans find it so hard to stay with truth when it is against them. That is the reason I'm so interested in having all the facts as we know them available. Maybe I am a nut on the subject. If I am I hope you'll bear with me.

Historians, those who edit news stories and even men who think they know facts, have to be studied and their errors put in the proper light.

I sent the wire day letter.

Sincerely,

Harry Truman

The Western World *article Truman refers to was titled "A Vital Necessity for America and Europe."* Western World, *which advertised itself as "the first bilingual transatlantic magazine," was published in Brussels, Belgium, from May 1957 to March 1960. It was absorbed by the* European Atlantic Review *in January 1961. He actually read a condensed version that ran as a syndicated column, titled, "Is NATO a Lost Cause? Kill NATO and Doom Europe, Ex-Secretary Acheson Says." Acheson argued against the point of view, recently put forward to former State Department colleague George F. Kennan, famed formulator of the Truman administration's containment policy, that Germany should be neutralized and unified, and that the United States and the Soviet Union should both withdraw from Europe.*

August 5, 1957

Dear Dean:

Your article from *The Western World*, of which I have just received a transcript, is a great one.

Whenever you put out something of this kind, it is always great, in my book.

Sincerely yours,

Harry S. Truman

Acheson asks Truman to write to certain congressmen in support of President Eisenhower's budget request for the Development Loan Fund, which was the agency charged with what was called Point Four foreign aid to underdeveloped countries during Truman's administration. Truman immediately did as Acheson asked. Albert Sidney Johnson Carnahan was a Democratic Representative from Missouri.

August 6, 1957

Dear Mr. President:

We must, I believe, strike another blow to help this incompetent administration by getting some obstreperous Democrats back on the reservation. The enclosed memorandum explains the situation which has arisen in the House concerning the proposed Development Loan Fund in the Mutual Security bill now before the Congress.

It would be most helpful if you would make a statement on the Fund after the Conferees have reported and before the bill comes to the House floor. This probably will be Thursday or Friday of this week. I have attached a draft for you to consider.

The statement might be made in reply to a request made by Speaker Rayburn, John McCormack, or Representative Carnahan, who handled the bill on the floor for the Foreign Affairs Committee and is a member of the Conferees and, presumably, will handle the Conference reports. Carnahan will give me a specific recommendation tomorrow which I shall pass along to you.

Your generous note about my article has just come. It has given me a real lift.

Sincerely,

Dean

Acheson writes Truman about legislation that became the Civil Rights Act of 1957, the first civil-rights legislation passed since Reconstruction. Congress had refused, despite Truman's most ardent efforts, to pass civil-rights legislation during his administration. Truman was able to desegregate the armed forces and the government civil service through executive order.

August 14, 1957

Dear Mr. President:

Thank you very much for having sent the letter to Congressman Carnahan, with copies to Sam, Lyndon and John McCormack.

After I wrote you, as a result of Sam's canvassing the field it was decided to strike out the loan authority altogether, and merely authorize appropriations for two years. All those concerned, therefore, thought that as this rather disappointing compromise would go through Congress without much help, they would not use your support now but would save it for what may be the very tough period when it comes to the actual appropriation itself. When the time comes they are to let me know and I shall get you on the telephone. The same letter can be used with some very minor changes toward the end of making it appropriate to the new situation. Everybody is most grateful for your willingness to help.

I think you will be interested in a copy of a letter to Lyndon which I wrote him today at his request. He and Sam have been having real difficulty with some of the Northern liberals, although I think most of them are now beginning to see the light. He wanted a letter which would express what I had been saying to him the other day, that the bill is not a mere compromise, not a second-rate article which has to be taken in lieu of something better, but is in reality a better bill than the one originally proposed. It will be a tragedy of the greatest order if well meaning but ignorant people are made the dupes of cynical politicians to destroy this really fine effort.

Alice is trying to get Clifton to come down this fall to speak to the Women's National Democratic Club. To this end she is hoping to induce Margaret and Clifton to stay with us. I pointed out that this is a delightful idea but leaves out one member of the family of the greatest possible importance.

With warmest greetings.

As ever,

Dean

Truman asks Acheson whether he should accept an invitation to speak at Yale University, Acheson's alma mater. The NANA article concerned the Eisenhower Doctrine and the Middle East.

August 21, 1957

Dear Dean:

I am enclosing you a copy of a letter I received from the Yale Political Union.

If you think it is a good thing, I will do my best to fit it into my schedule.

I am a little vague about the meaning of a "tri-partisan" debating society. "Bi-partisan" is, of course, within my scope of comprehension.

Your letter of the 14th was more than appreciated, and I read your message to Lyndon with the greatest interest. You told him exactly what he ought to hear.

I just happened to have a copy of my latest article for NANA which I will enclose. It covers the pending situation in the Near East, which, between you and me, I think we have lost.

Sincerely yours,

Harry

My best to Alice.

The new book that Acheson was working on was eventually titled Power and Diplomacy. *He chides Truman for some too-simple argumentation in his recent NANA article. Truman, now as earlier, was more willing than Acheson to advise Congress to give the President the powers he was request-ing to commit American forces to the Middle East.*

Dear Mr. President: August 28, 1957

Alice and I are off tomorrow for a vacation of three weeks visiting children and seeing friends—not that the children are not friends.

I am hastening this note in answer to yours of August 21st before we leave. My advice would be to pass up this invitation from the Yale Polit-ical Union. You have far more important things to do, and some day I want you to come to Yale for a stay of some days, under the auspices of the University itself and not of a particular under-graduate group.

The "tri-partisan" idea puzzled me too. However, my son, David, offers illumination. The Political Union did not exist in my day, but he seems to have been President of it in his. I gather from him that there are three parties in the Union, covering the spectrum—the Conserva-tive, the Liberal, and the Labor parties. So I think that neither of us need feel—at any rate we won't feel—that our intellectual powers are slipping because we did not know what the writer meant.

The letter to Lyndon, slightly recast to put it in the form of an article, will appear in *The Reporter* issue of September 5th (to go on sale August 29). In the next issue I have another article—a frivolous one, but I think you and Mrs. Truman will get a chuckle out of it.

Today I am in a state of exhaustion, having finished the first draft of my lectures at the Fletcher School, which will come out in book form in the spring. The title might be—but probably won't be—"An Ameri-can Looks at the World." It is an attempt to survey the world situation as it is, the two opposed systems which are in process of formation, and what we are called upon to do economically, militarily, and politically, if the free world system is to be viable and defensible. It is quite a mouthful. When I get a revised clean draft, sometime in September, I shall send a copy on to you.

I have read with great interest your last article, which you were kind enough to send to me. It lays down some truths which need to be said and resaid. Its abbreviated form necessitated stating some things as absolute, which I hesitate to think are quite so clear.

Our love to Mrs. Truman.

Sincerely yours,

Dean

Truman mentions that he is still settling in to his new office at the Truman Library. He would report for work to that office essentially every day for nine years when he was not traveling or ill.

August 31, 1957

Dear Dean:

Your letter of the 28th was most highly appreciated, and just as soon as I can get straightened out in my new office, I will sit down and write you a real letter.

Thank you for that information on the "tri-partisan" situation. When something of that kind puzzles my Secretary of State, who is never puzzled by anything (except, perhaps, the supposititious inclusion of an issue of the *Milwaukee Journal* in the library cornerstone), my confusion no longer troubles me.

I will try to get copies of the September 5th and immediately following issue of the *Reporter.* I may ask the old man to send it to me all the time. I used to get it when it was first started and I was making contributions, but he cut me off when I had to stop.

I am looking forward with longing and tremendous interest to the publication of your series of Fletcher School lectures. I see no reason why you should not call it *An American Looks at the World.*

The Boss was highly pleased to have an opportunity to read your letter, and she joins me in the hope that you and Alice will have a wonderful vacation.

Sincerely yours,

Harry

Truman tells a story on himself that features Senators Rufus C. Holman of Oregon, Owen Brewster of Maine, and Monrad Wallgren of Washington. The "PBY" was a flying boat, "PB" standing for "patrol bomber." Truman also bemoans the damage the United States is suffering internationally from Arkansas Governor Orval Faubus's use of the National Guard to prevent nine African American students from attending Central High School in Little Rock.

October 7, 1957

Dear Dean:

I've been thinking about you and present developments. Just received an invitation to attend some lectures you are giving at Tufts U. in Medford, Mass., Oct. 23rd, 24th, 25th. Wish I could be present. Will you send me the lectures? I'll read them and some day those back brain cells of mine may come up with a plagiarism!

I can't be in Washington on the 19th and 20th. The daughter of Mrs. T's favorite cousin is to be married that Saturday and we must be present.

You never in your life, I'm sure, have seen the like of invitations. Tomorrow I must go to Texas for Sam Rayburn's library dedication: As you know he came to mine and so did you. One of my cousins made a colored picture of you out in front of our old house. It was a good one.

November 1st I've accepted a trip to Los Angeles to "draw" So[uthern] Cal[ifornia] Democrats to a $100 dinner for the purpose of raising funds to put that great Crackpot State in a corner where it has always belonged. I'm like Sen. Holman when he went to Attatuck [perhaps Adak, or another of the Aleutian Islands] with Mon Wallgren and Brewster on an investigation which I was making in Seattle. The three went in a PBY and were shot at by the Japs. Sen. Holman in his high pitched voice said to Mon—"Ain't a man a damn fool to do this when he doesn't have to?" Well, "Ain't He."

The Russians and Arkansas seem to have the Chief Executive, Mrs. Dulles and the country over a barrel propaganda wise. It sure beats hell how things happen.

Wish I could sit and talk with you for an hour or thirty minutes or even for five minutes. My morale would go up 100%. When will I get one of your good, uplifting letters?

My best to Alice. Hope you won't throw this in the "Round File."

Sincerely,

Harry Truman

The dedication of the Sam Rayburn Library in Bonham, Texas, which Truman attended, was on October 9, 1957. Thomas G. Corcoran ("Tommy the Cork"), an official during the Roosevelt administration, was at this time a Democratic Party operative. The "renegade Democrat" Acheson refers to was Secretary of the Treasury Robert B. Anderson. Acheson looks forward to presenting a foreign-policy statement to the Democratic Advisory Council later in the month. He worries that Eisenhower's inattentive and ineffectual leadership, as demonstrated in the Little Rock crisis, could eventually cause the country to stumble into war. For the first time in this correspondence, Acheson seems truly concerned about the drift of foreign policy in the face of a serious worsening of foreign relationships.

October 8, 1957

Dear Mr. President,

Your good letter tells me that you are off to Sam Rayburn's Library opening. Tom Corcoran asked me to go on a company plane, but I passed it up. Why did Sam have to get a renegade Democrat to be paired with you as a speaker? If he was going to have a Republican he might have had the real thing, as you did with Uncle Herbert Hoover.

I shall miss you at the Council meeting on the 19th but approve your choice of a wedding to a wake. For me it will be another Post week-end. At least my role of presenting the Foreign Policy statement will have the merit which John G. Johnson found in staying at the bar instead of accepting Cleveland's offer of a place on the Supreme Court. "I would rather talk to the damned fools," he said, "than listen to them."

We have worked out a pretty good statement with some sense to it. But I suppose your brethren will want to clutter it up with a lot of words about peace, disarmament, Israel, Poland, etc., to produce the old futile attempt to appeal to nationality groups—like the 1956 platform.

We are, I think, getting in bad shape internationally. The combination of distrust of Dulles, our defense policy, which more and more rests on a relative nuclear position which we do not have and can never have, and no economic policy for the undeveloped countries is isolating us. It could easily pave the way for a quite unmanageable international situation.

This frightens me because of the lesson of Little Rock—a weak President who fiddles along ineffectually until a personal affront drives him to unexpectedly drastic action. A Little Rock with Moscow and the S.A.C. in the place of the paratroopers could blow us all apart.

My lectures try to get at the inwardness of our predicament and suggest lines of policy. Sometimes I am frankly over my head. But as I study I become increasingly depressed. The escape from Götterdämmerung will take vigor of mind and leadership which I do not see in either party, even on the distant horizon. And for three years it seems impossible to do anything at all. God rest ye merry gentlemen!

This is hardly a gay letter. But you are proof against depression.

Our warmest greetings to you and Mrs. Truman.

As ever,

Dean

Acheson discusses an invitation to Truman from a Yale University professor to speak to students and faculty. Acheson had written this professor in 1954 about Truman's coming to Yale: "Mr. Truman is deeply interested in and very good with the young. His point of view is fresh, eager, confident. . . . He has learned the hard way, but he has learned a lot. He believes in his fellow man and he believes that with will and courage (and some intelligence) the future is manageable. This is good for undergraduates. . . . It is not what he says but what he is which is important to young men. . . . [He is someone who could] give our undergraduates more sense of what their lives are worth . . . than anyone I know."

October 21, 1957

Dear Mr. President:

Some time ago you wrote me about an invitation you had from a student organization at Yale to speak there. I advised that you should not do this, but that if the University authorities should ask you I would most earnestly hope that you could go. During my last visit to New Haven President Griswold spoke to me most enthusiastically about your coming, and I have just had a talk over the telephone with Mr. Thomas G. Bergin, the Master of Timothy Dwight College, one of the under-graduate residential sections of the University, asking me whether you would consider coming for the inside of a week as what is known as a Chubb Fellow. I told him that I would immediately write you about it, preparing a way for his invitation which will follow soon upon my note.

Two years ago I went to Yale as a Chubb Fellow. It is an ideal way to meet and talk seriously with college students without getting into the big prepared lecture, which, unless one wishes to put it later into book form, is a trial and a nuisance.

The Chubb Fellow receives a pretty good honorarium and his travel expenses. He is given a suite in Timothy Dwight College—bedroom, bathroom, sitting room—he has his meals in the College and usually dines with the Master in the Master's house. A schedule is arranged for him, which is entirely subject to his approval.

When I was there I met with the boys who live in Timothy Dwight after dinner one evening. There are about 250 of them. We met in the common room, and this is very informal. The boys sit on the floor and stand against the wall. I talked for about ten or fifteen minutes to start them off, and then had questions until the Master had to break it up. Another evening, after dinner, we met in the Fellows' room with those members of the faculty who are attached to the college. We sat around with a drink in one hand and had a fine evening's talk. During the day I met on occasions with somewhat smaller groups who were studying government or foreign affairs, often with foreign students, for informal discussion. Once or twice I went to the larger classroom and discussed the subject which the boys were studying. On one occasion it was the influence of Europe on America, which gave a fine chance to talk about ideas, good and bad, received in the colonial period, the effect of our long isolation during the peace of the nineteenth century, and our abrupt awakening to the facts of life in this century. You can do as much or as little as you like. The boys are eager for informal conversation, and I think you would feel, if you did it, that you had had a contact with the younger generation which will give you a good deal of satisfaction in return for the very great help which you will give them.

If you want to talk with me more about this when they write you, please do.

In the meantime, let me give you a laugh for the day. When the Advisory Council was discussing the statement on foreign affairs which you very helpfully approved, it was opposed by Mr. Adlai E. Stevenson, who said that it was far too restrained and thoughtful, that no part of it would be published, and that it had no voter appeal. He was ultimately overruled, and turned out to be slightly in error about its newspaper prominence. However, the last touch was furnished by the *New York Times* editorial this morning, which begins, "The Democratic Advisory Council, employing a style greatly influenced by one of its members, Adlai E. Stevenson . . ." I am waiting with some interest to see how adaptable Adlai's mind really is. Perhaps in a few days he will imagine that he did write the statement, or I may get a note saying that his judgment is not infallible. Which side of the bet do you want to take?

With warmest regards.

Sincerely,

Dean

"Our friend the Governor" is Adlai Stevenson, whom Acheson playfully maligned in his letter of October 21.

October 29, 1957

Dear Dean:

Your letter of the 21st was most highly appreciated, and I hope that I can arrange a visit to Yale as a Chubb Fellow. After our correspondence on the subject, it seems to be the proper way to meet the situation. You will hear from me a little later on.

Never having been able to comprehend the attitudes of our friend the Governor, I cannot with certainty determine his reaction to the reception given your statement on foreign affairs. Painful prejudice, however, tempts me to believe that he might be willing to assume authorship.

Sincerely yours,

Harry Truman

Acheson reports on an attempt by John Foster Dulles to co-opt "our Peerless Leader"—Adlai Stevenson—into doing the Eisenhower administration's bidding. Christian Herter was now Undersecretary of State, as well as a noted internationalist and former governor of Massachusetts.

November 1, 1957

An Eyes Only Message

Dear Mr. President:

You were very kind to telegraph the Fletcher School as you did. I deeply appreciated what you said about me, as, indeed, I always do. It caused no little comment, too, and for this reason. Ike had promised one of the Trustees of the School—his host on his last fishing trip to New England—that he would send a message. Word then came that he would not. The trustees at once got in touch with their former Governor, and an alleged friend of mine, Chris Herter, who agreed to oblige. He did. He sent a message praising the School and Will Clayton, but omitting reference to the lecturer. So, when your warm reference was read, there was both applause and well bred chuckles at Chris Herter's awkward predicament. It seems to me that he is too much of a gentleman to have been a party to discourtesy of this sort without orders from above—he, also, has not enough backbone to disregard them.

(I now shift from office to house and a change of paper.)

Yesterday our Peerless Leader came to see me and later talked with me from New York. Since he is contemplating an act of unusual folly—even for him—I want you to know about it (how confidentially, I leave to you—the newspapers are already full of rumors). Dulles, he said, has asked him to come on, and had talked with him the previous evening. The Peerless Leader (P.L. to us) had with him when he saw me two pieces of paper. The first a copy of the Eisenhower-Macmillan press release on which Para. 5 had underlined three numbered "policies or purposes" according to the P.L. They were (1) that all of our allies who wish to should know more of the capabilities of security, which we had, in being and prospect, (2) a "greater opportunity should be provided to assure that this power will, in fact, be available in case of need for their common security" and (3) "that it will not be misused by any nation for purposes other than individual and collective self-defense, authorized (sic) by the Charter of the U.N."

Also a sentence was underlined that we and the U.K. regard our possession of nuclear weapons as held in trust—(for purposes which I forget).

The other paper was a draft press release announcing that a Mr. X, which the P.L. reluctantly admitted was supposed to be none other than his peerless self, would become a special assistant to the President to devise and negotiate, internally and externally, policies to carry out the underlined policies (1), (2) and (3). The problem, it had been explained to him, was that for some reason our allies had lost confidence in our capacity and intentions. The P.L. was to be given the job of restoring their confidence in both.

He felt that he should do this—or something like it. What did I think?

I thought it was a prescription for suicide. He was to sell our allies confidence in statements which were lies, to dilute—if he could—the growing distrust of Dulles, at home and abroad (while the grounds for it would remain true); he would embrace, for himself and the Democratic Party, a false and fraudulent policy and one which was certain to fail; and he would assume for all of us, the responsibility of devising steps which would not be taken, and which, if taken, would fail. The failure of foreign policy would be deftly transferred from Dulles to Stevenson.

I said that Dulles was smarter than I had thought. (You and I were pikers in trying to get Dewey to go to London.) I added that the real task was to pressure this decadent outfit into new and vigorous steps to (1) step up both our nuclear and conventional forces and research, (2) to have a vigorous program of economic cooperation (i.e., export of capital goods) to countries ready for them and subsidy for some others, (3) political policies which would tie the Western hemisphere and Western Europe together—the others would have no choice but to follow, in their own interest. To join this administration in telling others that we had military power which we do not have, and a resolution which does not exist, was inexpressibly foolish and wrong. Talk about bi-partisanship was cheese for a silly mouse.

Of course, he didn't like it. He is almost irresistibly drawn as a monkey to Kipling's boa constrictor. He wants to lay down conditions, to make policy—without knowing that to do this in such a field requires the vast knowledge and help of departments of Government which are at sixes and sevens and to which he would have no access, or knowledge as to how to use it, if he had it.

I write you this long and dreary story because although I have given him pause, he is clearly an eager beaver advised by junior grade Machiavellis and may well end up as a sort of reincarnation of Walter George and/or Dick Richards—only dragging the party into complicity for failure and frustration.

I do not intend politeness to inhibit me from calling god-damned nonsense, at least, folly; and I hope you will be careful not to let the silken cord of bipartisan honey talk bind you.

Enough of this. You know my thoughts and blood pressure.

As ever,

Dean

Truman raises the topic of his middle initial about which he never seems to have fully made up his mind. Should the "S" have a period or not? The original December 5, 1957, letter is not in Acheson's papers. Truman kept a carbon copy with, at the bottom, Truman's printed signature stamp— which includes a period after the S.

December 5, 1957

Dear Dean:

With reference to the attached, do you know the word meaning an initial standing in a name but signifying no name itself, as the "S" in

Harry S. Truman

Truman hopes to join Acheson at Yale to deliver lectures. Acheson later called Truman and arranged that he come to Yale the following April.

December 18, 1957

Dear Dean:

I have been trying to get things arranged so I could be with you at Yale, and it seems to me that the dates which you set out, the second Friday and Saturday in February, that is the 14th and 15th of February, would be most satisfactory to me, if that is all right with you. I don't want to be there unless you are there.

I hope you will write and tell me just exactly what I have to do. I have a couple of lectures which I have delivered around to the various schools on "Hysteria" and on powers and duties of the President of the United States as set out in the Constitution. I also have a lecture which I have delivered on the first Ten Amendments of the Constitution from the viewpoint of a layman not fully educated in the law. Do you think any one of these would be right and proper for us to use at the time you suggest. I'll be glad to do everything I can to keep you from being embarrassed by this old retired farmer from Missouri.

You tell Alice that her picture has a place of honor in my reception room and as soon as I can get a plaque made for it to tell what it is, what it stands for and where it came from, it will be labeled so everybody who comes in here can see just what sort of a Secretary of State I had by proxy.

Sincerely yours,

Harry Truman

[Handwritten note by Dean Acheson:] Arranged by telephone for HST to arrive N.H. Apr 8 and leave for Washington Apr 11th.

Acheson reaches some witty conclusions regarding Truman's middle "S." Acheson seems to be making a point here of not putting a period after the S, both in his quotation of Truman's letter of December 5 and in the address line at the bottom of the page. Acheson enclosed the December 11 memorandum from Elizabeth Finley with this letter.

December 20, 1957

Dear Mr. President:

In your letter to me of December 5, 1957, spurred by your incurable (thank God) curiosity, you asked me this question:

"Do you know the word meaning an initial standing in a name but signifying no name itself, as the 'S' in

Harry S Truman"?

You know, and so do I, how to get at a question of this sort. In my youth an advertisement used to say, "Ask the man who owns one." So I asked the two people who might know—and, of course, they were women— Elizabeth Finley, the librarian of Covington and Burling [law firm], past-president of the law librarians of the country, and Helen Lally of the Supreme Court library. Their reports are enclosed.

The essence of the matter is that we are blind men, searching in a dark room for a black hat which isn't there. The "S" in Harry S Truman (no period after "S") does not "stand for anything." Therefore, it cannot have a descriptive noun—"vacuum," "nothing," etc., are already pre-empted. But, more positively, it is something—not representatively, but absolutely. You are "S" (without a period) because it is your name. For instance, you appointed an Associate Justice of the Supreme Court (may God forgive you) whose name is "Tom." Now "Tom" usually stands for "Thomas." But not in this case. There it stands for nothing—absolutely nothing—except, of course, Tom himself, which may—who knows?—be the same thing.

So, you see, "S" is your middle name, not a symbol, not a letter standing for nothing, but an inseparable part of the moniker of one of the best men I have known in a largely misspent life. The same, for that matter, could be said of "Harry."

"Harry" stirs all my deepest loyalties. The senior partner, who brought me up, was christened "J. Harry Covington"; and what a man he was! After years in Congress (he was one of the men who, in 1912 in Baltimore, brought about the nomination of Woodrow Wilson), he had a phrase which to me epitomizes the political obligation, perhaps among the most honorable obligations because resting on honor alone. He never said of an obligation—"I have to do it." He always said, "I have it to do." What a vast difference! In the first, one is coerced into action; in the other, a free man assumes an obligation, freely contracted.

This has a good deal to do with politics—about which you have always thought I knew nothing—in those reaches of it which fit men for government. There are some reaches which unfit them. Honor is a delicate and tricky concept. It does not mean standing by the unfit because of friendship. But it does mean standing by in time of trouble to see a fair deal, when the smart money is taking to the bushes. All of this I learned from the old judge, and relearned again from you in unforgettable days.

So I say that "S" is a good name as it stands, and I am for it. Should either of us have the good fortune to have another grandson, let's agree to persuade his parents to a middle name of just plain "S" with no period, and no explanation.

Indeed, no explanation is possible, because it is the most truly international name. In 1200 B.C. it appeared in the Phoenician as a sort of wobbly "W", but was, unhappily, pronounced sin. By 900, in the Cretan, it looked like a 3 and had become san, a great improvement. For the next 500 years the 3 was turned around. Then the Latins, Irish, and Saxons, for some odd reason, turned it into a "V." Finally, the British, as they have so often done, got the thing straight in a wiggle, from right to left to right, but not until our colonial ancestors, Ben Franklin included, printed it half the time as an "f" to you and me.

That again is why I like "S" for you. It has had one hell of a tempestuous life.

As ever,

Dean

December 11, 1957

MEMORANDUM FOR MR. ACHESON

Despite diligent research, I have failed to turn up any word which means the use of a letter instead of a name. I even asked assistance from the Library of Congress to no avail. I did find that catalogers, faced with such a name, enter a foot note on the card saying "alternate pseudonym", but that is because catalogers are a special breed. They cannot endure an initial standing alone.

However, in Mr. Truman's case, I understand his parents christened him Harry S; the "S" was not something he added himself just because he did not like the looks of a two letter monogram on his handkerchiefs. Parents can name their child anything they please, and if they choose to name him X, then X is his name. I think S is Mr. Truman's middle name, as defined by Webster, "the title by which any person or thing is known or designated."

On the other hand it seems a pity to offer nothing to an ex-President. Why not make up a word? I suggest sic, meaning "so in christening."

Elizabeth Finley

Dean Acheson, Harry Truman, and others at the construction site of the Harry S. Truman Library in Independence, Missouri, in 1954.

6

January 1958 to June 1959

*Meetings in New Haven, Kansas City, and Washington,
D.C. – A Political Season – A President Who Doesn't Know
Where He's Going – Three Foreign-Policy Crises – Truman
Is "Steamed Up" – A Grand Birthday Celebration*

*A*s the 1958 midterm elections approached, Truman and Acheson increased their political activity, Truman as inveterate political campaigner and also as author of a new syndicated newspaper column, Acheson as a member of the Democratic Advisory Council and author of influential foreign-policy position papers. The presidential election wasn't far away, and Truman and Acheson were already worrying about finding a good Democratic presidential candidate. They met on three occasions during this period—at Yale University in early April 1958, in Kansas City later that same month, and in New York and Washington, D.C., in early May 1959. All three occasions included, in addition to a personal get-together, speechmaking and other formal activities. Truman's trip to New York City and Washington, D.C., was especially eventful. First he met with and spoke to students at Columbia University for three days, and then he attended a number of events at which his seventy-fifth birthday was celebrated in grand style. During all this, he was preparing to help his wife through a serious operation later in the month and to celebrate the birth of his second grandson. He fretted that his schedule did not permit him to visit with his old friend Winston Churchill, who was in Washington and New York on the same dates.

Truman's and Acheson's letters were, as usual, full of criticism of Eisenhower. Truman thought Eisenhower was following the same big-business economic policies that the Republicans had disastrously followed in the 1920s. There were three serious foreign-policy crises during this period. Truman and Acheson found themselves disagreeing in public about two of them: Eisenhower's actions in Egypt—the so-called Suez crisis—and in what at the time was called the Formosa Strait, involving the small islands of Quemoy and Matsu. Acheson was strongly critical of Eisenhower's responses to both crises, whereas Truman's instinct was to support the commander in chief in times of peril and to advise all Americans to do so too. Acheson wrote him very cross letters about the wrongheadedness of the position he was taking.

. . .

Truman has been reading Acheson's book Power and Diplomacy, *which was based on his William L. Clayton Lectures at Tufts University. Truman also refers to his upcoming speech, on February 22, at a Democratic National Committee fund-raising dinner. In the phrase "Humphrey-Mellon program," Truman means Eisenhower's Secretary of the Treasury George M. Humphrey and Andrew Mellon, Secretary of the Treasury under Presidents Harding, Coolidge, and Hoover. The country was in recession in early 1958, brought on, Truman believed, by the typical big-business policies of the Republican Party.*

January 24, 1958

Dear Dean:

I've been reading the lectures you delivered for the Will Clayton set up and for the benefit of Harvard, Tufts, et al. Those lectures are history at its best. I hope you'll keep the fires burning on foreign affairs. John Foster needs guidance just as his boss does. When I said that all the toady columnists had spasms! Shows it needed to be said.

John Knight, believe it or not, took it for what it meant. Even Hearst could not refute it. Let's keep needling them. Sam Rayburn asked Charlie Murphy to urge me not to needle Ike too much in my Feb. 22nd speech. Shows what's going on. My Sec. of the Treasury, John W. Snyder, has refused to be mixed up with me on a financial article about the Humphrey-Mellon program which brought on the recession. Now they found what happens when the N.Y. Federal Reserve Bank discount committee has charge of things financial. For three years that outfit tried to influence me to do what the former Sec. of the Treasury did (Mellon).

Now the Seventh Fleet has been returned to the Federal Reserve Bank, not only in D.C. and N.Y. but even in this backwoods, long horn, cattle, hog and hay capital known as Kansas City—the biggest suburb of the capital of Jackson County—Independence, Missouri.

In every instance where Ike, et al. have tried to discredit you or me they've had to back up.

Take care of that area and remember we have those tickets sold out here. We'll have a reunion around Feb. 22 in Washington.

Sincerely,

Harry

Acheson has finally succeeded in arranging a "distinguished visitors" program for Truman at Yale. It is not clear what the enclosed column was about, but the reply (see the next letter) indicates the subject was presidential disability.

March 25, 1958

Dear Mr. President:

I am enclosing the revised schedule for the three days, April 8, 9, and 10, in New Haven.

You and I will both be staying with Mr. and Mrs. Thomas Bergin at the Master's House of Timothy Dwight College. This is one of the ten residential colleges in which Yale undergraduates, except Freshmen, live. Professor Bergin is a genial host and an Italian scholar of considerable eminence. Mrs. Bergin you will find a delightful lady.

In making out the schedule, I have insisted that you must have a nap every afternoon. If, as seems likely, they have crowded you a little, we will stretch it out again.

All of your engagements on the list, with the exception of the Law Journal Banquet, are with small seminar groups, enlarged a little for your visit, but not too much, say, fifty or sixty students. The Law Journal Dinner is the annual event given by the high-standing men in the Law School who publish their monthly Journal. I am to introduce you and you are to speak. There is no occasion for a lecture or any written speech. As I said over the telephone this morning, the ideal thing would be for you to take an important presidential decision—we talked this morning of Korea—and trace through how a President meets this responsibility and comes to his conclusion—how the facts, uncertain at first, gradually develop, how and from whom the President gets counsel, and how finally he does what only he can do, come to a decision. This can be fairly short, and I think I would keep it to twenty minutes.

In the seminar groups, the subject matter of which is fairly well indicated on the schedule, either the professor in charge or I will break the ice with a few minutes of chatter, and then ask a question ourselves or stimulate the boys to begin. Once they begin, the meeting rapidly becomes very informal and a great deal of fun.

The train which you should take from New York on Tuesday morning, April 8, is the New York, New Haven and Hartford train No. 8, leaving from the Grand Central Station at 8:00 a.m. You will be met at the New Haven station. I will arrive as soon thereafter as my plane can get up and get in, and probably will meet you at Mr. Bergin's house around noon.

They will arrange at Yale for your transportation to Washington so you will get there in time for the luncheon. This will be either by the Federal Express from Boston to Washington, which has a New Haven car, or by morning plane as the weather seems to indicate.

You will need to bring dinner coat and black tie.

I talked this morning with President Griswold, whom you will like very much. He is looking forward keenly to your visit and to having you to dinner.

Sam Rayburn has already said to me that the enclosed column of mine shows mental deficiencies which cause him grave worry. Since you are the other "eminent" man referred to, you had better see how stupid I am as soon as possible.

With warm regards.

As ever,

Dean

Truman talks about both his and Acheson's recent articles on presidential disability and succession. Truman, who served without a Vice President during his first term as President, believed that the Speaker of the House and the president pro tempore of the Senate should succeed to the presidency ahead of the Cabinet officers. This order of succession became law in the Presidential Succession Act of 1947.

March 28, 1958

Dear Dean:

I appreciated your letter of the 25th and will arrange to arrive in New Haven at the time set.

The suggested program suits me perfectly, and thanks to you I will remember to bring my dinner jacket.

I read your article on Presidential disability. I wrote one myself for the North American Newspaper Alliance in which I included the Speaker, the President pro tem of the Senate, and the leaders of the Majority and Minority in both houses in a group to pass on the disability of the President.

As you know, the difficulty between Thomas R. Marshall and Woodrow Wilson arose from Marshall's statement that there was only one heart beat between him and the White House. It was said as a joke, but I do not believe Wilson appreciated jokes which affected him.

I made another suggestion regarding the death of the President and the taking over of the office by the Vice President. It seems to me that it might be a good plan to have a constitutional arrangement whereby the Presidential Electors would meet, on the death, or perhaps the disability, of the President and elect a new Vice President, in which case there would be no necessity for a bill on succession. But I will talk it all over with you when I come back east.

Sincerely yours,

Harry

My best to Alice.

Truman left Independence for Yale on April 6. He arrived in New York City the following day and visited his daughter and son-in-law. On April 8 he took the train to Yale. After a day of tours and social events, he spent two days meeting in informal settings with students, talking about the presidency and American history. Acheson joined him for most or all of these gatherings. Truman left Yale for Washington, D.C., on April 11 and, after two days of social gatherings, left for home on April 13.

Acheson on April 15 delivered a speech titled "Factors Underlying Negotiations with the Russians" at the second memorial Eddie Jacobson dinner in Kansas City; Edward Jacobson was Truman's former business partner.

April 16, 1958

Dear Dean:

I don't know how to express my appreciation for your visit here. Your foreign relations speech was a knock-out. I have never listened to a more logical approach than the one you delivered. I was exceedingly anxious for you to speak here, because this place in times past was a strong center of isolationism.

I have heard nothing but praise from everyone, and I have talked to a surprising number of people this morning who are well-informed on foreign affairs and half of whom are not Democrats.

The only person who was not pleased was Mrs. Truman, and that was because she was not there to hear you. Although she seemed to be feeling somewhat better this morning and I wanted to be at the airport to see you off, I thought I should stay with her.

I hope you can understand how very much I enjoyed my visit to Yale. I have never had a better time anywhere. It is what I have always wanted to do, but the opportunities were too infrequent. The visit to Yale and a recent one to the University of Oklahoma were, I believe, most successful. . . .

Sincerely,

Harry

Acheson refers to dental problems Bess Truman was having. He also discusses an encounter with a Turkish journalist who believed that Eisenhower administration officials concerned with Turkish affairs did not measure up to Truman's ambassador to Turkey during the early years of the Cold War, Edwin C. Wilson, or to George C. McGhee, who coordinated the distribution of U.S. foreign aid to Turkey from 1947 to 1949 and who served as U.S. ambassador for about a year at the end of Truman's presidency. Neither Acheson nor his informant would have known of a secret National Security Council document, "U.S. Policy Toward Turkey," issued in June 1957, which advised the U.S. to be wary of attaching conditions to its aid to Turkey to avoid impinging on that country's sense of sovereignty. Presumably Edwin C. Wilson and George C. McGhee were not hampered by such a policy prescription during Truman's administration.

April 18, 1958

Dear Mr. President:

Thank you very much for your reassuring letter about my speech in Kansas City. At the time it seemed to me that it was not the speech for that gathering, but, if you approve, that is enough for me.

I am glad that you stayed with Mrs. Truman and did not come to the plane. Please give her the most sympathetic and affectionate messages from Alice and me. I hate to think of all the discomfort and worse through which she has been.

This morning I have had a most interesting talk with a Mr. Yalman, a Turk, who is the editor of the Turkish newspaper *Vatan* and who is on a tour of this country. He is the great advocate of the western position in Turkey and carries with him several bullets which were put into him by some communist rowdies during the troubles which your Greek-Turkish Program helped to bring to an end. The great days of U.S.-Turkish relations, he says, were under your administration, when Ed Wilson and George McGhee were venerated and powerful in Turkish affairs. Since then we have drifted with men who are afraid to interfere in "internal affairs of Turkey," which, Mr. Yalman says, ought to be interfered with continuously, but tactfully. He is most eager to pay his respects to you, and will be coming east from San Francisco at a time when he could stop in Kansas City on May 12 if you could receive him. I am enclosing an envelope and a card. Would you note on it whether or not you could see him? . . .

With warm regards.

Sincerely,

Dean

April 30, 1958

Dear Dean:

. . . I am still thinking about the wonderful time you and I had at Yale and the fine speech which you made here for the Eddie Jacobson Foundation. It is the book on that subject, and I expect to use it, with your permission, all during the coming political campaign—if I am asked to participate.

I thought it was proper for me to do just what I did in the Arthur Krock matter. If the Republican Congressman who asked me the question had quoted more than just two sentences from the interview, I believe I would have remembered it, but whether or not it reflects on me, I believe my action was right, and I am glad you approve.

Bess is still having trouble with her dental affairs but seems to be improving gradually.

Please give my best to Alice, and my best to you, as always.

Sincerely yours,

Harry

May 15, 1958

Dear Dean:

I am very grateful to you and Alice for remembering my birthday. It was a happier one because of your kindness.

You are very thoughtful people, and I wish I could hear from you and see you more often. I cherish our good, and bad, times together and wish we could relive them all.

Sincerely yours,

Harry

Yale still rings in my ears. What a time we had!

This is a transcript of a call Truman made to Acheson to ask for his advice on what to say to the press about President Eisenhower's sending of thousands of marines to Lebanon. The Lebanese government had requested American troops in the wake of a military coup in Iraq and to prevent a feared invasion by Syria.

July 15, 1958

The President: How are you, Dean?

Mr. Acheson: I'm just being cross-examined by the Army.

The President: By whom?

Mr. Acheson: By the United States Army . . .

The President: What I was interested in . . . I have talked to Sam Rayburn and Lyndon Johnson about the meeting last night authorizing the sending of the Marines into Lebanon, and, of course, I am being harassed by people who want statements from me, and I was anxious to talk to you before saying anything publicly. I would like to know your reaction, if you want to tell me.

Mr. Acheson: You mean the agreement that Dulles made? Is there a proposal for a joint resolution in . . . ?

The President: Yes, in the Security Council of the UN, just like the one we got for Korea, only this comes after the fact.

Mr. Acheson: But the United States Marines are not in there, are they?

The President: Yes, 6,000 of them are now in Lebanon, at the request of the President of Lebanon, and the reason I wanted to talk to you is that I didn't want to go off half-cocked or do anything to upset any policy affecting the peace of the world.

Mr. Acheson: Well, if that has been done, the only thing we can do is support it, but I think it's probably a mistake. I don't think they should have done it.

The President: I don't think they should have done it before the fact, either—I mean, before the UN approved it.

Mr. Acheson: I think the President having taken this step, all of us have got to see him through, that under the circumstances, the President had no other choice. The peace of the world is at stake.

The President: All I intend to say is that he had no other choice. . . .

Mr. Acheson: I don't know if I would say "He had no other choice." My suggestion is to say something to the effect that the President, as the Commander in Chief and the head of the nation, is taking this step, and you think it's the duty of everyone to stand by him. That just underwrites what he has done. He is the one who had to make the decision. We don't approve or disapprove, but we stand by him.

The President: I hope you're having a good time up there.

Mr. Acheson: I just came up to speak to the Army at their meeting on weapon development. You know, this is a very surprising thing. I didn't know we had landed Marines.

The President: I have talked to Sam Rayburn and Lyndon Johnson about it. Sam was at the conference that authorized the thing at the White House, and he made quite a statement that [Lebanese President Camille] Chamoun asked us to come in, so we are not barging in. . . .

Mr. Acheson: But the landing has taken place?

The President: Yes, it's civil war in a way, with outside help coming in. . . . (The President proceeds to quote Rayburn's statement to him on the subject.) This thing was done at the request of Chamoun without the endorsement of the UN, and now they're trying to get the endorsement of the UN. The Congressional leaders went along with the President on the subject.

Mr. Acheson: Are they going to have a Congressional resolution?

The President: Neither Sam nor Lyndon said anything to me about it. They are trying to get one from the UN, just as we did before Korea.

Mr. Acheson: I think the whole thing's a terrible mess. Lebanon has been left and probably the whole thing will blow up. I think if you make this statement, it's the right one.

The President: I'll do my best to get one together. Don't worry about this; it's not our responsibility this time. I will be back in Washington on the 26th, and . . .

Mr. Acheson: I am just here for today, and will be back tonight. . . .

The passing of Acheson's mother made Truman think of his own mother. He was always very sentimental on the subject of mothers. General Harry H. Vaughan was a Truman confidant.

July 29, 1958

Dear Dean:

I have received a letter from Henry [Harry] Vaughan dated July 26th enclosing a clipping from a Washington paper about the death of your mother.

I'll never forget my experience back in 1947. So you very well know that my sympathy is heartfelt. There is no supporter like your mother. Right or wrong from her point of view you are always right. She may scold you for little things but never for the big ones. Wish I'd known about it sooner. You'd have heard from me sooner.

Sincerely,

Harry Truman

The Former Presidents Act of 1958, which was introduced in 1955, gave Truman a pension of $25,000 and an allowance for his office staff.

August 2, 1958

Dear Mr. President,

Thank you so much for your warm and understanding message about Mother's death. What you say is very true—particularly of mothers like yours and mine who had such quality and strength.

I am delighted to see that the Presidential Pension bill finally passed the House; you will get some help now in dealing with the mountains of mail you get—and also with the grocery bills. What an outrage that it has to take so long and that small minded men had to oppose it. However, they told me what I did not know—that you are an oil magnate!

With deepest thanks for your note.

Faithfully,

Dean

Truman sends Acheson a speech he had given on August 6, in Chicago, to the Fraternal Order of Eagles. His theme was the Cold War and the need for the United States to make a great effort to resist the Soviet threat. He warned against "peace at any price" demagogues and said that, in perilous times, "it is better to take too much action than too little."

August 7, 1958

Dear Dean:

Here's what I talked to you about.

After what you told me on the telephone, I believe you will like it.

Sincerely,

Harry

The people mentioned in this letter were with the Democratic National Committee and its Democratic Advisory Council. Eisenhower's speech to the United Nations, which Acheson ridicules, was on August 13. "Conversion of salt water" refers to Dulles's proposal to finance condensation plants for producing fresh water from sea water in the Middle East.

August 14, 1958

Dear Mr. President:

Thank you very much for your speech to the Eagles in Chicago, which you sent along to me in your note of August 7. I both agreed with it and enjoyed it.

The statement on the Middle East which you and I liked was strongly approved by Hubert Humphrey and Tom Finletter. However, Paul Butler, Charlie Murphy, Phil Perlman, and Averell opposed it, with the result that Charlie Tyroler did not issue it. They opposed it on what I thought was a silly ground—that it was not constructive. Why one has to be constructive in criticizing a fool step by someone else I do not know.

I said at a luncheon meeting of Civitans today that in one respect, which a lawyer could appreciate specially, Eisenhower's speech to the UN was excellent. It adhered strictly to the principle that if one's case is too weak to talk about, talk about something else. Apparently his principal plan to save the Middle East is by conversion of salt water.

As ever,

Dean

"Krusie" is Soviet Premier Nikita Khrushchev. Sherman Adams, Eisenhower's chief of staff, was forced to resign on September 22, 1958, as a result of allegations that he had accepted favors from a businessman who was being investigated by the government. Allen Dulles, brother of John Foster Dulles, was at this time director of the Central Intelligence Agency.

August 19, 1958

Dear Dean:

It has been some time since I've written you a long hand letter. I'm glad you liked my speech to the Eagles in Chicago. I made them "scream" but not in the usual way. I've made that speech many times before and the smart news men never seem to recognize it.

William J. Bryan made the "Cross of Gold and Crown of Thorns" speech three or four times before he had the chance to make it in Chicago in 1896. I'm of the opinion that the repetition of what's right is just as important to the minds of men as perhaps the lies of Hitler, Mussolini, Stalin and Krusie are. Sometimes I'm not so sure about that.

You were right about Ike's speech. It is in the same case situation as was Sherman Adams. The plan to take Sherm off the front page was Lebanon. I wonder if Korea was in that class also? I've never thought so. It seems now that "my war" in Korea may have been necessary!

This President doesn't know where he's going nor why. Allen Dulles came to see me a day or two ago and wanted me to read the President's speech before he made it to the U.N. I refused to look at it. I had no right to pass on his innocuous remarks and then give him hell about them.

I wonder just where we are going and what we'll do after we arrive, if we ever get there.

Guess I'm becoming a pessimist. Hope I'm not. This G.D. Dem. Committee has been trying to schedule me for a number of appearances. Guess I'm a weak person and will probably take on most of them for no good reason.

My best to Alice and to you.

Harry Truman

On August 23, the People's Republic of China (PRC) began shelling two islands near the mainland coast, Quemoy and Matsu, which were occupied by the Republic of China (ROC) on Taiwan. Eisenhower took measures in support of the Taiwanese government, and it seemed possible the United States might go to war with the PRC over the two small islands. As had happened during the Suez crisis almost two years earlier, Truman's instinct was to support the President in time of peril. Acheson writes from London to ask if Truman's statement as reported in the British press is accurate and complete, and to try to persuade him that the United States should not risk war, possibly nuclear war, over an unimportant and indefensible position.

September 16, 1958

Dear Mr. President,

As the last paragraph of this dispatch in the *Manchester Guardian* suggests I am somewhat bewildered, but most of all, eager to know what you said *in full*. Could you send it to me in Washington? My secretary will forward it to me.

I thought that we were in complete agreement on my statement. Does your statement (quoted) refer to the offshore islands Quemoy & Matsu? If so no amount of unity in the country can make a spot, as weak as Quemoy, strong. The Administration should not be encouraged to make the stand here. It would be a disaster involving, as it well could, defense by atomic weapons.

I have just been at a conference called by the Prince of the Netherlands, some fifty or more people. A secret questionnaire was issued on the Formosa Straits issue. Of those who answered only two, one American out of twelve including members of this administration, & one European out of thirty, thought Eisenhower should be supported on these small islands. All the rest believed that the position had to be, and could be, liquidated at an acceptable price.

Please don't be hooked on one of their "my country right or wrong" gambits. In this way Foster can always drive us like steers to the slaughter pew.

I eagerly await a word from you.

Affectionately,

Dean

Acheson writes Truman a punishing letter that must have shaken the former President. Acheson has now seen Truman's full statement on the crisis over Quemoy and Matsu, and he disagrees with his position in very strong language. The enclosed dispatch might have been Joseph Alsop's "Quemoy: We Asked for It," published September 3, 1958.

September 17, 1958

Dear Mr. President,

Just after writing you yesterday the *N.Y. Times* (European edition) brought me your statement or rather article on the Far East. It was so far from our telephone talk that I am quite at a loss to know how our earlier agreement comes now to be complete disagreement. I can only suppose that you have had second thoughts. I am writing again only because the consequences of error here can be so disastrous, and because I think you have encouraged very grave error.

The point is not that the Chinese Reds have taken the initiative, or that their purpose (and Moscow's) is to cause us the gravest embarrassment and divide us from our friends—all this is true. The essential point is that it is unwise, indeed reckless to make a stand over Quemoy. Consider why.

First, our position in the eyes of our friends whose security we are risking. We say that the question of Quemoy should not be settled by force. We then say that we cannot negotiate away what belongs to Chiang. And Chiang says he will never yield Quemoy. So what we really say is that Chiang must have an island which blocks Amoy harbor and which Chiang insists is an invasion base. Not even you can defend this position with all the high regard you command.

Second: The military realities. Chiang says (see enclosed dispatch from Alsop) that the talks are a mistake and that the only defense of

Quemoy is an attack on the mainland. This latter is true. It is also true that Chiang cannot succeed in this. The U.S. must join in the attack. It may well be that a conventional bombing may not be possible. Perhaps nuclear weapons will be used from the start. The attack may succeed; or the conflict may expand. If it succeeds now, the issue will arise again. The Reds cannot accept for any time what we demand that they accept—a blocked harbor, an invasion base four miles away, a continued humiliation. If the conflict expands what do we risk and what do we stand to gain? In our present state of readiness do we want to precipitate a nuclear exchange?

There are many statements in your article which I think are gravely wrong. For instance, that Chiang cannot start a war and that only Russia can—but the central one on which my letter is based is your assertion that "Whenever and wherever we are challenged by the Communists" we must meet the challenge. You cannot mean this. Certainly you did not want to fight in Hungary. This opposition to Russia is a dangerous business which requires lots of sense and coolness in making decisions of where and how.

You say that the mistakes of the past are not important now. They are vitally important. This crisis arises because of the fraudulent and wrong actions of 1953 which put Chiang's army on Quemoy to make a pretence at invasion. To go on perpetuating this error even though to isolation and war is simply not sense. It has got to be reversed.

Your attitude seems to insure that Foster is to be given united support to continue every folly he commits provided only the results are bad enough.

I am getting off that band (or funeral) wagon now. Please, Mr. President, reflect and do not continue this line, or listen to those who urge you to do so. It is a grave disservice to the country; and it makes the Democratic Party wholly useless as an opposition and brake upon wrong policies.

Yours as ever,
Dean

Truman sends Acheson his two most recent NANA articles, thinking they will demonstrate that the two men don't seriously disagree on the Quemoy-Matsu crisis. The articles, however, suggest a considerable distance between them regarding the crisis. The first article, from early September, argues that as long as the communist countries remain expansionist, "we have no other choice but to meet them and thwart them at every point where it is necessary," including at Quemoy and Matsu. Acheson did not agree. The second article, from early October, argues that the United States must present a united front to the world with respect to such crises, and that Democrats and Republicans must join together in a bipartisan foreign policy. Acheson probably wouldn't agree with this either; Truman in this letter seems to change his view regarding the need for a bipartisan foreign policy.

October 14, 1958

Dear Dean:

I have been trying to get a chance to send you a longhand letter ever since I received yours of September 16th, and I am still going to write you in more detail than I am now.

I am enclosing you copies of the two last articles which were gotten together on the foreign situation and while they are not exactly in conformity with the conversation which you and I had over the telephone, I did a lot of thinking after I talked to you, which no doubt I should have done before, and came to the conclusion that my fight for bipartisan foreign policy ought to be rather consistent and I think if you will read these statements you will find that you and I are not more than an inch or two apart on the subject. I am sure that the foreign policy of the United States is in the doldrums and has been ever since you and I left the White House.

When Eisenhower went to Korea and surrendered, that is what caused the present trouble. You remember the fiasco of the 7th Fleet when they pulled it out and in three weeks put it back. It was like the Frenchman marching up the hill and right down again.

I have been going around over the country listening to what people have to say. They are entirely confused by the procedure of the present administration on foreign policy and I have made press statements time and again. If we ever could find out what the foreign policy of the present administration is, then we could decide whether we want to support it or not.

I repeat, the bi-partisan foreign policy has never been in existence since you and I left the White House.

I was hoping that I would have a chance to see and talk with you personally in Washington the evening of the 17th, when Stanley Woodward is giving a small dinner for us.

We are going back there for the Women's Democratic dinner and then I am going to New Castle, Pennsylvania, Boston, Massachusetts, and maybe to Delaware. After that I hope to spend two or three days with the young man in New York who is beginning to walk and talk. His mother says that he is just like his grandfather—he never walks—he runs—and talks all the time.

Please tell Alice to help me keep in the good graces of the former Secretary of State.

Sincerely yours,

Harry Truman

Acheson, still in England, expresses relief at receiving Truman's letter of October 14, the first in almost two months. He has been worried that perhaps he offended Truman.

October 24, 1958

Dear Mr. President,

Today your most welcome letter of October 14th reached me. I had begun to wonder whether perhaps I had offended you by disagreeing with your first article, but I never really believed this, because it would be so unlike you.

I think that perhaps we are a little further apart on the Quemoy issue than your letter suggests, but it is of no moment. What seems to me of importance in this issue has a dual aspect. In the first place, in some way or other, we ought to end up after a respectable time by having Chiang Kai-Shek off these islands which present such a continuing hazard. In the second place, we ought to so arrange it that Foster has to clean up the mess which his own policies have created. It would be too bad if this had to be done by the Democratic President in 1961, with all the opprobrium which this would bring upon him.

However, I think we have both said enough so that we know one another's position, and I am delighted that our affection for one another remains as I know it always will, proof against any passing differences of view.

My stay in Cambridge has been a delight. Alice joins me today for a final weekend, and then we fly home in time to vote. She has been traveling in Ireland with our daughter, Jane, and having a glorious time. She tells me that she was received by President O'Kelly of Ireland, who immediately addressed Jane as "darling" and Alice as "dear." After this I think that she will regard your form of address as very formal indeed.

If Alice were here she would want her love sent to Mrs. Truman, as do I.

As ever,

Dean

Truman reassures Acheson. He goes on to indulge in a "spasm."

October 31, 1958

Dear Dean:

You'll never know how very much I appreciated your letter of Oct 24 from King's College at Cambridge. There's no way in the world for you to offend me—even if you'd hit me in the nose. I was very much afraid the offender had been this old man.

You know national political approaches are somewhat complicated. Especially is that true in foreign affairs and the touchy and soft feelings down south [in Latin America]. When we have a Secretary of State whose experience has been altogether in dollar diplomacy, a Democratic national Chairman whose experience has been in northern Indiana and Michigan State, you can see what we are up against to maintain somewhat of a balance for the welfare of the whole country.

"Professional liberals" are a pain in the neck to me as are "professional conservatives." To make them understand that the welfare of the whole country and the leadership of the free world is more important than some crazy local idea, is more important and is a chore for honest to god leadership.

We just haven't had that since 1952. To the so called conservatives high interest rates make the money lenders more bloated, make the borrowers not only subject to increased fundamental rates, but to commissions and palm grease for the lender—well, you can see what happens. The Home Owners Loan Corp. bought out all the busted house owners in the end with a profit. The Federal Housing Adm. gave the small family a chance to own a little farm. The Reconstruction Finance Corp. gave the little business man a chance to run without having his financial throat cut by a greedy banker when his inventory was too large.

Andrew Mellon taught me that lesson in 1922 when he broke me and thousands of others just like me.

Now are you bored enough? I get so steamed up when I view what these executive numb skulls have done to a foreign policy that you and I left to them and a domestic policy that took twenty long years of sweat, *blood* and tears to establish.

I hope Alice will still plead my case in spite of the Irish! How I would like to see you both. Just talked to the "Boss" and she wants to be remembered to both you and Alice.

When you want the next spasm just call for it.

Sincerely,

Harry

Truman visited Washington, D.C., for a week in early January to see members of Congress, and especially to welcome the many new Democratic members elected in the 1958 midterm elections. He had dinner with Acheson at his home in Georgetown on January 6.

January 7, 1959

Dear Dean:

Never have I had a more pleasant evening than the one at your house last night.

It was more than a pleasure to talk to you and Stanley about conditions facing the country. The Democratic Party must face up to its responsibilities. Let's hope it will.

I'll be in touch with you after my merry-go-round here this week. Maybe I'll do no good but a man can't be prosecuted for trying.

May you have the best of everything in 1959.

Sincerely,

Harry

Truman is venting again about the press. The Cabell Phillips article he mentions, "Dean Acheson, Ten Years Later," is an appreciative account of the life, ideas, and accomplishments of its subject. James J. Rowley was a member of Truman's Secret Service detail during his presidency. "Mr. P." means "Mr. President." The "Armenian Camel Thief" is Anastas Mikoyan, the first deputy premier of the Soviet Union, who had recently visited the United States. The "suburban scandal sheet in K.C." is probably the Kansas City Star.

January 22, 1959

Dear Dean:

I've just read the *New York Times Magazine* of the 18th. You see these damned newspapers and nutty columnists eventually have to admit the facts. Don't know when I've had as much satisfaction as when I read that Cabell Phillips article.

It is most difficult for a person in a place of terrible responsibility to take some of the things a so called "free press" insists on publishing. Sometimes I've been so worked up about what was published about you and General Marshall that I'd have been glad to punch the publisher. Luckily I couldn't get to him.

Jim Rowley once told me when I said to him that any SOB who tried to shoot me would get the gun shoved up his behind and I'd pull the trigger, "Mr. P. you can't get to him." I always remembered that. After about forty years of taking it and not taking it I've found that sometimes the facts come out and it's best to give them a chance. Hope you noticed that "no comment" was my answer to the Armenian Camel Thief. That's what Stalin called him.

You and General Marshal took it much better than I did and now you are both reaping the proper reward. I'm still after them. Just told my suburban scandal sheet in K.C. what I thought of them. One good thing there's nothing new it can say.

Tell Alice I'm still appreciating that grand dinner and the opportunity to talk to you.

Sincerely,

Harry

Acheson is concerned that Eisenhower is responding weakly to Soviet Premier Khrushchev's announcement in November 1958 that the Soviet Union intended to repudiate the right of the Western allies to occupy West Berlin, and to his proposal that all foreign troops be removed from Germany. The section of the Constitution Acheson mentions addresses impeachment of a President for "treason, bribery, or other high crimes and misdemeanors." Secretary of State Dulles was terminally ill with cancer. The " 'off the record' appraisal" to which Acheson refers was made at a luncheon address in Washington to the Harvard Law School Association. The luncheon was a private affair and Acheson's remarks were, as he says, off the record, but reasonably complete and accurate accounts of his remarks quickly made their way into the press. One newspaper called Acheson's performance "an astonishingly candid appraisal of Democratic presidential possibilities." "Stu" is Missouri Senator Stuart Symington.

January 27, 1959

Dear Mr. President,

You are very good to write me so warmly about the Cabell Phillips article. What you wrote gave me a good warm glow all the way through. When Cabell showed me the parts attributed to me, I remarked about the reference to drinks of whisky which seemed a bit overdone. I also said that, as he then had it, I was doing all the drinking and apparently hadn't offered him a drop, whereas in truth he wasn't one swallow behind. So he did change it to "another round of drinks." Some of my more suspicious friends claim that the whisky was what produced the favorable tone of the article. A gross slander.

At present I am at work on a piece on Berlin for the *Sat. Eve. Post.* When I get it done I'll send you the text. The effort is to wake the country up to the true gravity of the Berlin crisis, what is involved, and the soul searching decisions which may go by default, or be made in ignorance. If the words of the Constitution in Article II, Section 4 mean anything Ike ought to be removed from office.

We have two pamphlets for the Advisory Committee in the press now. One takes Dulles apart in a way you will like. If he will only stay well for two weeks, we're in business.

An "off the record" appraisal by me of the Democratic candidates made the press in a big way two weeks ago. It was all right with me except that only a part of what I said about Stu was printed, which made the tone unfavorable, although what I said was quite the reverse. But I have straightened Stu out and all seems to be well. Adlai will never forgive me. Are you making progress in consulting the leaders on candidates?

Alice is well. We talk often about our delightful evening with you. We must have Bess the next time.

Our warmest greetings to her and to you.

As ever,

Dean

Acheson sends Truman an advance copy of his article "What About Berlin?" in which he says the current Berlin crisis may be the gravest test of the Western allies' will since the outbreak of the Korean War. Acheson refers to his differences of opinion with Truman over U.S. policy during the Suez and Quemoy-Matsu crises.

February 12, 1959

Dear Mr. President:

So you will know what I have been up to before it comes out in the *Saturday Evening Post* the first week in March, I am enclosing a copy of a piece which I have written for that magazine on Berlin. We have had rather bad luck in getting on opposite sides of foreign policy questions recently. Maybe this will help us in keeping that from happening now.

I am off for Yale today and then on Sunday Alice and I leave for two weeks at our favorite vacation spot, Antigua, in the British West Indies.

Our warmest greetings to you and Bess.

As ever,

Dean

General George C. Marshall, very ill at this time, died later in the year.

February 19, 1959

Dear Dean:

Your letter of the 12th and the enclosure arrived over the weekend and I couldn't make the phone people fix things so we could talk.

You had left Yale and Miami. Florida central told me that lines to your winter resort were so busy I had no chance to get through to you! What would have happened in that case in 1949?

The piece "What about Berlin" is excellent. So what you are "up to" reads all right to me.

Now Dean there has never been a serious difference between us and there never will be if I can help it.

What I was anxious to talk to you about is General Marshall. I had talked to Mrs. Marshall before I called you and she had told me not to come to Ft. Bragg because the General couldn't recognize me. She and I spent the most of my call weeping. But I still hope he'll come out of it.

You know we fixed things for General Pershing about four times.

Hope you and Alice have a grand vacation and a good rest. Some day

I hope I can try out a real vacation. I have my doubts about ever getting one.

Harry Vaughan took the *Saturday Evening Post* (Curtis Pub. Co) for $10,000.00 for libel and slander the other day. They owe you twice as much and me too.

Hope they are meeting the situation on this good piece of yours.

The Madam joins me in the best to you and Alice.

Sincerely,

Harry

Truman mentions Acheson's letter to Dr. Philip C. Brooks, director of the Truman Library, concerning Acheson's donation of his papers to the library.

April 10, 1959

Dear Dean:

Dr. Brooks has just handed me a copy of the letter you addressed to him on April 1st. I more than appreciate it.

I expect to be in the Capital City from April 30th until May 7th and hope that you will be available then for a conversation or two.

All this ballyhoo about my 75th birthday is beginning to embarrass me a little. As you may realize, it embarrasses the Madam even more, but I suppose we will have to go through with it.

I had a grand trip to Crackpot City, California, but returned with one of their brand of flu bugs. It is responding to the usual medication.

Sincerely yours,

Harry S. Truman

It surely was good to talk to you on "another birthday." You expressed my opinion about birthdays.

"Supreme Headquarters on P Street" was Acheson's home at 2805 P Street in Georgetown.

April 16, 1959

Dear Mr. President:

I was just about to write you to find out your dates in Washington when in came your letter of April 10 with the answer—from April 30 until May 7. Alice and I have to start off for St. Paul's School [in New Hampshire] on April 30, but will be back the morning of May 4.

I have been instructed from Supreme Headquarters on P Street to ask you and the Boss to dine with us there on Wednesday evening, May 6, at 7:45, Black Tie. If you are engaged for that night, could you come on Monday the fourth? Same hour, same clothes. Either day is convenient for us, but Alice thinks you will not get as good a dinner if she only has one day to work on it. With this view I don't agree. So either day is fine for us.

You were very thoughtful to call me on my birthday. It was a great joy to have a gossip with you.

With most affectionate greetings to you both.

As ever,

Dean

The "rat-race at the Waldorf on the 8th" that Truman refers to was his grand seventy-fifth birthday dinner on May 8 at the Waldorf-Astoria Hotel in New York City.

April 22, 1959

Dear Dean:

You do not know how very much the Boss and I appreciated your letter of the 16th.

Margaret, as you know, is in an expectant condition, and the Boss has made up her mind to stay in New York while I come down to Washington. But if you and Alice would consent to my coming to your house for the evening of May 4th, I certainly would like to do it.

I have to return to New York on the afternoon of the 6th, because it will take me all the following day and most of the next to get myself ready for the rat-race at the Waldorf on the 8th.

It is always a disappointment to miss an opportunity to be with you and Alice, and if Monday evening, the 4th, will not cause you too much trouble, I will be there. Please tell her not to worry about things to eat. I am not a hearty feeder anyway.

Sincerely,

Harry Truman

But I always eat everything she's responsible for on the table.

Dear Mr. President: April 24, 1959

Hooray! You are ours for the evening of May 4. We agree that Margaret's claim on the Boss is greater than ours, but this concession we make only under the present circumstances. On the next visit we will put in our claim again.

We shall try to get some congenial friends together for the 4th.

Sincerely,

Dean

Truman's East Coast trip extended from April 27 to May 9. He first spent three days speaking to and with students at Columbia University. Then in Washington, he spoke before committees of both houses of Congress, advocating repeal of the Twenty-second Amendment (which sets a term limit for the presidency) and supporting the Mutual Security Agency, made the dedication speech at the National Guard Memorial, and attended reunion luncheons with his White House staff and the members and staff of the Senate Truman Committee. In between engagements, he joined Bess Truman at the side of their daughter, Margaret Truman Daniel, who would give birth to Truman's second grandson, William Wallace Daniel, later in the month.

Dear Dean and Alice: May 14, 1959

Thanks for the lovely evening. What a grand time I had!

If only Bess could have been there. I'm taking her to the hospital today for a check up. So you know I'm somewhat upset—and can't show it and won't. You'll hear from me as things develop.

Sincerely,

Harry

Bess Truman underwent an operation to have a growth removed from her breast on May 18. The growth was benign.

Dear Mr. President,   May 20, 1959

This morning's paper brings us two bits of very good news—one, that our hopes about the boss have been confirmed; the other that

Margaret has another boy. I know how happy both of these have made you; what a weight of worry has been lifted from you.

We rejoice with you. Please give Bess our deepest affection and Margaret our warm congratulations.

For your amusement I am sending on to you my latest venture in the field of literature, a short story in the June *Harpers*. This ends me as a serious character & puts me down, to the surprise of a good many people, as the frivolous fellow I really am.

The day seems bright for the good news of both your girls.

Affectionately,

Dean

Acheson formulates the outline for a speech Truman was invited to give at the Air War College at Maxwell Field in Montgomery, Alabama (today's Maxwell Air Force Base). Truman did not accept the invitation.

May 26, 1959

Dear Mr. President:

A week or so ago the Executive Officer from the Air War College at Montgomery, Alabama (Maxwell Field), called me up to ask whether I would intercede with you to get you to come to the War College to speak. He wanted you to speak about the appeal of democracy. I said that this was a stupid subject and that I would not urge you or anyone else to speak about it. This, of course, led him to ask and me to tell him the sort of thing which would be helpful if discussed by you. He went off to discuss all of this with the commandant and returned to accept the suggestion.

The suggestion was to discuss the problems of a democracy and how to solve them in its struggle with a great totalitarian power, all as seen from the vantage point of the chief of a democratic state. In order to make it as concrete as possible, he worked it out in this way:

The title of the speech would be "The Office of the Chief Executive of the United States in the Current World Conflict." The content of the speech would discuss:

(1) What are the problems that the great democracies face in meeting the challenge of the totalitarian governments? (These problems, I think, are first identifying the nature and extent of the challenge and then summoning and maintaining the continuous will and effort required to meet it.)

(2) What are the methods available to a democratic nation in thwarting communist designs? (I think that these are the methods in the political, economic, and military fields which you used during your administration.)

(3) How can the leader of a democratic government obtain the support of the people of his country in dealing with the aims of communism? (No one knows this better than you.)

(4) Does the office of the Chief Executive have adequate power for the exercise of timely and forceful leadership in today's world?

> (a) If not, what changes would you recommend in the relationships between the three branches of the government?

> (b) What structural and administrative adjustments would facilitate the functions of the Executive? (In my judgment, this is chiefly a matter of personality and not machinery.)

(5) Can Democratic nations take the initiative in the current world conflict or must they react? (Initiative about what? The Marshall Plan and Point IV were cases in which you took the initiative. Democracies cannot take the initiative in attacking someone else or increasing world tensions.)

With this kind of a speech, which I hope you would deliver largely from notes and not from a written text, I would urge you to consider going. They will invite you formally if I give them any encouragement at all. They would hope that you could do it in the last week of October or the first week of November.

They have a class of about 300 who are all Colonels in the Air Force or Army and Captains in the Navy or people of equivalent rank in the State Department and CIA. They would like to have you speak for an hour; then take an hour off with a few people in the library, chatting and resting; and then another hour receiving questions from the whole group and dealing with them.

I go once a year to the Air War College. They fly me down the afternoon before I speak, put me up comfortably in the Bachelor Officers' Quarters, with meals at the Officers' Club, and fly me back again.

I think you might enjoy it. If, however, you have a lot to do at that time and feel that it would be a strain, please turn it down without further thought, and I will get you out of it. A word to me at your earliest convenience will dispose of the matter.

Sincerely,

[Dean]

Acheson worries over Winston Churchill's disappointment in not seeing Truman during his recent trip to the United States. Churchill was in Washington and New York City from May 4 to 10, when Truman was also in those cities but could not escape his heavy schedule to meet with Churchill. Truman had already sent Churchill a letter, on May 27, explaining, "I had no intention of appearing discourteous to you." Kay Halle was a well-connected Washington resident who had many friends on both sides of the Atlantic.

May 29, 1959

Dear Mr. President,

I have a letter from Kay Halle from London who hears much of Sir Winston's disappointment that he did not see you on his farewell visit. When we lunched with him at the Embassy on May 7th he spoke of it. I told him of your being swamped by the jubilee festivities and held out hope that you might see or talk to him in New York. Apparently this was not possible. Now the old man seems to brood about it as he is very fond of you.

Would it be a good idea to drop him an affectionate line? I think he would treasure it. It would be too bad for him to get the wholly wrong idea that you didn't care about seeing him.

Probably you have written him already and I should have minded my own business. But you have had enough on your mind to have driven out such ideas altogether.

We hope the boss continues to make great progress. When does she come home? Our most affectionate greetings to you both.

As ever,

Dean

June 2, 1959

Dear Dean:

You'll never know how very much I appreciated your letter of May 29th.

I had worried about the situation to no end. So I wrote Winston about my difficulties and you should see the answer. It was heart warming.

Don't ever "mind your own business" where I'm involved. I'm hopelessly dependent on you for good advice. Sometimes I don't take it, but it's always good and appreciated.

My best to Alice. The Boss will be home tomorrow, thank God.

Sincerely,

Harry

*Harry and Bess Truman with Dean Acheson at the Truman Library site
in Independence, Missouri, on February 12, 1955. Also pictured is
David Lloyd, executive director of the Library Committee.*

7

June 1959 to November 1960

A Candidate for 1960 – George Marshall's Death – The U-2 Incident – Sit-Down Strikes – A "Treaty on 'Don'ts'" – John F. Kennedy and the Democratic Convention – The Campaign

*B*eginning in the summer of 1959, the approaching presidential campaign became the dominant topic in Truman's and Acheson's letters. Acheson worried that Adlai Stevenson might again be the Democratic nominee. He had never much liked Stevenson and didn't believe he could win in 1960. Truman worried that Nixon, a man he despised and thought dangerous to the country, might become President. He was also troubled by doubts about John F. Kennedy, whom he thought too young and inexperienced, and too linked with his rich father, Joseph P. Kennedy. He wanted the Democratic convention to be open and free to choose the best candidate—which would presumably be someone other than Kennedy; Truman favored Missouri Senator Stuart Symington—but as the convention neared, it was evident to Truman that Kennedy's people were controlling it and that the outcome was almost predetermined. Acheson worried about what his beloved but sometimes problematic old boss would say and do during the political season, and he sent him the most remarkable letter in all their correspondence (June 28, 1960) in an attempt to head off any embarrassing or harmful behavior on Truman's part. Truman, despite a somewhat rocky performance during the period leading up to and during the Democratic convention, was a loyal party man afterward, enthusiastically committed to John F. Kennedy, at least publicly. Acheson advised him to go on the attack against Nixon during the campaign. Truman did this especially effectively in one of his most unusual and whimsical speeches—which Acheson partially wrote for him—given in California near the end of the campaign.

Two other important events that appear in Truman's and Acheson's letters from this period are the death of General George C. Marshall and the shooting down by the Soviet Union of an American U-2 spy plane.

When the hectic campaign season was over, Acheson traveled to Independence to give a speech, and he and Truman enjoyed a quiet visit together.

· · ·

Truman did not accept the invitation from the Fletcher School of Law and Diplomacy to deliver a series of lectures. Acheson is worried about finding a winning Democratic presidential candidate for the upcoming campaign. "Writing for the Russian vote" probably refers to Averell Harriman, a candidate for President, taking a soft line in U.S.-Russian relations. The "military pamphlet" that columnist Walter Lippmann likes is one of the pamphlets Acheson, and his friend and colleague Paul Nitze in this case, prepared for the Democratic Advisory Council. Titled The Military Forces We Need and How to Get Them, *it argues that the country's defense forces were in desperate need of modernization and increased funding.*

June 25, 1959

Dear Mr. President,

I am turning into a nuisance for you. It all comes from people wanting me to intercede for them with you in cases where I should not do so but do not have the courage to tell them so. Now my good friend and old colleague at the State Department, Bob Stewart, Dean of the Fletcher School of Law and Diplomacy, wants you to give the Clayton Lectures next fall or winter. These are three connected lectures on three successive nights for a fee of $1,500 and expenses and a book published by the Harvard Press. I started these off in 1957. Mike [Lester B.] Pearson followed in 1958. Now they want you—very wisely from their point of view. They speak of getting some one to help you if you wish. Bob sent his letter to you via me.

This is a lot of work. I did it only because I had some ideas which I wanted to be driven into writing by a deadline and finishing. As of today

I would not do it. Probably when you write another book you will want more time and quiet than 1959–1960 are likely to provide. But if you have some ideas that would, without excessive labor, make a little volume of 200 pages, this is a dignified and worthy way to get them before the intelligent public.

That is about the story. I will not harass you more about it.

I am depressed by the shadow of things to come. It looks to me that, as I feared, drift is the master of our fates. That master seems headed for a ticket of Stevenson and Kennedy. No one else seems to be catching on; and none of our boys have the aura of victory about them. Have you any word of cheer for your despairing friend? Averell seems to be writing for the Russian vote, not that it is not all probably true. I just don't see where it takes him, though I think I see where he would like it to take him. But not with Adlai as President!

Please give your patient the most affectionate and solicitous messages from Alice and me. We hear good reports of her.

Did you see Lippmann this morning on the military pamphlet? He was positively lyrical about it. We must be slipping.

Affectionately

Dean

Truman is also thinking about the 1960 presidential campaign. Democratic National Committee Chair Paul Butler had recently attacked the congressional leadership, suggesting, some thought, he would try to lessen the grip of congressional Democrats such as Sam Rayburn and John McCormack on the running of the upcoming Democratic National Convention in Los Angeles. This might give some of the more liberal candidates, including the twice-failed candidate Adlai Stevenson, a better chance. "Soapy" is G. Mennen Williams, governor of Michigan.

Dear Dean: July 12, 1959

My so called promptness is gradually going into the slow-up stage. I am as sorry as I can be to admit it! My darned mail ran up to some 12,000 items when I had a birthday, Margie had another baby and the Boss had to have a ten or twelve pound tumor removed. Then to top it off I had to send my only sister in for a check up and the smartest of the smart M.D.'s could not decide what the trouble is! She is improving and now maybe I can begin to think—if I ever could!

I am very much interested in the Fletcher School of Law and Diplomacy, at Tufts University. Will try to appear. You put me out front at Yale and then Colorado came along and I'm going to have one hell of a time to maintain my standing. I've been to Un[iversity] of Cal[ifornia] and Harvard and Missouri and Kansas and Oklahoma and haven't been shot at yet. But that doesn't mean I won't be.

Next week I'm going to try and work things out and you'll hear immediately soon as it's done.

Hope you've noticed Mr. Butler's shot from the hip. Sam and Lyndon are boiling over. Humphrey, Stu, Kennedy and Soapy are upset because they didn't think of it first. Let the pot boil. It won't hurt anything. Later we'll try to obtain two men who can lead us to victory—and that we must have.

My best to Alice and all your family. Hope all are well.

Sincerely,

Harry

Truman frets about his relationship with Winston Churchill, about Paul Butler's leadership of the Democratic National Committee, and about Eisenhower and Nixon. But he had no need to worry about Churchill, who had in fact sent a very understanding letter (May 21, 1959) in response to Truman's apology letter (May 16, 1959) for his inability to visit Churchill in New York or Washington earlier that month. Three months later, Truman and Acheson had apparently both forgotten about Churchill's letter. William E. Jenner was a Republican Senator from Indiana and a McCarthy follower. The name "Alibi Ike" probably came from the 1935 movie of that name, which features a baseball player who is always making excuses. On July 9, 1935, when the movie was playing in Washington, Truman wrote to Bess Truman, who was in Independence, "I wanted to see Joe Brown in Alibi Ike *but didn't." Truman and Acheson did not quit the Democratic Advisory Committee, which became moribund once the Democratic National Convention met in July 1960. It went officially out of existence early in the Kennedy administration.*

August 22, 1959

Dear Dean:

I'm in a very bad position. When Winston Churchill paid his last visit, it was not possible for me to be present at the White House, because the invitation came too late—as intended. Then he was in New York as the guest of our "old friend" Barney Baruch.

Averell Harriman called me at the last minute and asked me to go with him to Barney's house where Winston was a guest. I couldn't go because I was at that minute packing up to take a train home. Mrs. Truman was due for an operation. So was Margie.

I wrote Winston and explained the situation. Haven't heard from him and probably won't. He thinks very much of old man Baruch and I don't. Of course he's fond of Ike because he thinks Ike saved the world in 1945. So I suppose I've lost a friend whom I have on record as just that. To hell with all that.

Now I have another problem.

You and I are on the advisory committee of the National Democratic Committee at the request of Paul Butler. I was never for him as National Chairman of the Democratic Committee. He owes his position to Sam Rayburn and Lyndon Johnson. He is organizing the L.A. Convention for Stevenson. What can we do? If we don't have a winner this time, it will take another F.D.R. to put the country on the right track. We are on a switchback now.

Butler was elected at New Orleans on the basis of a statement which he made to the southern block. Now he says he didn't mean it. He agreed to the Los Angeles site and now he says he didn't.

Seems to me the Chairman of the Democratic Committee should try to keep things in such shape as to nominate a man who can lead the people to believe that the Democratic Party will give them the best government, nationally and internationally.

Mr. Butler has not done that and as far as I can see does not intend to do it. I suppose we'll just have to let him lead the party to defeat — but I don't want to be a party to it.

Ike's gone to Germany, France, Britain and Russia. He sent the Vice President ahead of him. Mr. Nixon's background is one of sabotage. By misrepresentation he was able to beat a good Congressman, a good Senator and make himself Vice President. As representative of the President he ran up and down the country calling Democrats, me particularly, traitors. That was in 1954. Ike stood on the platform in Milwaukee and allowed Jenner and McCarthy to call Gen. George C. Marshall a traitor. It was my privilege to peel the hide off him for that in Colorado Springs.

Now Tricky Dick and Alibi Ike are trying to take me into camp. I won't go. Maybe I'm wrong. But I'm one of these contrary Kentucky feudists by inheritance. We don't forget our friends and we remember those who lied about us—and I'm afraid don't forgive them—especially if the objective is to use us to get right with God!—for a purpose.

Should we quit the Advisory Committee or should we not? If Butler has his way we'll nominate a loser and elect Nixon for President.

I'm against it!

Sincerely,

Harry

My best to Alice in which the Boss joins me.

Acheson analyzes the possible outcomes of the nominating process at the Democratic National Convention. Significantly, he picked Johnson and Kennedy as the most likely winning ticket in 1960, but in reverse order from the ultimate result. "Ziffren" is Paul Ziffren, a California Democratic party leader. Edmund G. "Pat" Brown was governor of California. Florence S. Mahoney was an advocate for health research and programs; her home in Georgetown served as a sort of salon for politicians and scientists. Adlai Stevenson is "this paunchy quipster." The recent Truman article to which Acheson refers was a NANA syndicated column that ran on or about August 25, in which Truman opposed Eisenhower's trip to Moscow to meet with Khrushchev and said that if Russia really wanted peace, it should bring its plan before the United Nations. Acheson, who once derisively called the United Nations "the international orphan asylum," might not have agreed with this view. The "triptych" enclosure Acheson mentions has not been identified.

August 31, 1959

Dear Mr. President:

I find it hard to believe that Winston would be so silly and so rude as intentionally to ignore your letter. He was certainly far from mentally acute when I lunched with him at the Embassy and it seems far more likely that he has forgotten it or that some secretarial failure is responsible. My suggestion is to get Rose to remind you well in advance that Sir Winston's birthday is Nov. 30 and write him a note in the course of which you can say again how sorry you were to miss him and hope that he got your letter explaining why. Then, at least, you can rest in the belief that you have done all you could to put things right.

I spoke to Sam Rayburn today about your concern over Paul Butler. Sam said he knows that Adlai was right when he wanted to fire Butler and thinks less than nothing of him and of his friend Ziffren of California. But the gossip Sam hears is that neither of them are for Stevenson. One of his authorities for this, so he said, was Pat Brown. Pat told me that the only Democrats who could carry California—aside, I imagine, from himself—were Kennedy and Stevenson.

My mind goes back to our talk the Sunday we lunched together with Florence Mahoney that the fruit of drift would be Stevenson. It still seems to me to be the most likely outcome, and I agree with you that it seems more likely than not that he would be defeated by either Nixon or Rockefeller. My analysis of the convention is that John Kennedy must win, if he wins at all, on a very early ballot. If he does not, there seems to me to be only two realistic next choices, Adlai and Lyndon. Humphrey is only an heir to Stevenson; and Symington, to Johnson. Stevenson would certainly get it if Kennedy would agree (having lost on his bid for first place) to run with him. Tom Corcoran tells me that the only person with whom, according to Joe Kennedy, John would run under the circumstances is Lyndon. If, therefore, Kennedy threw his strength to Johnson, Adlai might be stopped and the Johnson-Kennedy ticket might be nominated. Lesser combinations seem to me of only theoretical interest, because they cannot win.

To me a Johnson-Kennedy ticket would have much more appeal than a Stevenson-Kennedy ticket, though the polls would give the latter a better chance. But the polls gave you no chance in 1948. I say, to hell with the polls, if we have the real stuff against them.

Lyndon is the ablest man in national public life today. He has thousands of faults. But when we really take our hair down, he is a giant among pigmies. So I feel confident that if, with strong support and a united party, he took on the campaign, especially with Kennedy, we would have a chance for a fight in which I could join whole heartedly, because there would not only be a real chance to win, but to win under circumstances where victory might really turn the tide for the great struggle of our time. My constant worry about Adlai is that all we accomplish by electing him is to accept formal responsibility for ultimate defeat. Surely this is better than Nixon or Rockefeller, the inevitable figureheads of the futility and incapacity of the American managerial interest whose Pope is George Humphrey, but it isn't very good.

If I thought that it might even usher in a golden age before the twilight, like the 30 years of the Antonines, it would be worth while. But this paunchy quipster is no Marcus Aurelius.

As you know, I agree with you about the dangers of the forthcoming visits, though I advised against either of us opposing them now. Because of Ike's neglect for the basic realities of power he has been forced to substitute improvisation for planning. He feels, as a beautiful woman might, that his charm must carry all. But as Norman Hapgood said of Maud Adams in *Chanticleer,* "charm never made a rooster." Averell thinks your recent article was a mistake and that, of all the trips, Ike's to Russia may be the most important in undermining the picture of the U.S. which Mr. K has been selling to his people and limiting his capacity to build up war scares. But I have told him that he takes too serious a view of the effect of your piece and not to worry himself or you about it. The article has about it some of the mystery of the Virgin birth. I wonder what inspired it.

My own writing is taking varied forms.

I have done an article for *American Heritage* about Arthur Vandenberg. Another for the *N.Y. Times Magazine,* called "Time to Think," stimulated by Ike's speech on thinking in "the highest echelons" to the Foreign Service Institute. Both of these you will get in due course. Then I have written another story for *Harper's* about Italy like the one I had in last June's issue. It has kept me busy and my mind from rusting. I hear that you are to write two books. This is real ambition and energy.

I am enclosing a triptych which came to me in the mail showing you in the company of your successors. How about a good law suit out of this?

We are off on Sept. 13th for Italy, Germany, and England, part vacation, part meetings. We look forward to it eagerly.

Alice sends her love; and much of it to Mrs. Truman. (I always stumble over calling that dear lady, Bess, as she has bid me), and to you, Excellency and Friend, as do I.

As ever,

Dean

General George C. Marshall, who served President Truman as Army Chief of Staff, special envoy to China, Secretary of State, and Secretary of Defense, died on October 16, 1959. Truman in 1947 judged him "the great one of the age" and greatly valued his friendship and unwavering support. Truman has just read Acheson's recent article about Marshall—"Homage to General Marshall," in The Reporter *(November 26, 1959).*

November 24, 1959
Dear Dean:

That article in the *Reporter* about General Marshall was "just out of this world."

I sat and read it and read it again because my spectacles became clouded the first time. Do you suppose any President of the United States ever had two such men with him as you and the General? In my history studies of the Presidency, I haven't found a single case like it. Presidents had one on whom they could rely—but not two.

I'm getting sentimental again. Please forgive me. My best to Alice and I hope I can see you again soon.

Sincerely,

Harry

Happy Thanksgiving.

Acheson spoke before the fifth annual conference of parliament members of the NATO nations on November 18. He advised the Western alliance not to succumb to meretriciously attractive invitations to negotiate the situation in Berlin and Germany proposed by the Soviet Union. He ridiculed "the incredible view that any sort of a negotiation is good per se." Acheson regarded "the spirit of Camp David" as a "feel good" concoction that obscured the issues with the Russians. Camp David, in Thurmont, Maryland, on Catoctin Mountain in the Blue Ridge Mountains, was the weekend White House where Eisenhower had extended hospitality to the Russian leadership. Truman and Acheson would be together in New York City on December 5, 6, and 7 for meetings of the Democratic Advisory Council.

November 30, 1959
Dear Mr. President,

Your letter about my tribute to General Marshall and your words about me are about the most cherished that have ever been said to me. I cannot tell you how much they mean to me. In the next mail came a letter from Mrs. Marshall saying that my article "expresses a knowledge of my George that few people had." I was delighted to have been able to bring her some comfort that others who did not know him could get some understanding of his nature.

To have you class me with him is enough praise for one life time. And it came when it helped a lot—just as I was getting a good measure of abuse for my remarks about Ike's junket and my speech to the NATO

Parliamentarians, which *Pravda* printed in full. Thank God the Russians say that I have none of the spirit of Camp David. I wonder where the world would be—or, rather, I don't wonder—I know—where the world would be now if you had had the spirit of Camp David from 1945 to 1953?

I am looking forward to seeing you in N.Y. next weekend. Can we keep Adlai and Co. from "grabbing the peace issue"?

Alice and I send much love to the boss and to you.

As ever,

Dean

December 15, 1959

Dear Mr. President:

When I was walking down 22nd Street to the office this morning, a small, elderly colored man accosted me and challenged me to say who he was. Of course I failed in this endeavor and he told me that he used to open the west door of the White House for me many times a week.

I told him I had seen you very recently and gave him a good account of your spirits and fighting trim. This delighted him.

I had only gone a few yards down the street before he called after me and came running up to say that his name was Harry, too, and to ask me when I wrote to you to tell you that you were his boy.

Do you remember him?

Please give the Boss especially affectionate messages to add to the warmth of the Christmas Season and to those which usually go to you both.

Sincerely yours,

Dean

At a dinner tribute in New York City for Eleanor Roosevelt on December 7, Truman introduced the Democratic presidential candidates, including John F. Kennedy and Hubert Humphrey, and gave a speech in which he said that, for the Democratic candidate for President in 1960, "we need a vigorous, fighting, genuine liberal, and not a hot-house liberal, who talks the game but doesn't play it."

December 22, 1959

Dear Dean:

I appreciated your letter of December 15 telling about the messenger boy who stated that he was in the habit of meeting you when you came over to my office from the State Department Building. To tell the truth, I cannot remember him either. We had two men who usually looked after those doors at that office; one, by the name of Jackson and the other was John Mayes and both are dead now. I do not recall this man but I might have been able to if I had seen him. There seems to be a tendency nowadays for everybody who was in sight of the White House at the time you and I were there to give the impression they were exceedingly interested in our welfare. Well, maybe they were.

It certainly was a pleasure to see you at the meeting the other night and I do not know when I have had as good a time as I had introducing the candidates for the Presidency. As you noticed, I have placed a statement in the speech regarding the synthetic liberals which covers the situation in which you are interested.

I am hoping to be in Washington for the meeting on January 23 and I certainly want to have a chance to see you and Alice. I do not know whether or not Mrs. Truman will be with me. It will depend upon how she feels after the visit with these grandchildren of ours. She is having a good time with them and so am I, but we are not in the same position we were when Margaret was their age and we cannot go quite so fast. However, I expect you have had the same experience even though you are a good many years younger than I am.

Sincerely yours,
Harry

Truman encloses an article about an exhibition of works of art, all gifts to Truman, at the Truman Library. Alice Acheson's Bus Queue *was one of the works on display. Truman had lunch with Acheson at his home on January 24. He was in Washington to attend the 1960 Democratic Presidential Campaign Kick-Off Dinner. The artist Thomas Hart Benton painted the mural* Independence and the Opening of the West *in the main lobby of the Truman Library.*

February 5, 1960

Dear Dean and Alice:

I am as tardy as I can be writing you about that lovely luncheon. Don't know when I've had a more enjoyable one—not since your last one.

Glad I was tardy because here is something Alice will like, I hope. This place has stepped up a notch. Even Tom Benton admits it!

Hope to see you again soon.

Sincerely,

Harry

The madam gave me "what for" because I'm late. The best to both of you.

April 10, 1960

Dear Dean:

Haven't heard from you for some time. I'm at the office in the Library signing piles of mail the girls typed yesterday, sealing them and shall take them to the post office in Kansas City so they'll go out. You know this five day week doesn't work with me. I guess I'm old fashioned. I work every day and Sunday too even if Exodus 20:8, 9, 10 and 11 and Deuteronomy 5–13 and 14 say I shouldn't. I think probably those admonitions were the first labor laws we know about—and see how they've made contributions to the greatest Republic in history. But someone has to fix things so the rest can work five days—coffee breaks and all. I've often wondered what would have happened to me when I was receiving $35.00 to write up checks for collection on a 12 hour day if I'd stopped at 10 A.M. for a Dutch lunch. You know the Dutch farmer in our old neighborhood had a breakfast at 4:30 A.M., a lunch in the field at 10 A.M., dinner at 12 noon—and it was a dinner, lunch at 4 P.M. and supper after sundown.

That $35.00 was per month—not per day.

I expect to be in Washington the last week in April, probably some time on the 27th. The Boss and I are going to New York tomorrow because Cliff and Margie are going to Europe a couple of days after we arrive. Bess thinks she'll baby sit while Margie's gone. They have a wonderful nurse but I wonder how long that "baby sit" will last.

I have a lecture date at Cornell on the 23rd and one at Syracuse U. on the 18th but after a trip home I'll be in the Capital City, I hope, on the 27th.

I've been having a grand time with "sit downs" and broadcasters, foreign policies and Presidential candidates. I want to see you.

Sincerely,

Harry

Adele Lovett was the wife of Robert A. Lovett, Truman's last Secretary of Defense. Felix was Justice Felix Frankfurter. When Truman heard news of sit-down strikes in segregated Southern eating places, he said publicly that if he owned a store he would throw anyone out who disrupted business. About two years later, he wrote to the head of the United Auto Workers union on this subject. " . . . I don't like sit-down strikes. . . . When you destroy a man's business, especially a little man, it just isn't right and you know it as well as I do."

April 14, 1960

Dear Mr. President,

I shall look forward to April 27th. Would you have dinner with me on that night or the next one? Alice is away on a trip with Adele Lovett to Greece. But we still manage to eat pretty well. If you are free, shall we have a stag party or give the ladies a break?

Your schedule sounds as though you were headed for trouble with the Boss. I have been running a pretty hard one myself and got pretty tired. While Alice is away I am going to ease up a bit and play a bit of hookey out at the farm to which spring has eventually come. One most interesting experience I had in March was a week of lecturing seminars and student consultations at Knox College in Galesburg Illinois, where—as you know—the fifth Lincoln[-]Douglass debate took place and where Carl Sandburg was born. It is a fine and gallant little place, though the town is pretty bad. There were all Republicans when I got there. But we certainly changed that.

What is all this anti-sit-down attitude of yours. Felix was asking me the other day, saying that his brother Whittaker takes the same view. I told him that Missourians are Confederates at heart, and that while they—or some of them—accept the Constitution, and even defend it vigorously, they won't go a step further. There's nothing in the Constitution about how to run a drug store's lunch counter. Only we New England abolitionists find that reasoning irrelevant. Am I about right in my diagnosis.

Now for a prophecy. If Jack Kennedy stubs his toe in West Virginia or elsewhere, the candidate will be Stevenson. I hate to say this but I think the only possible alternative is Stu and I doubt very much, though I am for him, that he can make it. He just doesn't seem to catch hold. Maybe we should all give Jack a run for his money—or rather for Joe's.

My warmest greetings to the Boss and to you.

As ever,

Dean

Truman's response to the question about his "anti-sit-down attitude" makes clear that he thought of himself as a Southerner. Truman spoke at Cornell University on April 18.

Dear Dean:
                                                              April 20, 1960

I am also looking forward to April 27th. The dinner invitation is accepted for that night. I shall miss Alice but I'm betting on your cook! I envy her that trip to Greece. Bess is not coming to Washington. Grandma has to oversee and sometimes sit with a couple of obstreperous young men who want what they want when they want it and usually get it. So if you want to make the party stag that will be fine.

Your lecture tour must be as interesting as can be. Wish I'd been in the audience at Knox College. I'm sure I could have cribbed a good lecture for future use. You tell his Honor Felix that your diagnosis of my case is correct. I sometimes become so upset by the yellow half breeds from New York and Chicago that I almost go segregationist. If they'd stay up north and let those of us who know the problem settle it—we could and would do it.

I'll tell you about a plan when I see you. My meeting at Cornell was a humdinger: 9,900—at the lecture 90% students. Sounded like a Dem convention when I appeared and when I went away.

I'm looking forward to a grand visit with you. That letter of yours gave me a real lift.

Sincerely yours,

Harry

Truman is worried about events in the Caribbean and in Asia, and about how Eisenhower handled the downing of an American U-2 spy plane by the Soviet Union. Acheson's dinner—a black-tie event—took place on April 27.

Dear Dean:
                                                              May 9, 1960

I have been reading the results of our situation in Asia east of the Caribbean Sea and I am very much worried.

It seems to me that the President of the United States ought not to admit that he doesn't know what is going on. It looks as if we are in a very ridiculous position with our friends. We have always been known for honest and fair dealings as a nation and I really don't know how we are going to recover from this last blow.

I am still thinking about that wonderful dinner you had and what a grand time I had with you. I wish it were possible for the two of us to sit down and discuss the situation and see what we can do to remedy it. I don't know whether there is anything that can be done or not. As you know, I am a natural born optimist but I am pessimistic on this situation.

Sincerely yours,

Harry

Acheson analyzes Soviet motives for using the U-2 incident to prevent the convening of a summit conference at Paris in mid-May. Eisenhower had been humiliated by Khrushchev over the incident, and tried to deny the mission, but then the Russians produced the captured American pilot. The article Acheson sends to Truman is "The Persistence of Illusion: The Soviet Economic Drive and American National Interest," by Townsend Hoopes.

May 23, 1960

Dear Mr. President:

The first sentence of your letter to me of May 9 is a real puzzler. "I have been reading," you say, "the results of our situation in Asia east of the Caribbean Sea and I am very much worried." I have been worrying for some time that the Asia problem was creeping up on us, but I had not realized how close it had approached, and here it is now just a bit south of Bermuda. So I am worried too.

However puzzling your geography may have become, your meaning is perfectly clear, and I agree entirely that the President of the United States ought not to admit that he doesn't know what is going on. And, even more important than admitting this fact, it ought not to be a fact.

The day that our admission about the U-2 flight came out I was lecturing at the National War College and a madder and more disgusted group of officers I never saw. There used to be a saying around in my youth that the Lord took care of children, drunks and the United States of America. But it seems that now we are over-taxing omnipotence.

Shortly before the Summit meeting the official attitude around the State Department was that the Summit would be a pushover.

Khrushchev, they said, was under such pressures at home that in order to have a political success he must get an agreement and have Eisenhower in Moscow. So he would agree to a nuclear test ban and then adjourn the festivities to Moscow. I produced a great deal of merriment around town by predicting that the Summit would not last two days. I seem to have overstated it by one.

The official version has now changed. It is still said that Khrushchev was under great pressure, but this time it was pressure in the opposite direction. The State Department tells us that the pressure was not for a success but for a failure and came from the Army and the Chinese allies. Having learned of the firmness of Mr. Eisenhower and the unbreakable unity of the Allies, he had to end the Summit without a test of strength, and, in seizing upon the U-2 incident, he has overplayed his hand.

I think this is as erroneous as the first view. Mr. Khrushchev knew exactly what he was doing, and he was playing the game of the protracted conflict, as the Russians have always played it, alternating tension with detente. Peaceful coexistence is now abandoned for a renewal of the cold war, but the purpose is the same. It is to get us out of Berlin, get Germany out of the Western Alliance, and to get the United States out of Europe.

My guess is that, under the cover of the commotion which will be going on in the U.N., the East Germans will begin to tighten up on civilian traffic with Berlin, and sometime, when we are sufficiently distracted by attempts to prevent majorities or two-thirds majorities in the Security Council or the General Assembly, the treaty with the East Germans will be made.

Mr. Eisenhower, like a weary fighter, is maneuvering for the bell; and, whatever happens, he will do nothing about it, leaving these problems for his successor. The enclosed article from the *Yale Review* seems to me a pretty sound statement of the situation as it stands at present.

Most sincerely,
Dean

Truman is pessimistic about the situation in several parts of the world. He tells Acheson he's going to the Democratic National Convention in Los Angeles.

May 27, 1960

Dear Dean:

Yours of the 23rd gave me quite a lift. That sentence should have read "west of the Caribbean Sea." I was thinking of Panama, Guatemala, Chile, Indonesia, Indo-China and the riots in Japan. What started my train of thought was this whiskered nut in Cuba.

He's buying oil from Russia shipped in Russian ships when his neighbors could furnish it for maybe half the price! He's selling sugar for a pittance to Kruchie's agent for less than 3 cents a pound which is sold in Soviet Land for a dollar!

Panama wants to steal the canal as Nasser stole Suez. Chile our former good friend kisses in with our world enemies. Venezuela spits on our Vice President while the President of the United States receives the same treatment in Paris. I'm not a pessimist as you very well know.

But how the hell could we come to this international debacle? And you and I are in a fix where we dare not kick the guy in the ass who is to blame. I wrote an article last September which came out in October I think in which I said what I did yesterday—if the United Nations is expected to work summits are a farce. Now Ike's reading a prepared U.N. speech.

I'm going to L.A. as a delegate and I suppose I'll be tongue tied.

It's a hell of a situation!

You'd better cheer me up or there'll be a personal explosion.

My best to Alice.

Harry

Acheson had trouble writing this remarkable letter reining in Truman so as not to damage their party's chances of winning the presidency. He first handwrote a draft, which he heavily altered. He had the edited draft typed, and then handwrote a slightly altered version that he sent Truman. Acheson also telephoned his friend to talk over, perhaps in softer language, what he had said so bluntly in this letter. Acheson's new salutation "Boss" suggests that Truman had said something to activate this new familiarity, possibly first names, which would have made Acheson very uncomfortable. Hence the compromise: Boss.

June 28, 1960

Dear Boss,

As the Convention approaches and you are likely to become, shall we say, emphatic in your statements to the press, could we make a treaty as to what we shall not say?

On the positive side we can, and doubtless will, say that our candidate—yours and mine—has all the virtues of the Greats from Pericles through Churchill. St. Peter and the Pee-pul. Forgive this innocent though improbable hyperbole. But there are some things that no one should, and few will, forgive.

These fall into several groups, but the common denominator is the harm that comes from allowing the intensity of the personal view to dim a proper concern for the common cause. The list of the "It's not dones," as I see it, goes like this:—

I. About Other Democratic Candidates:

(a) Never say that any of them is not qualified to be President.

(b) Never say that any of them can't win.

(c) Never suggest that any of them is the tool of any group or interest, or not a true blue liberal, or has (or has used) more money than another.

The reason: At this point public argument is too late. Deals may still be possible. I just don't know. But sounding off is sure to be wrong. If our candidate is going anywhere—which I doubt—it will not be because of public attacks on other candidates. And such attacks can do a lot of harm when they are quoted in the election campaign.

II. About the Negro Sit-in Strikes:

(a) Do not say that they are communist inspired. The evidence is all the other way, despite alleged views of J. Edgar Hoover, whom you should trust as much as you would a rattlesnake with a silencer on its rattle.

(b) Do not say that you disapprove of them. Whatever you think, you are under no compulsion to broadcast it. Free speech is a restraint on the government: not an incitement to the citizens.

The reason: Your views, as reported, are wholly out of keeping with your public record. The discussion does not convince anyone of anything. If you want to discuss the sociological, moral and legal interests involved in this issue, you should give much more time and thought to them.

III. About Foreign Policy

(a) For the next four months do not say that in foreign policy we must support the President.

The reason: This cliché has become a menace. It misrepresents by creating the false belief that in the recent series of disasters the President has had a policy or position to support.

This just isn't true. One might as well say "support the President" if he falls off the end of a dock. That isn't a policy. But to urge support for him makes his predicament appear to be a policy to people who don't know what a dock is.

So, please, for just four months let his apologists come to his aid. We have got to beat Nixon. We shall probably have to do it with Kennedy. Why make it any harder than it has to be? Now if ever, our vocal cords ought to be played by the keyboard of our minds. This is so hard for me that I have stopped using my cords at all. By August they will be ready to play "My Rosary."

So I offer you a treaty on "don'ts." Will you agree?

Most sincerely,

Dean

Truman takes Acheson's strong medicine graciously. He had, however, already violated the "treaty on 'don'ts.'" On July 2, in a televised press conference at the Truman Library, he had said he would not attend the Democratic convention, which was taking on aspects of a "prearranged affair." He then addressed John F. Kennedy directly. "Senator, are you certain that you're quite ready for the country or the country is ready for you in the role of President in January 1961?" He asked Kennedy to put aside his personal ambition and allow the convention to select a candidate "with the greatest possible maturity and experience." He gave a long list of potential candidates who he felt had these qualities, including his own favorite, Missouri Senator Stuart Symington. Truman says in this letter to Acheson that he will depart for the convention the next day, but he did not go.

July 9, 1960

Dear Dean:

You'll never know how very much I appreciated your call and good letter. I tried my best to profit by both. Whether I did or not is up to you to decide.

Anyway it looks as if things have, to some extent, slowed down and the band wagon isn't running so fast. I've never been so wrought up and if you and the "Madam"—the "Boss"—had not put the brakes on I'd have blown my top—maybe!

Now Butler, the permanent Chairman, the temporary Chairman, Sam Rayburn and all the rest of them are spending money on long winded telegrams urging me to be present at the Convention.

I am taking a plane tomorrow evening for L.A. and intend to have a lot of fun with the guessers and the prophets.

It may not amount to much but you never can tell.

When I return home I'll owe you more information.

Again thanks to a real friend and a real standby.

My best to Alice.

Sincerely,

Harry

The Achesons are at their farm in Sandy Spring, Maryland. Acheson is pleased—if only tepidly—with the outcome of the Democratic convention and is looking forward to a new Democratic administration led by Kennedy.

July 17, 1960

Dear Boss,

We are here for the summer, and I, a commuter. So your letter of July 9th, by virtue of your extravagance in putting a special delivery stamp on it, lay on the floor at P Street for about a week. Mr. Summerfield forwards ordinary mail but special delivery has him baffled, and it goes into oblivion through the mail drop until Alice or Johnson happens to go in to P Street.

But in this case it was just as well. Your letter told me of your penultimate decision to go to Los Angeles, which was happily reversed by the ultimate one, not to go. Had I gotten your letter I should have wasted the family substance on the telephone urging you not to do what fate was to prevent you from doing. I am sorry that your sister-in-law had to be sacrificed to keep you from so unwise a step. But it was in a good cause and I hope that she is now much improved.

I listened to your press conference and regretted that you felt impelled to say anything, though what you said was better than what you first told me that you intended to say. It seemed quite inevitable that Jack's nomination would occur and that all that you and Lyndon said you would both have to eat—as you indeed have.

Poor Lyndon came off much worse, since he is now in the crate on the way to the county fair and destined to be a younger and more garrulous—if that is possible—Alben Barkley. It is possible that being a smart operator in the Senate is a special brand of smartness which doesn't carry over into the larger political field. Lyndon certainly behaved like a high school lad running for class president in 1956, and seems to have retrograded by 1960. Jack and his team were the only "pros" in Los Angeles, so far as I could see.

The ticket seems to me the best which under the circumstances—by which I mean Jack's determination to go all out for it and the absence of any opposition of comparable capacity and determination—the Party could put up. It will not raise great enthusiasm, but neither could any other ticket, and neither will Nixon on the other side. So far as a Kennedy administration is concerned, it would, I think, be better than what we have, than what Nixon would give: and I see no solid evidence on which to found a belief that Stu or Lyndon would do any better.

One current belief seems to me quite unfounded, that Lyndon as VP will continue to run the Senate and have great influence with Sam. I remember on the Hoover Commission urging on President Hoover that the V.P. should be selected and set up to be the Administration's agent on the Hill. The old man said, "It won't work. That is what I thought when I selected Charlie Curtis to be my V.P. But I found the day after the inauguration that no one, including his Senate colleagues, wanted to talk to No. 2."

Well, we're off to the races, after a little breather and a little more vulgarity and foolishness at Chicago. I hope that it is still true that the Lord looks benignly after children, drunks and the U.S.A. But he may think it about time that the last of the trio grew out of irresponsibility.

Our warmest greetings to Bess and you.

As ever,

Dean

Truman is unable to accept Kennedy completely as the Democratic presidential nominee or to like the process that selected him. The "Governor of Connecticut" is Abraham Ribicoff.

August 6, 1960

Dear Dean:

Well, you told me what I ought to listen to—and don't. Your letter of July 17th was a classic. It was most highly appreciated. What I want to know is how much of a damphool can a man be—and still think he might be right. That's this old man—and he can't help it!

Now we have the devil and the deep blue sea to choose from and I suppose we'll have to take the devil. Maybe he won't be so hard on us as Galilee was to the pigs that were drowned.

You were right, that I would have been in a better position if I'd said nothing. But, Dean, what can you do with a talker when there is a chance to talk. Well, here we are with two men who are problems.

You and I are not able to vote for Nixon. So I suppose we'll have to vote for the "ticket." Lyndon has been to see me and the Governor of Connecticut is coming here on Wednesday the 10th to try to persuade me to campaign with Kennedy. Kennedy is expected on the 21st to "pay his respects." I wonder what I can do that won't hurt the Party and still be right!

My mail gets bigger and bigger—and most of it is crackpot—but I rather like to read that sort. They'd never let me see it in the White House. It is sometimes entertaining and most times makes you want to aim a good punch at the proboscis—but you can't.

Hope you'll always be patient with me because I love your letters and you too.

Sincerely,

Harry

August 12, 1960

Dear Boss,

Your delightfully contrite letter has disarmed me wholly. To add to this, Alice and I read your letter just after looking at the *N.Y. Times* picture of you and Governor Abe under the caption "Truman Will Stump Coast to Coast for Kennedy." So I offered the thought that if the Lord is accurately quoted as having remarked "Vengeance is mine," He probably has a copyright on "I told you so," also. So I say no more. You have said it all, and said it with all your wry good humor.

Now you are in for it. Just don't exhaust yourself through sheer nonsense. Here is a thought which you might work in to get you onto the merits of the Party as such. In the U.S. the registration is something like 60–40 in favor of the Democrats. When it comes to enlisting Americans of brains and character for all the multifarious tasks of democratic government, the Republicans proscribe all Democrats. This brings them down to 40% of available material—a minority to start with. Then they proscribe all Republicans who had worked for the Government under Democratic administrators. This brought them down to about 20% (the inexperienced fifth). You were old fashioned enough to believe that all Americans were needed and eligible for the great task which faces our country and you used them all. The Party will do this again. We don't have a means test in reverse, nor are we limited in our choices to big business executives who can only "afford" a year or two for public service—though that may be all the public can afford of them.

Well, you see. This is known as the "high road." But it really is, you know. (You have to be ready to explain that Ike and Foster got by, even though they had worked for you, but getting out in time to denounce you.) All of this may make no sense but it could upset the calculation of the "truth squads" which the newspaper tells me will follow you around and read your preconvention statements about Kennedy. As for those, they were obviously made by another fellow of the same name.

I have a very depressed letter from Dirk Stikker. You remember him. He was the Dutch Foreign Minister from about 1949–53, was then Ambassador to London and is now the Dutchman on NATO. He says that the alliance—the only hope against Mr. K.—is floundering for lack of U.S. leadership Spaak tells him the next ten months will decide NATO's fate. In the absence of U.S. leadership, de Gaulle, Macmillan, and Adenauer each take their crack at some new idea which weakens the basic conception that it is Europe AND North America which is needed to deal with the U.S.S.R. He urges that both candidates make strong statements that no plans for NATO can or should be made now but that immediately after Jan. 1961 the new president will confer with the NATO powers on an urgent and far reaching strengthening of the alliance.

I have some ideas as to what this should consist of, but now is no time for this sort of thought and, perhaps, ideas from me will not get very far at any time.

So far in 1960 Jack Kennedy seems to have handled himself very well. In his match with you, in his handling of Lyndon (who made quite a goat of himself), Adlai and the whole convention I find it hard to fault him. This is by no means the same thing as saying that he arouses enthusiasm. Neither candidate does that. If their joint appearances don't stir some interest the campaign may turn out to be one of these pitchers' duels where neither side gets a hit and the paying customers go to sleep. If enough of us stay awake we can still win.

Alice is 18 today.

Affectionately,

Dean

During his meeting with Governor Ribicoff on August 10, Truman agreed to campaign for John Kennedy, and he arranged with Ribicoff to meet with Kennedy at the Truman Library on August 20. Kennedy flew to Kansas City from Washington that day and met privately with Truman for about thirty minutes. Afterward, they joined Senator Henry M. Jackson, the new chair of the Democratic National Committee, and Senator Stuart Symington of Missouri at a press conference in the library's auditorium. Truman took Kennedy by the arm and guided him to his place at the speakers' table. He announced that he would campaign for Kennedy and that, in the midst of an overall Democratic victory on election night, Kennedy would carry Missouri by an "overwhelming majority." Kennedy replied, "I am happy the President is going to join in, we need all good Democrats. I am delighted he is going to associate himself with us." When a reporter pressed Truman on his earlier statements about Kennedy's youth and immaturity, Truman responded tersely that such concerns were "solved by the convention. . . . That's all there is to it."

Acheson will be coming to Kansas City to speak to the Lawyers Association of Kansas City on November 30. Don Jackson is an officer with the association.

August 15, 1960

Dear Dean:

I am enclosing you a copy of a letter I have written in reply to one I received from Don Jackson.

I am as happy as I can be that you are coming here on November 30 and if there is anything in the world that I can do to make your visit pleasant, you may be sure I will do it.

Please give my best to Alice and tell her that the "Boss" is still in charge of my house.

Sincerely yours,

Harry

Acheson is becoming bored by the presidential campaign.

August 23, 1960

Dear Boss,

Many thanks for your letter about the Bar dinner on November 30. I accepted their invitation to get a chance to see you and Bess in Independence without the whole gang around which make Washington visits so hurried and hectic — except at P Street. So I shall get there perhaps the day before, or anyway early enough for a good visit with you.

Do you get a funny sort of sense that, so far at least, there are no human candidates in this campaign? They seem improbable, like very life-like puppets, who, or which, are operated by most skillful technicians. Both are surrounded by clever people who dash off smart memoranda, but it is not all pulled together, on either side, by and into a man. The ideas are too contrived. No one believes a congeries so suited to his apparent "voter need", as Madison Ave would put it. Even Bob Taft was heretical enough to be for government housing. These two are so perfectly suited to some one's idea of what they ought to be suited to that they bore the hell out of me.

This session of Congress seems to be bearing out a long held view of Alice's that Lyndon is not nearly as smart as he and [a] lot of his admirers think.

Whew! What a lot of subversive stuff!

Affectionately,

Dean

Truman wrote two versions of this letter, both presented below. In the second, shorter version, he removed his ramblings about former Presidents. Both versions express his lingering despair at the outcome of the Democratic convention. Regarding his account of earlier presidential elections, it should be noted that Winfield Scott ran for President only once, in 1852, losing to Franklin Pierce.

August 26, 1960

Not Sent

Dear Dean:

Your letters of the 12th and the 23rd really gave me the lift I needed. I have been as blue as indigo since the California meeting in L.A. It was a travesty on National Conventions. Ed Pauley organized it and then Kennedy's pa kicked him out! Ed didn't consult me!

That convention should have been helped immensely if it had been in Chicago, St. Louis or Philadelphia. But it wasn't held at any of those places. You and I are stuck with the necessity of taking the worst of two evils or none at all. So—I'm taking the immature Democrat as the best of the two. Nixon is impossible. So there we are.

When I took the stand I did I hoped to help—but I didn't. I look at history and the period after Madison and then the one after Jackson. After Jackson we had Martin Van Buren a smart fixer and then William Henry Harrison, a stuffed shirt who insisted on riding a white horse to the Capital—and a month later John Tyler was President. You know that old devil, who was my great grandmother's uncle, had some ideas of honor. He resigned from the Senate when he was not able to support Jackson's financial program. Then came James K. Polk, a great President. Said what he intended to do and did it. Then three months after leaving the White House went home and died!

Then old Zach Taylor came along, father-in-law of Jefferson Davis. He became famous at the Battle of Buena Vista by telling Captain Bragg to "give them a little more grape." Winfield Scott "Old Fuss and Feathers" as anxious as Grant and Ike to be President. Old Zach kept him out. But he ran again and was ingloriously defeated by one of his Brigadier generals Franklin Pierce—who always had the stomach ache or a pain in the neck when there was a shooting engagement in Mexico.

Franklin Pierce agreed to the repeal of the Missouri Compromise and signed the Kansas Nebraska Bill. With John Brown and his murders on the border between Missouri and Kansas these events caused the War Between the States—now officially called the Civil War, as was the War of the Roses in England.

I'm afraid I'm boring you but that is not the intention. I'm afraid that this immature boy who was responsible for picking out five great Senators may not know any more about the Presidency that he will occupy, than he did about the great Senators. Only one, Henry Clay, belonged in the list. I sent him a list of a dozen or so but it wasn't used. So, what the hell, you and I will take it and not like it but hope for the future.

Sincerely,

Harry

Dear Dean: August 26, 1960

Your letters of the 12th and 23rd really gave me the lift I needed. I have been as blue as indigo since the California meeting in L.A. It was a travesty on the Convention System. I don't think the end of Conventions is in sight, in spite of what Sam Houston said.

The California Convention was organized by Ed Pauley without any consultation with anyone. He lined 65% of the National Committee and then called me!

In my opinion the Convention should have been held in Chicago, St. Louis, or the "City of Brotherly Love." But it wasn't. You and I are stuck with taking the lesser or the worst of two evils—or none at all.

So, I am taking the immature Democrat as the best of what's before us. Nixon is impossible. There we are. I hoped my stand before the Convention might help—but it didn't. Maybe I should have been there.

Well, I've come to the conclusion that the devil has a hand in most things and he certainly ran the L.A. Convention.

When we look at the history of this great country, we wonder how the hell we arrived at the top notch of things where we are. I am sure that's what the oldsters thought in 1828, 1840, 1852 and sure enough in 1860. Well, we came out on top in all those dates. Let's hope to God we'll do it again. It is going to take Him to do it!

Sincerely,

Harry

The letter to Kennedy that Acheson mentions argues against a concept, much discussed at the time, that the Vice President should be a kind of prime minister, running most of the government's affairs and leaving the President primarily with the duties of commander in chief. Acheson advises Kennedy to "make it plain that you know enough about American history to know how idiotic this Prime Minister business is." The article Acheson sent to Truman is titled "The President and the Secretary of State" and concerns the relationship between the two officials. Mr. Citizen *was a collection of magazine articles written by Truman, published as a book in January 1960. Acheson's article was published in a book,* The Secretary of State, *ed. Don K. Price (Prentice-Hall, 1960).*

September 14, 1960

Dear Boss,

Thank you a thousand times for sending me *Mr. Citizen* with its most appreciated inscription. I read it at once and of course, with the greatest interest. It has a lot of you in it and while that has been known to bring mingled emotions, it is all to the good in this case. Alice, too, was touched by your reference to her in the inscription and her gratitude goes along with mine.

You may be interested in a letter which I have just written to Jack Kennedy and a copy of my article mentioned in it. I have not the slightest doubt that you will agree with every word of the article. Indeed, Mr. Hoover will too, for he expressed the same ideas when we were on the first Hoover commission together.

This campaign is so far a bust. If Kennedy goes on talking about this religious business he will gain few protestant votes and lose a lot of Catholic ones. His strongest point he can't make. He isn't a very good Catholic.

Affectionately,

Dean

Acheson advises Truman regarding his upcoming campaign tour. Edward L. Rodden was ambassador to Uruguay from 1951 to 1953.

October 3, 1960

Dear Boss,

Did Charlie Murphy read you a speech, originally written by Ambassador Rodden and revised by me attacking Nixon. I hope he did and that you will deliver it.

Your most effective role in this campaign will be attack. What you say in praise of Jack will carry no weight. But you have the truth on your side and no contrary statements to embarrass you when you lambast Nixon.

The speech is a good speech.

We are back in town today for the winter. It has been lovely in Sandy Spring.

Yours,

Dean

Truman's tour, which he called his "fall lecture tour," began October 8. He visited Iowa, Texas, Washington, D.C., North Carolina, and Virginia, then went to Tennessee, Missouri, Alabama, Mississippi, Louisiana, Washington State, Nevada, and California, and finally to New York and Pennsylvania. He completed the tour four days before election day with a speech in Pittsburgh on November 4. He gave eighteen speeches in fourteen states in a little less than four weeks. Perhaps Truman's most famous statement from his campaign tour was made in San Antonio, Texas, on October 11. "If you vote for Nixon," he said, "you ought to go to hell." John Kennedy claimed that when he heard about Truman's remark, he sent him a telegram that read, "I have noted with interest your suggestion as to where those who vote for my opponent should go. While I understand and sympathize with your deep motivation, I think it is important that our side try to refrain from raising the religious issue."

Truman promises Acheson to give the speech about Nixon, which Acheson partly wrote, in Nixon's home state of California.

October 9, 1960

Dear Dean:

I was happy to receive your note of the 3rd about the proposed speech on Nixon, which I am expecting to deliver in California without an erasure. It struck me and it struck Mrs. Truman as exactly what ought to be said, but I think California is the place to say it.

I am leaving tomorrow for Texas to talk principally to the Baptists in Waco, although I have an interlude meeting in Texarkana and one in San Antonio. Just bear in mind that I owe you a longhand letter in reply to your beautiful one about my book and as soon as I can sit down and attend to things as I should you will receive it.

I certainly do appreciate the trouble you have gone to to give the facts and figures on Nixon. He is a dangerous man. Never has there been one like him so close to the Presidency.

I had a wonderful farm meeting in Iowa yesterday. In Iowa, which was as enthusiastic as the labor meeting I had in Marion, Indiana, I was overwhelmed. If the Waco, Texas, religious meeting turns out all right I think we will then be on the road.

I have a schedule which takes me from Waco on the 12th to Washington, D.C., by regular plane. Then the next morning I am supposed to leave for Raleigh, North Carolina, and on the 15th I will go from Raleigh to Abingdon, Virginia, and then back home. I thought perhaps if I arrived in Washington at a reasonable hour you and I might have a session on the situation as I have found it, in the various places where I have been.

The trend is very substantially on the mend so far as our side is concerned but, of course, you must understand that this is a statement of a prejudiced witness, in fact a *very prejudiced witness*.

Please give my best to Alice and say I certainly will be happy when this *rat race* is over and we can have our usual associations, socially and otherwise.

Sincerely yours,

Harry

Truman gave the Nixon speech on October 28 in Oakland, California, without an erasure, as he promised, but with some additions of his own that increased its punch. He began by telling of many good people and things that come from California. "There is only one product of this state that does not measure up to its high standards," he said, "and that is Richard Nixon, Trickie Dickie, the political opportunist." He added the "Trickie Dickie" part in his own hand on the speech draft. He mentions Disneyland, favorably, and then launches on an extended fantasy. "Now I think I have discovered what Nixon can do," he begins. "He has considerable gifts of showmanship, and the ability to create all kinds of illusions. He should go into this amusement park business and open one of his own, which we could call Nixonland. . . . Nixon would be in charge of Nixonland personally, and he would be the guide for all the Nixonland rides. Which he would do very well—by the way—as he has been taking the American people for a ride for a good many years already." He goes on to describe many of the rides in Nixonland, including "the Nixon trip . . . through Communistland. And you would see stuffed Communists popping out from behind every bush. And Nixon would stand in the bow of the boat, and shoot them dead—with blanks." This Nixonland is fake, Truman warns. "So, I say, let us leave Nixonland behind us, and leave Nixon there, and face the real world and its problems. . . . Let us build for the future of the United States of America and for a secure and peaceful world with Jack Kennedy and Lyndon Johnson." One wonders what Tru-

man's audience thought of this peculiar speech, and how many votes Tru-
man won for the Kennedy-Johnson ticket that night.

On November 8, 1960, John F. Kennedy was elected over Richard Nixon.
Truman looks forward to a visit from Acheson, who is giving a speech in
Kansas City at the end of the month.

November 21, 1960

Dear Dean:

The campaign is ended and we have a Catholic for President. It makes no difference, in my opinion, what church a man belongs to, if he believes in the oath he takes to support and defend the Constitution of the United States. I have taken it twenty five or thirty times.

I didn't have to weigh what I was swearing in that oath. I believed in it.

If our new President works at the job, he'll have no trouble. You know, I wish I'd been young enough to go back to the White House and make Alibi Ike wear a top hat! He spent his time after the election in 1952 trying to show how good he could be. But why worry about what's past.

We are faced with a situation equal to any we've been up against in a hundred years.

I'm looking forward to a visit when you come out here on November 30th.

You know what the "Boss" has done? She's torn up the whole second floor of this old 1859 House of ours and we are in a hell of a fix. Mrs. R. had to stay at a hotel and I fear you will too. But maybe you and I can have a better time! Don't tell Alice but let's see what happens.

Sincerely,

Harry

Two weeks after the election, Acheson speculates about the close results.
"Schuman" was French statesman Robert Schuman, president of the Euro-
pean Parliamentary Assembly.

November 22, 1960

Dear Boss:

Many thanks for your post election letter which came this morning. First a word or two about your plans for our meeting in Kansas City. I am planning, if you approve, to stay over on Thursday, December 1st until the 4 o'clock through flight to Washington, to have some quiet time with you. The plane from here on November 30th will not get in until after lunch—1:54 P.M.—and WDAF wants me to record a television interview in the afternoon. So there won't be much peace on Wednesday.

If you are free on Thursday we might meet at your convenience say at the Library, and from there on do what you wish. If I could see the top Boss it would be a joy for me.

Alice is not coming as she did something to a muscle or nerve in her right leg which has been painful and incapacitating, though now yielding to heat and rest. She will send her messages and get her report through me.

This election is so unbelievably close that I wonder whether we really know the result yet. If the southern conspiracy should flower, and enough delegates—I mean electors—withhold their votes to prevent a majority of the total number, what then? Some electors are pledged by state law and some are not. Can they be ordered by mandamus to vote? To vote for the one to whom they are pledged? Suppose they violate the order and either refused to vote, or vote for Lyndon. What then? I suppose that the court could put them in jail for contempt, but it can't vote for them. If it invalidates the votes for Lyndon the election goes to the House and Nixon has a majority of states, with one vote each. Or perhaps if Lyndon were on the slate which went to the House he might get a majority should the Kennedy states switch to him.

It is all very speculative, but most interesting.

Do you really care about Jack's being a Catholic? I never have. It hasn't bothered me about de Gaulle or Adenauer or Schuman or De Gasperi, so why Kennedy? Furthermore I don't think he's a very good Catholic. But a Jehovah's Witness would bother me badly. The whole public health service would go to hell over night.

Another question. You are quoted as saying that you won't worry about the farmers any more because they voted for Nixon. But did they? A lot of people in the farm states voted Democratic. What about them? Guilt by association? That ought to stir up the animal.

Affectionately,
Dean

November 26, 1960

HONORABLE DEAN ACHESON
WILL SEE YOU WHEN YOU LAND IN OUR BIG SUBURB. WANT
TO HAVE GOOD VISIT WITH YOU THURSDAY. YOU WILL SEE
THE BOSS. SORRY ALICE IS NOT WITH YOU.
HARRY S TRUMAN

Harry Truman and Dean Acheson on February 17, 1955, during a press conference at the Muehlebach Hotel in Kansas City.

8

February 1961 to October 1971

JFK and LBJ – An Operation and a Fall – More Memoirs –
Deaths in the Family – The Last Letter

Once the excitement of the campaign season had subsided and the new, young, Democratic President had moved into the White House, Truman's and Acheson's letters to each other began to convey less mutual engagement in the nation's affairs. With Eisenhower gone, the two friends no longer felt an urgent need to join forces to try to change policies that they felt were deeply in error. They wrote fairly regularly during 1961, but beginning in 1962 the steady, and equal, flow of letters abated. In addition to this, with advancing age Truman was naturally becoming increasingly less interested in public life. In what is probably the saddest letter he ever wrote to Acheson, on July 7, 1961, he also worried about his ability to present himself in public as he should, and said he envied Acheson for being able to make an important contribution to the national life: "You are making a contribution, I am not. Wish I could."

Acheson was indeed making a contribution. President Kennedy had immediately brought Acheson into his administration as an adviser on NATO and Berlin, and Acheson wrote three important policy-review reports for Kennedy on these topics, as well as one on the country's balance-of-payments problem. During the Cuban missile crisis, the President included Acheson in the so-called ExCom group, which advised him on how to end the threat the Soviet missiles created without bringing on war.

Shortly after Kennedy's assassination on November 22, 1963, President Johnson called on Acheson to advise him on a number of foreign-policy questions, including U.S. policy in Vietnam, and although Acheson didn't write Truman in detail about all the highly secret work he was engaged in, he did share some gossipy accounts of Kennedy and Johnson. He called Kennedy "a sort of Indian snake charmer" who was too concerned with image and had trouble making decisions. Johnson, he said, "creates distrust by being too smart. He is never quite candid. . . . He yields to petty impulses."

The subjects of illness and death crept into the men's letters, often humorously. Truman especially attended many funerals. "At 79 you go to funeral after funeral of your friends," he wrote in May 1963, " . . . and you sometimes wonder if the old man with the scythe isn't after you." Both friends did write each other promptly to express heart-felt sympathy about these losses.

Acheson did not write Truman about the substantial relationship he developed with President Richard Nixon. Though Acheson had mixed feelings about Nixon, he admired him—and his National Security Adviser, Henry Kissinger—enough that on important occasions he advised Nixon and publicly supported his foreign policies. Truman had never forgiven Nixon for remarks he made during the 1952 campaign, in a speech in Texarkana, Texas. Truman, Acheson, and Adlai Stevenson, Nixon had said, were all "traitors to the high principles in which many of the nation's Democrats believe." On another occasion Nixon charged that "Mr. Truman, Dean Acheson, and other [Truman] administration officials for political reasons covered up the Communist conspiracy and attempted to halt its exposure." Truman had a long memory for this kind of attack on his patriotism and on that of loyal public servants such as Dean Acheson. When he was criticized in 1958 for insulting Vice President Nixon by calling him a "squirrel head," Truman justified his use of such a moniker by saying "character assassins cannot be insulted."

The two friends had several opportunities to honor each other publicly. On one occasion, Truman provided a heartfelt tribute about Acheson, Yale class of 1915, to the Yale Club of Montclair, New Jersey. "No one," Truman said, "has had a clearer sense of the times or the direction of the course this nation had to take in her relations with its friends and allies." When Acheson learned of this tribute, he wrote to Truman, "You always touch me by your faith in me." When Acheson's memoirs of his State Department years, *Present at the Creation,* came out in

1969, the book carried a brief but moving dedication: "To Harry S. Truman, 'The captain with the mighty heart.' "

. . .

Truman is not pleased with President Kennedy's new United Nations ambassador—Adlai Stevenson.

February 6, 1961

Dear Dean:

I have the urge to write you a personal communication, in the hope that there will be a chance to see you when I'm in Washington March 9th.

I am very much interested in what the new President will do. I hope he will do the right thing.

What a condition we are faced with! Cuba—the water shut off on our naval base, the dictatorship in Nicaragua, Santo Domingo, Haiti, Ecuador, Chile,—etc.

Wish you were the United Nations ambassador. I'm very much perturbed that Adlai Stevenson won't know what to do, and if he does he won't do it!

I'll be in N.Y. Feb 10th sail for Bermuda to see Margie and the two boys on Feb. 11th and be back in N.Y. Mar 2nd, then home and in D.C. Mar. 9th.

My very best to Alice, which includes Mrs. T.

Harry

Acheson again asks Truman to allow State Department historians to see documents relating to the Potsdam Conference in the papers from his White House office file that had not yet been turned over to the Truman Library. Acheson refers to his appointment as chair of President Kennedy's Advisory Committee on NATO. At about the time he wrote this letter, he submitted to the President a report titled "A Review of North Atlantic Problems for the Future."

March 23, 1961

Dear Mr. President:

This letter is outside the famous HST-DA series and has to do with a matter of business which Dr. Bernard Noble of State Department has taken up with me. Today he called on me and gave me the enclosed explanatory letter. He mentioned the fact that in connection with the Department's Potsdam papers, you had most kindly allowed offices of the Department to see papers in those files which you have not yet turned over to the Library and had given permission for some of these papers to be included in the official record. He now wishes to request similar consideration from you in regard to the regular historical series "Foreign Relations in the United States." The volumes covering the years of your Presidency will not be published for some time but the Department is already at work on them. He would like to have permission to look at the files which I have already mentioned and if any documents appropriate for inclusion in the official volumes are found to request your permission to use them. Not only would their use be contingent upon your permission but policy offices of the Government would examine them also to see whether there were any reasons for not making them public by the time the volumes should go to press.

I think that this is a fair and proper request and hope that you will grant it. It is most important that these official volumes be as complete as propriety permits. They are widely used by scholars throughout the world and will be an important source of understanding the years of your Presidency.

Your last visit to Washington came at a time when both Alice and I were stricken with the most virulent virus which has yet come our way. Poor Alice has had a wretched winter with one of these attacks after another. I joined her at the end of a rather splendid demonstration of my own. The result was that we missed you and were full of disappointment.

As you know, I have been drafted for a tour of duty on a review of NATO. This, I think, has been useful to President Kennedy and his Cabinet officers concerned with it. The first phase of my work is about at an end. Alice and I will fly to Amsterdam on the sixth of April for an argument which I have at The Hague Court beginning April 10. By the end of the month we should be back. I hope in time for a spring visit from you.

With most affectionate greetings to you and the boss,

As ever,

Dean

March 28, 1961

Dear Dean:

I appreciated very highly your letter of the 23rd and, of course, I will be glad to do whatever is necessary with regards to the request of Dr. Bernard Noble.

I am enclosing him a copy of this letter and you tell him he will be perfectly welcome here and I will do everything I possibly can to help him.

Sincerely yours,

Harry S. Truman

Those articles of yours are dandies. Will write you about them later.

"This asinine Cuban adventure" is the Bay of Pigs invasion by Cuban partisans, organized by the CIA, which was a humiliating failure. Acheson reminds Truman that they had rejected similar coup plots for Iran and Guatemala proposed by Truman's intelligence advisers. The book Acheson sent Truman is his Sketches from Life of Men I Have Known.

May 3, 1961

Dear Boss:

I am home just in time to thank you for your birthday note and to write you one wishing you all good things for this coming year and many to follow. I have seen some recent photographs of you looking sassy and full of fight.

Our trip to Europe was interesting, hard work and fun, all mixed together. The end of it, in which first our government and then de Gaulle's fell apart, had its grim aspect. Why we ever engaged in this asinine Cuban adventure, I cannot imagine. Before I left it was mentioned to me and I told my informants how you and I had turned down similar suggestions for Iran and Guatemala and why. I thought that this Cuban idea had been put aside, as it should have been. It gave Europe as bad a turn as the U-2. The direction of this government seems surprisingly weak. So far as I can make out the mere inertia of the Eisenhower plan carried it to execution. All that the present administration did was to take out of it those elements of strength essential to its success.

Brains are no substitute for judgment. Kennedy has, abroad at least, lost a very large part of the almost fanatical admiration which his youth and good looks had inspired.

Washington is a depressed town. The morale in the State Department has about struck bottom.

Nevertheless, I say again, "Many, many happy returns of your birthday."

As ever,

Dean

P.S. An inscribed copy of my book goes to you today.

Truman indulges a pet peeve about daylight saving time, which he feels ruins the time-zone system. He longs for a moment to return to the Senate, and refers to the appointment in September 1960 of Missouri Lieutenant Governor Edward V. Long to the U.S. Senate to replace the deceased Senator Thomas C. Hennings, Jr.

May 13, 1961

Dear Dean:

I'm sitting here this Saturday morning at eleven o'clock wondering what you may be doing at the same time maybe two hours later by that God Awful mixed up time under which we have to live.

You know it took about fifty or sixty years to arrange the time zones and now they mean not a thing. Maybe we should have a rod in our back yards with a couple of poles on each side of it, pointing to true north, if such there is, so we may be able to tell when it is noon by old sol. But I'm thinking of you, noon, one or two o'clock.

I've been reading Attlee's book and his opinions of some of his associates are as frank as I'd like to be about some of mine! Your statement about Iran, Central America and Cuba pleased me no end. You are as right as rain on "Brains are no substitute for judgment." Sorry Washington is so depressed. I'm to be there May 27th & 28th. We must have a go around for the benefit of both of us.

The autographed and inscribed copy of your book came and I've read it again, and believe it or not so has the "Boss." There has not been a better one on the people of your and my time. Sometimes I wish I'd gone back (if I could) and sometimes I wish I'd taken the appointment as Senator from Missouri a short time ago. But, I'm glad now that it didn't happen in either case.

Tell Alice her picture still hangs in my reception room right outside the door to the private office and hundreds of customers have commented on it favorably. Hope Alice will take it as a high compliment from the clod hoppers who come to see me. Their comments are worth more than Churchill's and all the modern artists, in my opinion.

Best of everything to both of you.

Sincerely,

Harry

June 6, 1961

Dear Mr. President:

Would you be willing to see a Sandy Spring neighbor of mine, his wife and two daughters, who will be in the vicinity of Independence between July 1 and July 5? Mr. William W. Miles is the principal of our Sherwood High School in Sandy Spring, and is a personable and persuasive man. Not only has he prevailed upon me to write you, but he had committed me to speaking to the graduating class on June 19.

He is planning to take his family after school on a motor trip through the Middle West. The Truman Library is one of the places of highest interest on their itinerary, and a chance to greet its high priest would add great joy to the interest. I do not know whether this is the sort of request you feel you can grant. If it is entirely out of line, please do not hesitate to tell me so. But if it isn't and you would let me know a time when they could come in to see you for a moment — or would tell them to have them call Rose Conway when they arrive in the area — they and I would be most appreciative.

With affectionate greetings.

Sincerely,

Dean

At the end of this letter Truman refers to an agreement he made with a production company, Talent Associates, Ltd., to produce a series of television films based on his life and career.

June 11, 1961

Dear Dean:

Of course I'd be pleased to see Mr. William W. Miles. He must be a great man and a persuasive one! It will be a pleasure to meet him. If he can come on either the 4th of July or the 5th it will be good for me. Tell him if he comes on the fourth, he'll have to listen to a speech by me! If he comes on the 5th he'll miss that ordeal.

I'll be here both days. Tell him on either day I'll personally give him the $5.00 tour for nothing—and since the tour is free to every teacher and student that is really no inducement. Tell him to call these numbers C.L[.] 21061 or C.L. 23678 and either Rose Conway or I will answer.

Dean, listen to me, you can't make a request, no matter when, where or what that I won't break a hamstring to meet. Hope you know about hamstrings.

I've been having a hell of a time. I've a fantastic offer to teach school on television and radio. If I can do it, it will save me a lot of running to schools and colleges. Hope I can. It will also finish the library building and furnish the Presidential historical gallery. Good things like that just can't happen to me, but I hope.

My very best to Alice,

Sincerely,

Harry

There ain't no $5.00 tour!

"My commencement speech" was at Sherwood High School, Sandy Spring, Maryland, near Acheson's farm. Mr. Miles was the principal. Acheson was working, at the time he wrote this letter, on a report on Berlin for President Kennedy. Soviet Premier Nikita Khrushchev had precipitated a crisis over the future of Berlin by announcing that the Soviet Union would sign a peace agreement with the German Democratic Republic (GDR, East Germany) in six months if the United States did not negotiate a new agreement regarding the Allied position in West Berlin. The Soviet agreement with the GDR, if signed, would have turned over the access routes into West Berlin to the East German government, which the United States did not recognize. Kennedy had met with Khrushchev in early June in Vienna, Austria, where they spoke openly of war. Acheson submitted his report, titled "The Berlin Crisis," to Kennedy on June 28. It recommended stern measures, including declaration of a national emergency and an immediate buildup of U.S. nuclear and conventional forces, to demonstrate the determination of the United States and its allies not to be forced out of Berlin.

June 24, 1961

Dear Mr. President,

How thoughtful you are of the simple and good people of this world. Mr. Miles, his wife and two girls are thrilled at the idea of meeting you.

They have consulted me about the protocol of addressing you and are, in the current jargon, well briefed. They will call up and make a date for the 4th or 5th. If you should answer the phone and hear a dull thud, it will be because he has fainted. I told him you were likely to do it.

My commencement speech turned out to be a great success because it was to be on a dull subject—"The Political Responsibilities of Young Citizens," of all things—and I hit on a happy device to deal with it. We have a very beautiful bit of country road leading to our village which is notoriously defaced by motorists throwing beer cans and all sorts of trash along the roadside, despite signs threatening horrendous penalties. I pointed out that the people who did this might technically be citizens but in reality they treated the home country as pigs treat their pen. But, I said, within the week I had seen truck loads of boy scouts, armed with shopping bags, picking up this trash and making land beautiful once more. They were learning the indispensable foundation of citizenship—to love some part of this land with all their heart and treat it with disciplined respect and tender care.

Apparently that meant something to the whole audience, children and parents, which generalities about patriotism and duty did not. They gave me a reception afterwards. On the whole, an interesting evening came out of an expected dull one.

I am working hard on plans to meet a Berlin crisis towards the end of the year. It is grim business, but I think that the Joint Chiefs and the State Department have now got the idea and that we shall make some progress. These Chiefs are not nearly as good as yours: nor are their staffs. In fact I am shocked and I think the Sec. of Defense is, also— at the shoddy work which comes out of the military. For what we spend on them we deserve something better than what we get.

Kennedy's performance worries and puzzles me. Somehow, he does not succeed in being a President, but only in giving the appearance of one, though he did do well with Khrushchev. Both Kennedy and Dean Rusk seem to me to be better when they make speeches than when they act. We have heard a lot about the necessity to make sacrifices but we haven't been asked to make any. There are plenty to make if the Administration would just get started. Time is running out.

With warmest greetings,

Dean

Age was taking its toll on the old President, and he felt unsure of his ability to present himself as he should. In this sad letter, he envies Acheson his ability to make a contribution to the national life. The "Pop" that he's afraid of is Joseph P. Kennedy, John F. Kennedy's father. Truman is reported to have said during the campaign, when asked about Kennedy's Catholic religion, "It's not the Pope I'm afraid of, it's the Pop."

July 7, 1961

Dear Dean:

I am sitting here at the desk and wondering about things political, both nationally and internationally. It is a hell of a thought provoking situation.

Mr. Miles, his wife and the girls came in and I had a good visit with them. At least it was good from my point of view.

There couldn't be any doubt how your commencement speech would turn out. Wish I could be as certain how my statement would come out. I have been calling off meeting after meeting on that account.

As you know I wasn't for Kennedy at Los Angeles. But when the Convention decided that he was "the man," what could I do but work my head off to elect him. I did just that—I'm still afraid of "Pop."

I have the same trouble with the "litter bugs" you wrote me about. They throw beer cans, pop bottles, lipstick wipers and anything else for the trash can into my front yard; from sidewalk and the street in front.

As an early riser I pick up the trash and take a walk with most unkind thoughts for the litter bug public!

As to Berlin and Laos and Indo China and Cuba we have problems and problems. May Almighty God help us to solve them! There have been times in the history of the world that I thought "He" was looking the other way. And I suppose "He" should have been!

The performance of our Chief Executive worries me, as the Chiefs of Staff do.

You are making a contribution. I am not. Wish I could.

My best to Alice.

Sincerely,

Harry

Acheson, from his vantage point within the Kennedy administration, is able to compare it with the Truman administration. He was clearly impa-

tient at the fumbling of the new administration. Robert McNamara was President Kennedy's Secretary of Defense. General Maxwell D. Taylor was at this point a military adviser to Kennedy.

Dear Boss: July 14, 1961

This, as you say, is a worrying situation. I find to my surprise a weakness in decisions at the top—all but Bob McNamara who impresses me as first class. The decisions are incredibly hard, but they don't, like Bourbon, improve with aging.

There is also a preoccupation here with our "image." This is a terrible weakness. It makes one look at oneself instead of at the problem. How will I look fielding this hot line drive to short stop? This is a good way to miss the ball altogether. I am amazed looking back on how free you were from this. I don't remember a case where you stopped to think of the effect on your fortunes—or the party's, for that matter—of a decision in foreign policy. Perhaps you went too far that way, but I don't think so. Our government is so incredibly difficult to operate that to survive in the modern world it needs the most vigorous leadership.

I will say for Kennedy that getting any good clear work out of the present Joint Chiefs is next to impossible. But McNamara and General Taylor can help him mightily; and, as Holmes said, every day we must make decisions on imperfect knowledge.

The great point is that we ought to be acting now to bring home to Khrushchev that we are in deadly earnest about Berlin, which is only a symbol for our world position. This is what Khrushchev has under attack.

Affectionately,
Dean

Truman believes his campaign appearances in several Southern states and Missouri may have helped Kennedy win those states.

Dear Dean: July 18, 1961

I don't know when I've had a letter I appreciated as much as yours of the 14th.

Your discussion of the "image" approach is correct and to the point. If you can't field that "hot drive to the short stop," no one can. Of course you pay me the high compliment of a tried and true friend—but, you must remember that I had no "yes" men around me, particularly was that true of the great Secretary of State.

I am frankly worried about the situation. When the young man came to see me before the Democratic Convention in L.A. I asked him if he felt he was ready for what faced him. There was no answer. When the rigged convention was over he came back and asked for help in the election. Since the Democratic Party had given me everything I ever aspired to from precinct to President, I did what I could.

I am egotistical enough to think that No. Carolina, Alabama, Louisiana and Texas were helped a little in their anti-Catholic attitude, and Missouri was just saved by an inch. The State ticket went over by about 330,000 majority—Kennedy by 35,000 or there about. Same happened in No. Carolina by about the same difference. Half the electoral vote was saved in Alabama and Huey Long's La. went in toto as did Texas. As you remember, I told the Baptists in Waco what I had in mind about their bigotry. Since I'm one myself they had to take it.

You know all this but I like to talk about it. It is like the old 88 year old who was being prosecuted for rape by a 20 year old. He made no defense. The Judge asked him why. "Well," he said, "it sounded so nice and I was wishing so much it could happen that I enjoyed it." He was not convicted!

Keep writing, it keeps my morale up—if I have any. My best to Alice—tell her I didn't say Mrs. Acheson!

I told Bess I was writing and she wants to be remembered to you both.

Sincerely,

Harry

Acheson's involvement with the Kennedy administration on the Berlin crisis continued through July. On July 25, President Kennedy, who had essentially accepted Acheson's recommendations regarding Berlin, announced on live television and radio that the United States would immediately strengthen its conventional forces and take other measures to resist any Soviet attempt to force a change in the Allied position in West Berlin. Acheson submitted his final report on Berlin to Kennedy, titled "Berlin: A Political Program," on August 1. After this, Acheson, as he tells Truman in this letter, decided to take a holiday from government work. He could not stop thinking, though, of all he had experienced in recent weeks and about what the future might bring. Shortly after Acheson left Washington for his vacation on Martha's Vineyard, the Soviet Union began construction of the Berlin Wall. In addition to Berlin, Acheson is also concerned about American policy toward Portugal and its African colonies. Besides his belief that the United States should support its NATO allies, including Portugal, he was personally fond of Portugal, and apparently also of its dictator, António de Oliveira Salazar, with whom he had had extensive dealings during World War II. Early in the Kennedy administration, the United States began supporting United Nations resolutions that denounced Portugal's policies in its African colonies. Acheson strongly opposed the American position. Adlai Stevenson was at this time United States ambassador to the United Nations, and G. Mennen "Soapy" Williams was Assistant Secretary of State for African Affairs. Both advocated American opposition to Portugal's colonial policies. Acheson deplores the new President's indecision and delay in foreign-policy decisions. David Bruce was U.S. ambassador to the U.K. "Mr. K" is Khrushchev, and Franz Josef Strauss was the leader of the Christian Social Union in West Germany.

Dear Boss,   August 4, 1961

I have just finished a job which I volunteered to do for Dean Rusk and am now going—in the current jargon—"to phase out" for a while. To work for this crowd is strangely depressing. Nothing seems to get decided. The job just finished was to get up a program of international political action—negotiation with its public opening, fall back, and very private position on Berlin and Germany, together with a propaganda campaign. The State Dept. has all sorts of suggestions but no definitive recommendations. This Rusk now has and I have bullied him into giving the President a copy. But I cannot get them to decide on this—or anything else—as our program to present to our allies. Rusk wants to approach everything piecemeal. But how you lead anyone unless you first know where you yourself want to go, I do not know.

I am told that the President wants to talk with me. But the man he ought to talk with is his Secretary of the ~~Treasury~~ *(a curious slip)* State; and he ought to demand a written program of action which he could approve, change or disapprove. Instead of this everything is kept nebulous. This is a good way to drift into trouble wholly unprepared. What is the new word? Disenchanted. I am becoming disenchanted.

So Alice and I are getting out of town. Our daughters are both going to be on Martha's Vineyard for the last half of August and we have decided to be with them but at the other end of the island so as not to be breathing down their necks. In the autumn we might go abroad. The Chancellor wants me to come to Bonn and I would like to see the Bruces and other friends in England. Finally it just might be possible to get both Salazar and Kennedy to make a little more sense about Angola. We are about to alienate a most essential ally by our silly attitude in the U.N.; and our ally is about to go bankrupt trying to suppress an uprising which it probably can't suppress. I think that we could help by trying to quiet things down on the basis of more participation in government by the blacks and economic development in both Portugal and Angola. This means some give by Salazar and a silencer on Soapy and Adlai.

But over all of this hangs Berlin. I don't want to be abroad if I have to defend action of which I do not approve. I do not agree with an alleged remark of yours that Mr. K is bluffing. He has, I believe, sensed weakness and division in the West and intends to exploit it to the hilt. It wouldn't take more than an error or two on each side to carry us over the edge into nuclear war. Or we could panic into an abject acceptance of K's terms. "We" includes our allies. Last weekend I had over seven hours of talk with Joseph (*Frantz Joseph,* to be correct) Strauss. It was not reassuring. Not that he was ready to quit, but rather he just hadn't thought the crisis through and was full of fears at one moment and utterly extravagant expectations of our nuclear power. In my judgment we shall have to run grave danger of war by preparations for ground action—in which most soldiers (Max Taylor excepted) do not believe—to convince K that by pressing too far he might force us into a nuclear response. Only in this way do I think that he can be brought to a truly sensible and tolerable negotiating state of mind.

With affectionate greetings
Dean

Acheson's outlook here is gloomy. Fortunately his fears were not realized, because of good luck. The three European leaders who Acheson feels are going to give in to Soviet demands regarding Berlin are Paul-Henri Spaak, the foreign minister of Belgium; Halvard Lange, the foreign minister of Norway; and Konrad Adenauer, chancellor of the Federal Republic of Germany (West Germany). John J. McCloy, a former U.S. high commissioner for Germany, was an adviser to President Kennedy at the time, and Walter Lippmann was the venerable Washington columnist.

September 21, 1961

Dear Mr. President,

This is a somber note. It is not intended to depress you, though it will. It is highly confidential. The purpose is to put you on guard for developments which neither you nor I can prevent, but which neither one of us should support or condone. Beware especially of the tendency to get you "to support the President" in syndicated newspaper articles.

I believe that sometime this autumn we are in for a most humiliating defeat over Berlin. Our own policy and preparations are increasingly weak and vacillating. Our allies are already in full retreat. Spaak is, or [will] soon be, in Moscow looking for terms. Lange of Norway will follow. The Germans are about to collapse. If Adenauer is allowed to stay on, which is doubtful, it will be only to sign the surrender. McCloy is everywhere urging an accommodation with Khrushchev. Walter Lippmann is the archangel of appeasement. The White House staff is already scuttling my recommendations.

The worst of it is not that eight years of Eisenhower inaction and one of Kennedy may have made the result inevitable, but that it will probably be dressed up as statesmanship of the new order, a refreshing departure from the bankrupt inheritance of the Truman-Acheson reliance on military power.

So count one hundred before you comment on anything, and don't let Bill Hillman write anything for you on foreign policy. The First Amendment protects silence as well as speech. I am going underground.

If you read today's U.S.-Soviet agreement on the principles of "general and complete disarmament" with the U.N. to have the only armed forces to be permitted, and look also at the Soviet demand for the Troika system and triple veto in the U.N., you will see the idiocy of our policy. No one means a damned thing which is said. We are all engaged in a propaganda battle of insincerities to create "images" of ourselves in the minds of people who don't count. If we get Barry Goldwater after this—as we well may—we shall thoroughly deserve it.

This is all for your most private eye. I hope I am wrong, but do not think that there is the remotest chance that I am. The course is set and events are about to take control.

Alice sends her love to you and the Boss.

As ever,

Dean

September 24, 1961

Dear Dean:

Your letter of Aug. 4th has been read and reread. I think it is a classic. It sets out the issues. What the hell are we to do? I don't know. Your letter sets it out.

For my part I'm happy you are trying to set the Administration on the right track. *Keep it up.*

I am supposed to be in Washington on the last day in October for a talk to the Washington Press Club. Then to stay all night at the White House.

I'll let you know what time the arrival will be made. My headquarters will be at the Mayflower. Don't know whether I should go to the White House or not.

Bess will be with me.

Sincerely,

Harry

Truman responds to Acheson's letter of September 21. He is, unlike Acheson, always an optimist.

September 25, 1961

Dear Dean:

Your somber note gave me the most depressing viewpoint I've had since Jan. 20th 1953.

I can't agree with you. We saved Berlin once. We will have to do it again. The Russian Dictator is one of those who can't face issues when they are met head on.

You must remember that our head of state is young, inexperienced and hopeful. Let's hope the hopeful works.

Was good to talk to you. Let's keep working for the country. We, I hope, can do it. You know what I told you. I'm always in your corner.

Sincerely,

Harry

Joe Brown, whom Truman mentions, was a personal friend; he had been vice president and general counsel of the Kansas City Southern Railway.

October 26, 1961

Dear Dean:

Yesterday morning I received a telegram from Mrs. Joe Brown telling me that Joe had passed away the night before.

I was very sorry to hear that and I know you will be. The funeral ceremony, I think, will be tomorrow. Her address is 1030 West 59th Terrace, Kansas City, Missouri.

I am hoping to see you when I arrive back in Washington and I hope we will have the usual good visit. I am also looking forward to the luncheon with you on the date you and the Madam set, which I believe is November 1st.

Sincerely yours,

Harry

On November 1 Truman had lunch with Acheson in Washington, had dinner with President Kennedy at the White House and spent the night there. On November 2, he gave a speech to the National Press Club, which had asked him to look back on his presidency. "I don't like to do that," Truman said, "because I always have looked forward." He talked mainly about the 1948 campaign, because his speech was on the anniversary of election day, 1948. He also mentioned how depressing his trips to Washington were during the Eisenhower administration, when he always knew the President was following misguided policies. He contrasted his current happy trip to Washington. Kennedy was President and the country was turning in the right direction. "I look to the days and months ahead with confidence," he concluded.

Chester Bowles, a successful advertising man, cofounder of Benton & Bowles, was regarded by Acheson as too intellectually soft to be suited to foreign affairs and was removed as Under Secretary of State but immediately named as a special adviser to the President on Asian, African, and Latin American affairs. German Chancellor Konrad Adenauer was eighty-five years old at this time and perhaps, Acheson observes, beginning to fail.

November 28, 1961

Dear Mr. President:

Mayor Richard Lee of New Haven has just passed on to me the transmission to you of his request that you speak at a fund raising dinner in New Haven. The funds are for his campaign for the Democratic nomination for U.S. Senator. The dinner could be held in late January, late February or anytime in March. Dick says that he has as yet no opposition and expects none unless Ribicoff wants the nomination. He (Dick) does not think that he does want it, but instead wants an appointment to the Supreme Court. I do not advise your doing this, since you have a good many more important things on your calendar. But if you have an urge for a political speech, here is a chance. What shall I tell him?

Washington becomes more and more puzzling to me. One day Bowles is kicked out of the State Department; the next day he is taken into the White House to advise on all foreign problems except those of Europe. Dear old Averell becomes, of all things, Ass't Sec. of State for the Far East where he has been once.

When Adenauer was here he asked me to see him alone, which I did. He had failed a good deal since last April. I thought that he did not make much sense. I gather from Paul Nitze that the Chancellor made the same impression in his conferences. The whole Berlin and German policy becomes bewildering to me. One of my friends will brief me on it soon and I shall try to give you a more coherent account than I could now.

Alice is hard at work for an exhibition of her new paintings here in January, early in the month. We plan then to go to Cambodia on Prince Sihanouk's invitation, and then on for a visit to Australia, principally to see Bob Menzies—and to get a month away from winter in Washington, a frivolous reason but the true one.

Affectionately,
Dean

At the Yale Club's annual dinner in Washington, D.C., on March 27, 1962, held at the National Press Club, Truman presented an award called the Yale Bowl to Acheson (Yale class of 1915). He gave a brief speech about his old friend, reading from a draft handwritten on hotel stationery. When he got back home, he handwrote a somewhat more polished draft of the speech and sent this to Acheson (reproduced below). Acheson in turn sent Truman the notes, quite rough in this case, which he had used in making his acceptance speech. Although Acheson began by saying he was going to talk primarily about Yale, he then spoke about "my beloved Chief" on the pretext that "Mr. T. is a Yale man by our adoption." He addressed the "mystery" of why Truman was such a great success as President, citing three reasons. First, his vitality, a priceless gift "for which ancestors, not he, are responsi-

ble." Second, the clear and competent decision-making procedure he followed. All the people involved in a decision understood their mutual
responsibility; all their points of view, including adversarial ones, were
heard in the presence of one another; the President worked hard to be well
informed on all issues; he made decisions promptly, clearly, and in writing;
and he adhered to his decisions once he had made them. The third reason
was Truman's combination of good judgment and good luck. "Judgment
easy to admire, but don't despise luck," Acheson concluded.

March 27, 1962

I am here this evening to perform a duty that I like very much. I
more than appreciate the privilege you have given me to help honor my
good friend of many years standing, the Honorable Dean Acheson.

Dean is one of the greatest men of this period and he will go down in
history as one of the greatest of the great Secretaries of State of the
United States. When history is written he will be placed in that galaxy
of the men who saved the free world.

He will be in the same class as Washington and his Secretary of
State, Thomas Jefferson, and as Lincoln and his great Secretary of
State William Seward.

He is among the greatest of the great public servants in every capacity in which he served—and he served in many capacities from the
1930s to 1953.

He furnished me with the information needed to end two wars—
one in Europe and one in the Pacific.

I wish I had command of the English Language such as Dean has, so
I could adequately state his record to this great government. Present
the bowl

Harry Truman

Truman did not accept the lecture invitation Acheson speaks of.

April 9, 1962

Dear Mr. President:

Ned Hall sent me a copy of his letter to you of April 6, asking you to
give a lecture at the Hill School in April 1963 on the new foundation
which they have gotten this year. He mentions in his letter that I did it
this year. So I am writing to say that indeed I did, and that Alice and I
enjoyed our experience very much. It is no trouble to get to the school,
which is only an hour away from Philadelphia by car, which the school

will provide. It is also a simple way to pick up fifteen hundred dollars without much pain.

I can't tell you what a delightful time we had with you and Mrs. Truman a week ago last weekend. It was wonderful to see you both looking so well and to have a chance for a little, though not much, talk. We must make up for the crowded scene by having some private talk when you are in these parts next.

Alice is off on Sunday for Cyprus and southern France. I join her in London at the end of the first week in May for a short stay there and then a visit to Sweden. We are really establishing the all-time record for travel in 1962.

Our warmest greetings to you both.

As ever,

Dean

Acheson came to the Truman Library on March 31 to attend a meeting of the board of directors of the Harry S. Truman Library Institute for National and International Affairs and the presentation ceremony for a bust of himself commissioned by the foundation that had raised the funds to build the Truman Library. Acheson also spoke at a conference of scholars held in conjunction with the board meeting. The bust of Acheson has been installed for many years in the Truman Library's research room, where scholars pore over the papers of both Truman and Acheson.

April 20, 1962

Dear Dean:

Miss Conway brought me the picture which you sent to her to be signed for Mr. Gardner Jackson and we are sending it to him direct, as you requested, in the self-addressed, stamped envelope you enclosed. I can't understand why in the world you would send a stamped envelope to one who has been signing his name in the right-hand corner and letting it go free.

You really made the meeting here for the Heads of the Universities and Teachers. Everybody in Independence is still talking about it.

I don't know when I will be in your neighborhood again but I certainly want to spend some time with you discussing conditions as they are and what they ought to be in the future. I have refused to give any interviews on the present administration as to the welfare of the country and the world. I always tell them we can't judge a President when he has served only one-eighth of his term.

I hope everything is going well with you and I sincerely hope, when conditions work out as they should, I will have an opportunity to have another visit with you.

Sincerely yours,

Harry S. Truman

David K. E. Bruce, with whom Acheson mentions having lunch, was the American ambassador to the United Kingdom. Archbishop Makarios III of the Greek Orthodox Church was president of the Republic of Cyprus at this time.

May 3, 1962

Dear Bobbi

Alice and I will be in London with the Bruces on your birthday. We shall drink your health and raise a loud cheer for you in the company of good men and true everywhere. All good wishes and many more years to spread the word and hearten the brave. We need it now more than ever these days.

I have a curious and apprehensive feeling as I watch JFK that he is a sort of Indian snake charmer. He toots away on his pipe and our problems sway back and forth around him in a trance-like manner, never approaching, but never withdrawing; all are in a state of suspended life, including the pipe player, who lives only in his dreams.

Some day one of these snakes will wake up; and no one will be able even to run.

So we are going away again. Alice has been in Cyprus doing some painting and being received by his Grace of the whiskers, Archbishop-President Makarios. (What a President you would have made if you had been an Archbishop into the bargain and had had whiskers down to your waist! The idea is a novel one but quite intriguing.) I am to meet her in London after she has a week or ten days in Southern France, in the small town of Vence near Grasse, a place for painters. After ten days we go on to Sweden when I attend a conference presided over by Prince Bernhard of the Netherlands. Then we shall both visit the Bohemans for a few days. You will remember him as the Swedish Ambassador, a tall able fellow who always believed that agriculture would prove the Achilles heel of the Soviet system—that is, the limiting factor.

Again our most affectionate remembrances and greetings go to you and Bess.

Most warmly,

Dean

Years before this letter was written, when Truman's presidency was into its sixth year and he was starting to think of his place in history, he wrote a memorandum to an assistant: "The lies are beginning to be solidified and made into historical facts. Let's head them off now while we can. The truth is all I want for history. If I appear in a bad light when we have the truth that is just too bad. We must take it. But I don't want a pack of lying so called historians to do to Roosevelt and to me what the New Englanders did to Jefferson and Jackson." Truman, who was a devoted reader of history and felt he understood something about historians, always worried that false or biased accounts of him and his administration would be accepted as factual.

July 6, 1962

Dear Dean:

Well, it came about at last. My historical outfit insisted that I call you. I did, and you answered as I knew you would.

But, Dean, if there is anything in the world I dislike to do, it is to put my good friends on the "spot." Under no circumstances would I have called you, but because I am most interested in having the facts properly stated for the future.

Andrew Johnson, James Monroe, James Madison, Rutherford Hayes, Grover Cleveland and even Calvin Coolidge have been placed in a most embarrassing position by people who want to make them appear as ridiculous characters.

Maybe I am one. But I am anxious that my good friends help me to prevent that from happening. You know, better than anyone, how hard I worked to meet the decisions it was necessary to make.

Now, articles are coming out, along with books, showing I could never make a decision unless some smart boy told me how to make it. That may have happened—but I didn't know it.

Dean, my best to you and Alice.

Sincerely,

Harry

Truman did not accept the invitation that Acheson mentions.

August 6, 1962

Dear Boss

Early in July Jack Wheeler-Bennett, the only friend I have with an office in Buckingham Palace, asked me to urge you to accept an invitation which he sent you on July 5th to give a lecture at Ditchley House next spring. I decided to mind my own business, an unusually rare and wise decision for me. Now he writes again asking whether his earlier letter went astray. Thus we are chivvied to chivy our friends.

But I do not urge you to do this, but only say that if you and the boss would like a free ride to Europe and back to fix up any damage that Ike may have done, this is a pretty painless way to get it. Ditchley House is a most beautiful eighteenth century great house, the Foundation represents the crème de la crème of England, and the subject they want to hear about you know backwards and forwards.

This does my duty and, I hope, puts not even the pressure of a thistle down on you.

Alice and I have been getting the greatest satisfaction from the first class job which our David has done for over a year now as U.S. attorney for the D.C. He is becoming a wise and effective force in the community, understanding the problems and respected by judges, police and citizens. It is very gratifying to see his fine qualities blossom.

With deep affection.

As ever,

Dean

August 8, 1962

Dear Mr. President:

Six years ago I took up with you, at Dr. Bernard Noble's urging, the request of the Department of State for access to your reserved papers relating to the Potsdam Conference, in aid of compiling for publication a volume or more of papers on that Conference. You readily agreed and were of immense help in the preparation of the work. In fact, it would have been woefully incomplete without your help.

Dr. Noble, who is retiring because of the trouble which we are all having with the calendar, now asks me to appeal to you in aid of another request—for access to your reserved papers for 1945 and

1946. The request for the former year is urgent. The professional staff of the Historical Section of the Department is now compiling the 1945 volumes of *Foreign Relations of the United States,* an official publication of this Government. Section officials have already gone through pertinent papers of the same character as yours in the files of the Department of State and the Roosevelt Library. The projected volumes cannot achieve the purpose for which Congress authorized them unless all repositories of relevant diplomatic papers for the period have been examined.

Dr. Noble is not asking permission to examine all reserved papers but only those pertaining to foreign relations in 1945 and, later, 1946. He is not asking authority to publish all that his section thinks relevant. Policy officers determine what it is in the public interest to publish, subject—if you wish it—to your veto over the publication of any of your papers.

You have always been the leading exponent of the view that the practice, sanctioned by history, which permits a retiring President to take with him the papers collected in the White House during his term of office is justified by preserving them in trust for the Government in the service of which they were created. So I know you will agree that, when that Government in the course of publication directed by Congress finds need to examine these papers, it should not be denied the opportunity of doing so.

Before he packs up and joins the "Has Been" Club, may I tell Dr. Noble that you will help him again? If you give me the word, his successor, Mr. William M. Franklin, will get in touch with anyone you say to arrange the working details.

We are doing what you never do—having a lazy summer. This year Washington, or rather Sandy Spring, has been an ideal resort, on many days almost too chilly to swim.

With warmest greetings.

As ever,

Dean

Homer Capehart was at this time a Republican senator from Indiana. Truman was on the campaign trail in, among other places, the senator's home state, where Capehart lost his bid for re-election. The "Mississippi situa-

tion" Acheson refers to involved the admission of African American James Meredith to the University of Mississippi. The governor of Mississippi for a time prevented Meredith's admission, but Attorney General Robert Kennedy persuaded the governor to allow Meredith to enroll and on October 1, 1962, a heavily guarded Meredith entered the university. A large, violent mob gathered, and President Kennedy had to send in federal troops to restore order.

October 8, 1962

Dear Boss,

I hope that you have not answered my note of August 8th because you have been so busy getting Senator Capehart's blood-pressure up, and not because you thought that I was off-side in pleading good old Dr. Noble's case for a look at your reserved papers for 1945 and 1946. If you are fed up with the whole subject, I shall not press it further.

Alice and I are off in two weeks for a visit to Berkeley and Pasadena (Cal. Tech) in both of which I lecture and then hold meetings and seminars with faculty and students. Then on Dec. 15th we go off for a month in the West Indies with the MacLeishes and the John Cowleses of Minneapolis. This shows, at least, that our life holds interest still.

The Mississippi situation was, I imagine, inherently pretty bad. But it seems to me that the mob was allowed to get out of hand by too long temporizing by JFK. He seems to have been thinking too much of possible criticism and not enough of the calming effect and vigor and decisiveness on those who are working themselves into hysteria. I hope he doesn't treat Mr. K this way over Berlin.

Cuba is a problem that I am glad I don't have to deal with. Two Presidents have pretty well messed it up.

Our warmest greetings.

Yours,

Dean

Truman cites instances from American history when Presidents—Andrew Jackson and Abraham Lincoln—took decisive action to force the South to obey the law of the land. Recent Presidents had not always, in Truman's opinion, been so decisive. The "damfool" comment in the postscript probably refers to his own foolishness in going on the campaign trail again, at age seventy-eight, when he didn't have to. This was to be his last trip along the campaign trail, and he cut it short because of the Cuban missile crisis.

"In calling off my appearances as a partisan Democrat," he said in an October 25 statement, "I appeal to everyone regardless of his party affiliation to support the Chief Executive and the Commander in Chief."

October 12, 1962

Dear Dean:

My being fed up with you is an impossibility. I have been from Philadelphia to San Francisco, Los Angeles to Boise, Idaho, and back again to Youngstown, Ohio—to Clarksburg, West Va., and Evansville, Indiana. All, I hope, in the interest of the Democratic Party. That's the reason you haven't heard from me.

You tell Dr. Noble to come to see me and he'll get what he wants. These archives boys are trying to obtain what Dr. Noble wants to see before I'm ready to turn them over. Dr. Noble will have no trouble—but tell him to come to see me—not the Archivists!

I'm glad you are going on a vacation—wish I could.

Arkansas and Mississippi are bad examples of what can happen when the man in charge (in Washington) is not sure of his powers. You remember what old Andy did to So. Carolina and what Old Abe had to do in '61.

As to Cuba the man in the White House when it started should have stopped it at the beginning. Grover Cleveland acted in Venezuela and without, I hope, your thinking I'm haywire and an egotist, Berlin, Greece and Turkey were in the same category.

Damn it, Dean, you are one man who can say to me what you please anytime, anywhere on any subject.

You and George Marshall had the keenest minds I ever came in contact with. What a hell of a fix I'd have been in without the two of you.

Most sincerely,

Harry Truman

"Ain't a man a damfool to do what I'm doing when he don't have to." That's a quotation from Sen. Holman of Oregon when I gave him permission to fly over Attu in World War II with Mon Wallgren. I stayed in Seattle and they went on a jaunt which they wished they hadn't taken. At least Holman thought that.

Truman did not accept the invitation Acheson mentions. "British Public Enemy No. 1" refers to the outcry in Britain over Acheson's recent speech at West Point, where he said, "Britain has lost an empire and has not yet found a new role. . . . Great Britain, attempting to work alone and to be a broker between the United States and Russia, has seemed to conduct policy as weak as its military power." Acheson had trouble understanding how a very small and not very important part of a speech delivered to a student audience could give rise to headline news expressing outrage and hurt pride.

December 14, 1962

Dear Mr. President:

I am for my sins Vice President under Chris Herter of the Atlantic Council of the United States, which is a merger of all the NATO and Atlantic Community organizations, brought about at the State Department's request.

It is giving on January 14 a dinner in honor of Laurie Norstad, the retiring Supreme Commander in Europe. Chris has asked General Eisenhower to come and has asked me to ask you. A formal invitation will be com[ing] along in course. I think this is a matter which you can deal with as most convenient to you. I see no pressing reason why you should turn from more important engagements for this salute to a retiring General. If it fits in with your plans and you would find it pleasant, everybody, including myself, would be delighted to see you there.

Alice and I are off today for a brief vacation in the West Indies to get away form this cold and feel the sun and water of the Tropics once more.

With warm greetings from British Public Enemy No. 1.

As ever,

Dean

The article Truman refers to is "My Morning in America," published in the Saturday Evening Post, on December 15. Truman and Acheson were both devoted autobiographers, and both possessed a streak of nostalgia for bygone days. The most personal and revealing part of Truman's memoirs is a long section about his early life. He also wrote several autobiographical manuscripts, the most important of which were published by historian Robert H. Ferrell as The Autobiography of Harry S. Truman *(1980). Acheson wrote two volumes of memoirs:* Morning and Noon *(1965), about his early life, and* Present at the Creation *(1969), about his State Department years. Truman acknowledges in this letter his debt to the many books he has read in his lifetime, particularly books of history and biography. "Ter-*

rible *trial"* refers to the burden of the presidency, which fell upon him on April 12, 1945.

December 18, 1962

Dear Dean:

I've been reading your *Saturday Evening Post* article. Tried to call you soon as I read it. It gave me many memories of my growing up.

We had almost the same experiences. Only your experiences were in the great state of Connecticut and mine were in Missouri. You had white people who helped out and we had black and brown—but the experiences were almost the same!

At the time of the Spanish American War, the twelve and fourteen year olds organized a company. That company marched, carried 22 rifles, killed the neighbor's frying chickens and camped out until our parents put a stop to it. Then I had to study whether I wanted to or not. Read the Old & New Testaments—King James translation—three times before I was fifteen, and all the histories of world leaders and heroes I could find. Our public library in Independence had about three or four thousand volumes, including the ten encyclopedias!

Believe it or not, I read them all—including the enclo's. Maybe I was a damphool but it served me well when my *terrible* trial came.

You know better than anyone. Hope your trip abroad was a happy one.

Sincerely, your friend and great admirer,

Harry Truman

December 20, 1962

Dear Dean:

If you are punished for your sins by association with Christian Herter—I am of the opinion that you are not punished! He needs your brains and ability. No one knows that better than an old man who—by accident—became President of the United States.

You were one of my greatest assets. Marshall was the other. How in the world could a man be as lucky as I was—with two such able men!

I don't know what to do about January 14th. I am told that the Dam Democrats at Kennedy's suggestion are putting on a $1,000 dinner! If and when that happens we'll quit being democrats with a little d!

I was not consulted about the "thousand dollar dinner." If I had been, I'd have told them that Democratic dinners should start at $25.00. A thousand seats at $25.00 would be $25,000.00, two thousand seats at $10.00 would be $20,000.00 and 4,000 seats at five dollars would still be $20,000.00. Therefore more real Democrats would take a hand! That's the way Democrats have won.

To hell with these multimillionaires at the head of things. Maybe I'm just a poor retired farmer.

Sincerely,

Harry S. Truman

Truman underwent an operation to correct an abdominal hernia on January 18. The vacation partners Acheson mentions are Mr. and Mrs. Archibald MacLeish. Acheson's memoir Morning and Noon *covered his life from 1893 to 1941. The two troubled alliances Acheson refers to are those of the communist nations and of the Western powers. Besides learning of Truman's operation in his morning newspapers, Acheson read about a fracas at the East German Communist Party congress, where a Chinese delegate said the "Tito group" of communists in Yugoslavia had "surrendered to the imperialists." This was understood to be a veiled attack on the Soviet Union's policy of peaceful coexistence with the West. Acheson also read about France's adamant opposition to British entry into the European Economic Community, a predecessor entity to the European Union. Jean Monnet was the intellectual father of the European unification movement, of which President de Gaulle was the chief enemy. Harold Macmillan was prime minister of Great Britain.*

January 19, 1963

Dear Boss:

I was distressed to read in the press that you were to fall victim again to Dr. Graham's sharp knives, and then reassured this morning that your condition was reported as "excellent." Alice and I send you a large case of love and devotion—all in full quarts—to take you home to a leisurely (I hope) recuperation. If I know Boss Bess, you are going to take a rest and a good one. Why isn't this the time for you both to visit Ed Pauley in southwestern sun? Alice and I are just back from three weeks in the West Indian sun, partly being lazy with the MacLeishes at Antigua, and part of the time cruising on a sailboat from St. Lucia to Trinidad through waters more exotic than any that Ulysses saw. So we are experts on the value of sun and relaxation.

Thank you so much for reading, liking, and writing me about the piece I wrote about my childhood. The memories it evoked from you about your own are fascinating. They confirm a suspicion about you which has been growing on me for over fifteen years. It is nothing less than that you are a shrewd old fraud. All this talk about you being a simple retired farmer, untroubled by what Cordell Hull used to call "book larnin", is part of a deep conspiracy to mislead the gullible electorate and probably violates the Hatch Act. Unless silenced by bribery of regular letters from you, I shall—at a moment carefully chosen to rock the John Birch Society to its foundations—disclose the shattering truth that you are, in fact, the most unmitigated intellectual, who, before he was out of short pants, had read four thousand volumes and three encyclopedias. One has to go back to Drs. Sam Johnson and Ben Franklin to equal that. If this is blackmail, as one of our patriots said to George III, make the most of it.

Today's press tells me also that both the alliances are in trouble. China is trying to divide the children of darkness; and France, the children of light. My guess is that neither will succeed. Jean Monnet has always said that the unification of Europe can only take a step forward in an atmosphere of crisis. At the urging of my German friends, and with the approval of the State Department, I have been urging Adenauer by cable to move General de Gaulle from the disastrous course he has charted, which, if followed, will go far to destroy the Chancellor's life work. My guess is that de Gaulle's purpose was to needle MacMillan into making the break. The General is too conscious of history's judgment to make it himself.

With all get well messages and our love to both bosses.

Yours,

Dean

February 15, 1963

Dear Dean:

You don't know how very much I appreciated your letter of the 19th, and I don't want you to consider this a reply to it. I just want you to know that I received your letter and it brought me much pleasure when I needed it most. I hope to get around in a week or two to answering it.

Mrs. Truman and the doctor are still insisting that I not do very much for a while longer, you will be hearing from me before too many days go by, in the manner in which you ought to hear.

Give my best to Alice.

Sincerely yours,

Harry

Truman sent with this letter his two most recent NANA articles, one on Cuba, which appeared on February 24, and one about France, which would appear on March 16. Truman argued that the United States had a responsibility to make the Cuban people free again. He imagined a conversation between himself as President and Castro, at which an understanding was reached that would result in free institutions in Cuba. He concluded that the recent Cuban crisis was useful in that it gave the United States an opportunity to show the Soviets that when a line was clearly drawn, as it was during the Cuban missile crisis, the United States stood firm. His article about France, though intended to reflect on de Gaulle's refusal to allow the United Kingdom to join the European Economic Community, was drawn largely from his presidential papers. He recounted de Gaulle's action at the end of World War II to establish by force an occupation zone in Germany around Stuttgart. The United States ordered him to remove his French forces, and when he refused, Truman cut off supplies to his troops. De Gaulle hadn't changed, Truman implied. Truman concluded by holding out a dream of "a unified international community under the United Nations—devoted to the common good of all people." Acheson would have liked the next sentence better: "As we keep on trying to organize the whole world for peace, we must remain alert to the realities of the situation—and that we live in a period of ruthless power."

March 9, 1963

Dear Dean:

Your good letter of the 19th was heartwarming. I have been working a couple of hours a day on a Cuban release and a De Gaulle squib. I am sorry to say I haven't had the nerve to talk to the White House. If you know of any reason why I should I might consider doing it.

Why in hell a successor would not consider things which happened three Presidential generations before hand—well, I'll never understand. I am sending you a copy of the Cuban release and one on De Gaulle which will come out a week from tomorrow. You see I kept a transcript of the conversations with the interim President of France.

What luck that was! De Gaulle has not changed from Stuttgart. He was told what was in view by all the people between me and what had to be done (I have the record!) and the President finally cut off U.S. Supplies to France and the Provisional President of France came across and moved to the occupation positions that France was supposed to take!

But Dean, why rehash all this past history stuff? I suppose it is because I want to show off to my able, distinguished and brainy Sec. of State! Please don't believe that. Dean, I never had a man in my immediate White House family or anywhere else in my political career that I thought more of than I did of Dean Acheson. You know why? Because he always told me the truth and the facts whether I liked it or not!

I'm still a little under the weather, seventy-eight is not twenty-eight—so—I'll have to stop. Don't you stop writing me those wonderful letters. My best to Alice. The "Boss" joins me.

Most sincerely,

Harry

Truman refers to a speech Acheson gave at Berkeley, California, on March 13, 1963, titled "Europe: Kaleidoscope or Clouded Crystal." Acheson argued that, despite France's unwillingness to be a cooperative member of the Western alliance, the United States' European defense policy "was right and should be continued." Truman's enclosure is apparently the article about de Gaulle enclosed with his March 9 letter but may have been slightly different or in a different format. Truman mentions the theft from the Truman Library of a very fine collection of coins, including a type set of every American coin made during every presidency. The coins have never been recovered.

March 18, 1963

Dear Dean:

It was with great pleasure and satisfaction that I read your Berkeley, Calif., speech on the "Great" De Gaulle. In return I'm sending you a release I made for the North American Newspaper Alliance on the same fellow.

Yours was much better than mine because it is a character analysis and mine is a historical statement of some years back.

Luckily I have kept those documents of that period—and they are available to you and anyone you suggest for any use you want to make of them. There were two sets of all these important reports of those important meetings in 1946–47–48–49 & 50. I've no idea what the State, Defense, Commerce and Agriculture did with their copies—but I have mine and expect to keep them for the use of my friends—you at the top of the list!

I said two sets—there were two official sets and copies for all the others interested. Every effort has been made by the General Services and some department to obtain my copies. Those copies are in an Archives Building for which I raised $1,750,000.00 to construct and for which Independence gave me a 13 acre site. I turned over 4,500,000 documents and more than $300,000.00 worth of presents which had come to me as President from Heads of State. They are now the property of the people and Government of the U.S.A.

But you understand the said Govt. of the U.S.A doesn't take very good care of the articles. A short time ago $50,000.00 in coins and engravings of the Presidents' pictures in whose time the coins were made disappeared from this Government Institution and have not been heard of since. The whole FBI has made an attempt to catch the thieves and are still working on it. They may catch the thieves but they'll never find the coins nor the pictures.

Looks to me as if the President of France is way out in field left of 3rd base and nothing to catch!

Sincerely,

Harry

Acheson had recently been working on a report on the United States' balance-of-payments problem for President Kennedy. He submitted the report, titled "Recommendations Relating to United States International Payments Problem," to the President on February 25.

March 20, 1963

Dear Boss,

Two letters from you in quite short order give me the comforting assurance that you are moving on to complete recovery from your recent operation. You please me very much by liking the Berkeley speech. I worked very hard on it, trying to cull out any distracting and troublesome statements, such as got into the West Point speech and prevented the main theme from coming though. As a result, it seems to have forced a good deal of attention onto the substance of what was said.

Your own historical review of your discussions with the General were most interesting to me. I do not remember having known at the time what you two actually talked about, so it had all the interest of new discovery.

You must have been very distressed at the theft of that most unusual collection of coins, which—as I recall—John Snyder gave to the Library. The whole thing, as framed, was so large that it seems almost impossible that it could be taken away without any alarm at all. The guards surely do not suffer from insomnia.

I have, at the President's request, been doing some work for him to get agreement within the Administration on a matter which might be regarded as outside my field of competence. But one can understand even unfamiliar subjects as no one knows better than you, if one works at them. So I went to work and soon was able to report that the departments concerned would go along happily with a paper I had prepared if the President crushed the first sign of revolt which all good bureaucrats try on just for luck. A big meeting was held, the rebel standard was raised, but the President did nothing. In no time at all the cell block was in a riot, and we are starting anew. I suppose it takes time to learn that just as there is a time to permit discussion, there is also a time to end it. Don't delay in reading the riot act too long or no one will hear it!

Alice sends her most affectionate greetings to you and the Boss, as do I.

As ever,

Dean

Truman was asked by the president of the Yale Club of Montclair, New Jersey, to provide a message for a ceremony at which Acheson would be honored. "The judgment of history . . . ," Truman replied, "will mark Dean Acheson among the top three or four of the great Secretaries of State. No one has had a clearer sense of the times or the direction of the course this nation had to take in her relations with its friends and allies, as well as to meet the threat from the new enemy."

March 29, 1963

Dear Dean:

I'm enclosing you a copy of the letter which I have received from the Montclair Yale Club of Montclair, New Jersey, and a copy of my reply to them.

Sincerely yours,

Harry S. Truman

A. Whitney Griswold was president of Yale. Acheson was the senior member of the Yale Corporation.

May 6, 1963

Dear Boss:

All hail to the 8th of May and your coming of age! I claim that you are a youth yet, and have two more years of your seventh decade. I, who have just turned seventy, am only completing my sixth. But we still aren't as young as we were, when we struck blows for liberty, are we? Alice and I send you—and Bess, who makes it all possible—our love, affection, admiration, and all wishes for years of usefulness to the nation and joy to your friends.

Friends report that you are disappointed that it has taken longer to regain your strength after the operation than you had hoped. I can imagine you fretting to get at those morning walks again and cussing fate. But the first article of my faith is that you are indomitable and that the day will come. When it does, compromise a bit with the army regulations. A hundred paces a minute is enough for a while.

The death of our friend, Whit Griswold, of Yale, was a hard knock for all of us at Yale, but especially for me, since I had been so close to him, worked at his side, and had come to be devoted to him. We spent the afternoon before he died together, his last clear hours. He was a gallant and most lovable man.

You were most kind to write to the Montclair Yale Club so warmly about me on the occasion of their dinner to me. You always touch me by your faith in me. There are times now-a-days when I have a longing that together we might take the wheel and the bridge just long enough to set a firm course and get the crew standing to quarters, confident in the course and the command. I do not believe that the situation is as puzzling as the Administration appears to think. Germany is the present key to movement in Europe, and, I think, is ready to act with us. Instead Rusk spreads suspicion with his futile talks with the Russians, and we continue to negotiate with ourselves in Geneva over a nuclear test ban which the Russians have no intention of accepting.

Every good wish!

Affectionately,

Dean

Truman has apparently not fully recovered from his mid-January oper-ation.

May 14, 1963

Dear Dean:

I understand that you are presiding at the dinner of the Washington Institute of Foreign Affairs, on May 28th. I certainly wish I could be with you but I just can't make it, much to my regret.

As you know, I am just as interested in what goes on now as I was when I was in the center of things but that old lady "Anno Domini" has been chasing me and I have to slow up a bit, particularly since she has a partner in Mrs. Truman.

Please remember me to Mrs. Acheson.

Sincerely yours,

Harry S. Truman

Truman presided over the twenty-second Truman Committee Anniversary Dinner in Washington, D.C., on June 13. He had headed the Truman Committee—or, more properly, the Senate Special Committee to Investi-gate the National Defense Program—from March 1941 until he was nomi-nated as the Democratic Party's vice-presidential candidate in the summer of 1944. Acheson was invited to the dinner, but did not attend. Nor did he and Truman have an opportunity to visit together while Truman was in Washington.

May 26, 1963

Dear Dean:

I have been reading again your good letter of May 6th a couple of days before I became within twenty one years of one hundred. If, as you suggest, I finish this 7th decade, as I hope, I am sure I can do the other twenty.

It reminds me of one of my old political stories, which my old Uncle for whom I'm named told me seven decades ago.

It seems that there was a contest as to who could eat the greatest number of roasting ears off the cob. Well, one old fellow ate thirteen. He had to send for his doctor and his doctor told him he should send for his Baptist preacher to pray for him. His preacher told him he'd have to pray for himself. The old fellow said, "I'm not in the habit of addressing the Lord, you do it." "No," said the preacher, "you'll have to ask Him for relief yourself."

Well, the old fellow got out of bed, got on his knees and made the following petition to the Almighty: "O Lord, I've eaten too many roasting ears—thirteen in fact. I'm not like these Damned Methodists, if you'll relieve me of seven ears I'll try to rastle around the other six." Wasn't that a fair proposition?

Now I'd like very much to trade Him two for twenty—can you help me?!

I was very sorry to hear of the death of President Griswold of Yale, because I knew of your close association. But, as you know, we have to meet them head on and you know how to do it.

At 79 you go to funeral after funeral of your friends, most of whom are younger than 79—and you sometimes wonder if the old man with the scythe isn't after you. I'm trying to out run him.

Your suggestion about a take over intrigues me. Wish we could try it. I'm egotistical to think the two of us together could do some good for the country. You could do it by yourself and I hope you will. It's always a pleasure to hear from you. Glad you were pleased with my letter about you. It wasn't as good as it should have been.

Sincerely,

HST

It looks like I'm stationery stingy—but I couldn't help stop! [Postscript written vertically in left-hand margin of letter. The last line of the letter and Truman's signature are squeezed tightly and awkwardly on the last bit of paper on the bottom of the page.]

I'm hoping we'll have a long time "get together" on June 13th. I'll be at the Mayflower all day. Get in the evening of the 12th rather late.

Truman suffered a serious fall in the upstairs bathroom at his home on October 13, 1964. He appeared never to recover fully from this fall. He grew thin and came to the Truman Library less and less often. The "bewhiskered prelate" is Archbishop Makarios III, of the Greek Orthodox Church, president of the Republic of Cyprus at this time. The Greek and Turkish populations of Cyprus had been fighting over the future of the island all through 1964, and the United Nations was attempting to mediate a peace between the two sides. Acheson spent the summer of 1964 in Geneva, where the United Nations–sponsored negotiations were taking place. Although he had no official role in the negotiations, through the strong support of the Johnson administration and the force of his personality, he came to dominate the talks. They collapsed in late August, and Acheson came home. Greece and Turkey were both NATO member states, and the problems in Cyprus threatened to weaken NATO's southeastern flank.

October 16, 1964

Dear Boss:

Now that I have made a determined start on the decade of the seventies you have confirmed a night mare fear—the ever lurking menace of the bath tub. Far more dangerous than the submarine or the bomb, nuclear or otherwise, it is a trap set for us old codgers. It is as dangerous to get into as to get out of, or to stay in. Recently when we built a new bath room onto our guest house at the farm, I refused to have any bath tub at all. Instead a gleaming white shower cabinet with a rubber floor. But still the wretched things lie in wait for us everywhere.

My heart goes out to you, battered, black eyed, lung congested, all to pursue overrated cleanliness. Remember the Eskimo! Not a bath from the autumn to the spring solstice. And now you are having what is worse than a tub bath—certainly more humiliating—those dreadful hospital baths.

Sympathy, affection, constant thoughts—all go from me—and from Alice—to you. And to Bess. We had an interesting and very pleasant summer in Geneva trying to do in the bewhiskered prelate. I failed but Alice did some fine painting.

Poor Lyndon! What a blow from fate!

Yours ever,

Dean

January 12, 1965

Dear Dean:

I was confronted with such an accumulation of matters which required my attention, when I returned to the office after my mishap, that I had to put off replying to my important mail. I am just now getting around to answering the ones in the special folder. I had hoped to write you a longhand letter, but I will have to dictate this one, and will send you a handwritten letter a little later.

I did not fall in the bathtub, as was reported by the press. I was going into the bathroom, caught my heel on the sill which caused me to fall and hit my head against the washstand. I wasn't satisfied with the one fall and proceeded to hit the tub on the rebound and broke some ribs as well.

It has taken me a while to come out of it but I am now getting along all right, although I must be careful for some time yet.

Best wishes to you and Mrs. Acheson for a Happy New Year in which Mrs. Truman joins me.

Sincerely yours,

Harry S. Truman

President Truman's brother, John Vivian Truman, died on July 9. The meeting with President Johnson that Acheson describes took place on July 8. The day began with a series of meetings of several elder statesmen, called the "Wise Men," with administration officials, who described the deteriorating situation in South Vietnam. At the end of the day the Wise Men met with Johnson. About three weeks later, on July 28, Johnson announced his decision to send American troops to fight in combat roles in South Vietnam. The Wise Men mentioned in this letter are former Secretary of Defense Robert Lovett, General Omar Bradley, and former Assistant Secretary of War and U.S. High Commissioner for Germany John J. McCloy. Henry H. Fowler was Johnson's Secretary of the Treasury.

July 10, 1965

Dear Boss,

Just a line to say that my thoughts are very much with you these days. I know how close you and Vivian have always been and that his death has been a sad break with so much that you hold dear. Alice and I want to send you a special message of love and devotion—a message which goes also to Bess.

On Thursday a few of us, whom LBJ calls his panel of advisors, met with him for three hours to talk about Europe, Latin America & S.E. Asia. We were all disturbed by a long complaint about how mean everything and everybody was to him—Fate, the Press, the Congress, the Intellectuals and so on. For a long time he fought the problem of Vietnam (every course of action was wrong; he had no support from anyone at home or abroad; it interfered with all his programs, etc., etc.). Lovett, Bradley, McCloy and John Coutes were there with McNamara, Rusk and Fowler. I got to thinking about you and General Marshall and how we never wasted time "fighting the problem", or endlessly reconsidering decisions, or feeling sorry for ourselves.

Finally I blew my top and told him that he was wholly right in the Dominican Republic and Vietnam, that he had no choice except to press on, that explanations were not as important as successful action; and that the trouble in Europe (which was more important than either of the other spots) came about because under him and Kennedy there had been no American leadership at all. The idea that Europeans could come to their own conclusions had led to an unchallenged de Gaulle.

With this lead my colleagues came thundering in like the charge of the Scots Greys at Waterloo. They were fine; old Bob Lovett, usually cautious, was all out, and, of course, Brad left no doubt that he was with me all the way. I think LBJ's press conference of yesterday showed that we scored.

I am reading the bound galleys of a biography of Roger B. Taney by a Walker Lewis, a very fine book on a man whom I have always admired. Houghton Mifflin is publishing it this fall.

As ever yours,

Dean

On July 31, President Johnson paid tribute to Truman's attempt during his presidency to pass into law a national health-insurance program, by coming to the Truman Library to sign the legislation creating Medicare. He came back to Independence several months later to present to Harry and Bess Truman the first two Medicare cards issued by the government.

August 4, 1965

Dear Dean:

Thank you for your interesting letter of July 10th. I appreciate your sympathetic message regarding the death of my brother Vivian. His passing has meant a great loss to me, but we have to accept those things when they happen—and I try to console myself by the fact that he had lived a long and happy life and had performed his public service honorably and well.

I read with interest about the meeting you described and appreciate the interest you take in things in which I am vitally interested. I believe that Johnson is doing a good job.

You heard, of course, of his coming here to sign the Medicare Bill. There were about 3,000 people on hand to witness it. We could only seat about 300 inside but the rest of them were on hand to witness his arrival and departure and I believe they felt as though they had been a part of the ceremony.

Bess joins me in warm personal regards to Alice and yourself and we hope an opportunity will present itself so we can have a visit again at sometime or other.

Sincerely yours,

Harry S. Truman

Truman has read a review of Acheson's memoir Morning and Noon, *dealing with his life prior to the Truman administration. The review, by Federal Reserve Chairman William McChesney Martin, is positive throughout and concludes that in his memoir Acheson "comes through clearly as a proud, tender and sensitive man of great intellect, whose contributions to our society are very real indeed."*

November 16, 1965

Dear Dean:

I have been reading a tear sheet from the *Washington Post,* called "Acheson's Contributions Reflected in Autobiography." It is a wonderful piece and one with which I completely and thoroughly agree.

I hope everything is going well with you and that it will continue to go that way.

Sincerely yours,

Harry S. Truman

The book mentioned is Acheson's memoir Morning and Noon.

December 1, 1965

Dear Mr. President:

The book about which you have been reading should have gone to you long since, and I thought it had from the publisher. That was an unfounded belief, and a copy is now on its way to you.

Alice and I are well and looking forward to our winter vacation in Antigua, beginning January 7th. We send our most affectionate greetings to you and The Boss.

Sincerely,

Dean

Truman's signature and his handwritten postscript on this letter are less bold and sure than they would have been in prior days.

December 10, 1965

Dear Dean:

I am happy to have your book *Morning and Noon*.

I started to read it and found that there are some things about you that I had not known. But, of course, you know there is nothing I could ever learn about you that would make me admire you any less.

Hope we can get together one of these days.

Sincerely yours,

Harry Truman

A most interesting book, I can hardly put it down!

Frank F. Jestrab of North Carolina asked Acheson where he should send a donation of fifty dollars, intended for a "Truman Memorial Center of some sort" that was being set up at a university in Israel. Acheson sent the letter to Truman. The former President, who did not like things to be named for him and usually denied requests to use his name in this way, allowed his name to be given to a Truman Center on the campus of the Hebrew University of Jerusalem provided that the center be devoted to the study of peace. The center was founded in 1966 and is today named the Harry S. Truman Research Institute for the Advancement of Peace.

June 8, 1966

Dear Dean:

Thank you very much for the letter from Mr. Jestrab and your reply to him. I do not know what disposition to make of the check. I assume that it was intended for the Harry S Truman Center for the Advancement of Peace, which will be built in an area within the complex of the Hebrew University in the City of Jerusalem.

As you may have read, the project was made possible by contributions made by forty citizens here and abroad, of $100,000 each, so that there is in excess of four million dollars presently committed.

I made it clear from the outset that this institution will be international in scope and operation and will have no connection with the government or nation of Israel, or any other government.

I would assume, therefore, that if Mr. Jestrab still wishes to make this tender, it should be made to the Harry S Truman Center for the Advancement of Peace.

Hope all goes well with you and that we can have a visit soon.

Sincerely yours,

Harry Truman

"Scoop" Jackson is Democratic Senator Henry M. Jackson of Washington, who chaired the Senate Armed Services Subcommittee on National Security and International Operations of the Government Operations Committee. Acheson provides a statement in support of NATO which he hopes Truman will send to Jackson. Truman sent a shorter and somewhat revised version of Acheson's draft to Jackson, though not for almost a month. Acheson had testified before the subcommittee on April 27. NATO was threatened at this time by France's withdrawal of its troops from NATO's integrated military command and its order that all non-French NATO troops leave France. Truman's fourth grandson, Thomas Washington Daniel, was born on May 28.

June 28, 1966

Dear Mr. President:

Soon I shall write you a gossipy letter about my three months' service in the State Department in the Johnson Administration. It has been quite an experience. Everything is different from when you-know-who was in the White House and in the State Department. The best description of its operation is in the words of the negro spiritual: "The

big wheel runs by faith and the little wheel runs by the grace of God."
But more of that in another letter.

Today I am bothering you at the request of "Scoop" Jackson. His
committee, as you know, has been holding hearings on the present
NATO situation. McCloy and others, including myself, have testified,
and "Scoop" has tried earnestly to create a record which will make
more sense than that provided by the group of screwballs who now
function as the Committee on Foreign Relations. Eisenhower wrote a
letter giving some rather confused views, but on the whole supporting
NATO. "Scoop" has asked me to ask you whether you would express
your views in a letter for the record.

As you remember from the old days, I tried never to present a problem without suggesting a solution. In this case I know that it would be
an awful nuisance for you to undertake from scratch a letter on the
present NATO situation. Therefore, I have tried my hand at a draft. In
it I have kept away from all controversy about General de Gaulle, about
where various headquarters should be transferred, and whether or not
the US contingent should be decreased or transferred in part to home
bases. I do think it would be helpful, since NATO was one of the great
works of your Administration, to have a word from you stressing the
essential foundations of NATO, which have not changed.

If this whole matter seems to you a burden, just let me know and I
will make everything all right with "Scoop." If you like the draft, use it
in any way you wish.

We congratulate you and the Boss on another grandson. Margaret is
the Mother of the Year.

With love to you both.

As ever,

Dean

Dear Dean: July 26, 1966

I was glad to comply with your suggestion and have written Scoop
Jackson urging continued support to NATO.

It is always stimulating to hear from you—and I hope you will write
again soon giving me your views on the shape of things.

Sincerely yours,

Harry S. Truman

Acheson's younger brother, Edward Campion Acheson, died in late September.

September 30, 1966

HONORABLE DEAN ACHESON
BESS JOINS ME IN SENDING OUR LOVE AND SYMPATHY TO YOU
AT THIS SAD TIME.
HARRY S TRUMAN

Acheson writes Truman the promised gossipy letter about Lyndon Johnson and his Secretary of State, Dean Rusk. For about three months, from April to July 1966, Acheson had coordinated the Johnson administration's response to the crisis within NATO caused by France's withdrawal. The book Acheson mentions is his memoir of his service with the State Department under Presidents Roosevelt and Truman. He titled it Present at the Creation.

October 3, 1966

Dear Mr. President,

The message which you and Mrs. Truman sent me was most kind and thoughtful of you, as you have always been to me. My brother, who was ten years younger than I, died very suddenly, as he was reading at home. He had no history of heart trouble, though he had been in poor shape for some years from progressive emphysema. One of his proudest memories was of holding the title of your "Personal Representative" in late '47 or '48 when John Hilldring sent him off to Scandinavia to buy fish for the Germans to eat on Fridays. Now I am the only one left of my generation in the family, although I was the oldest.

We had hoped to go to an Army dinner in honor of you and were saddened to get word that the Boss had wisely decided to save your energy for other things. It is too long since we have seen you. I do hope that you are coming back strongly from your illness.

This year I put in five months of what Lincoln called "unrequited toil" in the State Department for LBJ and Dean Rusk on the De Gaulle NATO crisis. I found it—between you and me—a most disillusioning experience in regard to both men. I recommended Rusk to Kennedy when he wanted to appoint, of all people, Fulbright; and had high hopes of him. He had been a good assistant to me, loyal and capable.

But as number one he has been no good at all. For some reason, unknown to me, he will not disclose his mind to anyone. The Department is totally at a loss to know what he wants done or what he thinks. All sorts of channels spring up between various people in the Department and White House aides which result in conflicting policies getting rumored about.

LBJ is not much better. He, too, hates to decide matters, is a worse postponer of decisions than FDR. The phrase for that now is "to preserve all one's options." That means to drift and let decisions be made by default. It passes for statesmanship in our town today.

Two other things about LBJ. He can't carry on more than a few matters at once. Now-a-days his preoccupations are Vietnam and the balance of payments. So Europe is forgotten and a great deal that you, General Marshall and I did is unraveling fast. For the Chief of the world's greatest power and the only one capable of world responsibility, this is a disaster.

The other is that he is not only devious but would rather be devious than straight forward. While I was doing my best to advise him on NATO, and while he was writing messages and making speeches I wrote for him, he was circulating rumors in the press that my views were not his. If they were not, a half hour talk could have gotten us together. But it was not until I blew up that we had it and then I never did find out what he wanted done differently.

At any rate, I am now a free man; writing a book about my years in the State Department and about another President who used to do things very differently.

It is really too bad about LBJ. He could be so much better than he is. He creates distrust by being too smart. He is never quite candid. He is both mean and generous, but the meanness too often predominates. He yields to petty impulses such as the desire to surprise everyone with every appointment. It is too childish.

Well, I have gotten a lot off my chest.

Alice who is blooming (can you believe that we shall have been married 50 years next May!) sends her love to you and Bess, as I do.

As ever,

Dean

October 19, 1966

Dear Dean:

As always I was glad to hear from you.

As you may well imagine I was disturbed by all you had to say about the situation as you found it after taking a good look at it! I can only hope that with experience and the conditioning and strength that comes to the man after he has weathered the storms of criticism, vilification, disappointments and betrayals that he will rise to the full measure of the great calling of that office.

Bess joins me in sending you and Alice our warmest greetings and our best wishes.

Sincerely yours,

Harry Truman

Joseph Alsop wrote a syndicated column called "Matter of Fact." One of these columns, titled " 'Never Again Panmunjom,' " likened the possibility of a cessation of American bombing of North Vietnam in order to facilitate the beginning of peace talks to a "standstill order" that Truman allegedly issued to General Matthew Ridgway, the commander of United Nations forces in Korea, at the time peace talks with the communists were beginning. "The results of President Truman's standstill order," Alsop wrote, "were two more needless years of war and some 90,000 additional American casualties. . . . The standstill order—really a unilateral cease fire—was, in fact, the worst mistake that President Truman ever made."

November 16, 1966

Dear Boss,

Will you please get Mr. Noyes to help me in a battle I want to fight to correct an error which Joe Alsop has now printed four times about you. I enclose his last rendition of it today. I think better of Joe than you once did—I remember your references to Alsop—but unless firmly corrected he will go on repeating an error until people begin to believe it.

Paul Nitze and I having compared notes, are sure that you never sent a standstill order to Ridgway. To accuse you of causing 90,000 needless casualties and two needless years of war is outrageous.

I am asking Bradley to search his memory and papers about this and also Joe Collins. Paul will have a search made in the Pentagon. Will you ask Noyes to see whether your papers show anything on the subject. I don't want to quote anybody or any paper. I only want to assert on my own authority that after inquiries which convince me that I know the facts that you issued no standstill order in connection with any armistice talks nor interfered in any way with military operations at that time. You followed at all times your normal relations with the Joint Chiefs of Staff and the Secretary of State and of Defense.

These columnists try to rewrite history as much as the communists.

I hate to bother you with this, but I do think that it is important not to let this repeated misstatement continue without correction.

Alice sends her love to you both.

All your successors demonstrate what rugged health you had—yet you were never paid for overtime.

Affectionately,

Dean

Truman asked his assistant David Noyes to look into Alsop's contention about a "standstill order." Noyes headed a search of Truman's papers and discovered much evidence that no such order was issued. Robert Dennison was President Truman's naval aide at the time of the Korean War. Sidney Souers, who was a special consultant to the President on military and foreign-policy affairs at the time the order was allegedly issued, confirmed with certainty that no such order had been issued.

November 21, 1966

Dear Dean:

I have no idea where or from whom Alsop could have picked up the notion of a standstill order or how he came to make the ugly charge in his column. It was bad enough when you and I had to put up with this sort of thing in the days when it was our responsibility—but to use it now in relation to the Viet Nam situation is a little hard to take.

Dave had dug up some passages from the documents which may help. We tried to reach Bob Dennison but he is out of the country. Sid Souers suggested that the most likely source for a final check would be Omar Bradley.

Bess joins me in sending you and Alice our best.

Sincerely yours,

Harry S. Truman

Acheson sends Truman a copy of a letter he received from General Mat-thew B. Ridgway regarding Joseph Alsop's allegation of a standstill order. Ridgway wrote Acheson: "My recollection is very clear and positive that no such order was ever given by the President or other competent authority." William Bundy, who was Acheson's son-in-law, was a State Department official during the Johnson administration who advised the President on the Vietnam War. James "Scotty" Reston was a journalist with the New York Times. *Eric Sevareid was a journalist with CBS News.*

December 5, 1966

Dear Boss,

I am most grateful to you and David Noyes for your letter and his memorandum on the Joe Alsop article. You will both be interested I know in the letter from Matt Ridgway which I enclose. It supports your recollection and your files in every way—so does the memory of Gen-eral Bradley and General Collins's search of the Pentagon files includ-ing the official army history of the Korean War not yet released for publication.

I have had a long talk with Joe Alsop who has been so far rather difficult, but will—I hope—on reflection be more straight forward. His attitude after I stormed his outer works is that if he is wrong about you, he will retract the personal attribution, but still asserts that the whole administration, military and civil, let the enemy escape destruction by way of a quasi truce for negotiation. This, I say to him, is false. Ridgway says that the enemy was not subject to destruction except by augmentation of our land and air forces and by tactics which no one, military or civil, advised—it is Joe Alsop against the world. We shall see. Perhaps, as in his very decent letter of apology to you which David enclosed, his more gentlemanly side—which exists—will prevail.

I will see Bob Dennison when he gets back—we had lunch just before he left—and get his recollections, too.

Europe is a very worrisome spot these days. Disintegration is going so fast that it would be hard to check; and no one seems interested in doing so. The sentiments are expressed in an orthodox way by LBJ and DR but their hearts are not in the expressions, nor are their backs in any determined push.

Our son-in-law Bill Bundy went off with Rusk yesterday for another ten day visit to Asia. This part of the world, which does evoke a great deal of hearty interest in the President and Secretary, is doing much better, though the worries are still great. If everyone would stop talking and keep on plugging the results might be great.

Today Reston & Sevareid said to me that LBJ could conceivably lose in 1968. I said that first they must think up some one to whom he could lose. I saw no one and didn't believe it anyway.

Alice joins in affectionate greetings to you and Bess. We are off to Antigua a month from tomorrow.

Yours ever,
Dean

In Joseph Alsop's "letter of apology," to which Acheson refers above, dated March 12, 1965, Alsop wrote to Truman: "My purpose is simply to apologize for the inexperience and bad judgment which led me to underrate your leadership of our country while you were in office. When I look back now, I must say with greater opportunities for comparison, your years in the White House seem to me a truly heroic period. Nowadays, I never lose a chance to say that in print. But I did not say it then, and that is why I think an apology is owed." Truman replied to Alsop on March 15, 1965: "There is something in my make-up that rebels at the thought of exacting an apology from anyone who has publicly disapproved of me—and I surely would not expect to receive one from so talented an observer as yourself. But I warmly welcome your reassessment of 'the period' and dare hope that it might be sustained by the ultimate judgment."

Acheson, in the midst of writing his memoirs, is trying to remember how he first came to Truman's notice. Matthew J. Connelly was Truman's appointments secretary from 1945 to 1953. George V. Allen served several roles in the Truman administration, including ambassador to Iran (1946–48), Assistant Secretary of State for Public Affairs (1948–49), and ambassador to Yugoslavia (1949–53).

December 17, 1966

Dear Boss,

May I plumb your memory? My own, I find, does unaccountable things—invents what never happened; forgets what did; gets times and places all mixed up, and so on.

For a long time I have believed that on the first morning of your Presidency, April 13th, Matt Connelly summoned me to the Cabinet room from across the street. There—so memory seems to record—he,

George Allen, and two or three other people were working over a statement of some sort for you. You, he said, had remembered me from a call I made on you at the Capitol about some rascality that McCarran was up to. You came in and talked with us for a few minutes and we soon finished whatever the task was.

The strange part of this is that although the picture of the scene is clear, I can find no verification of any part of it. You made no statement so far as your book and your Public Papers reveal until your address to Congress; and I am sure I had no part in that. Do you remember my doing any kind of chore for you in those first days?

I resigned as Assistant Secretary on August 8th and you accepted it on August 9th. I had barely gotten to Saranac Lake, N.Y., where Mary was on V.J. Day, when Jimmie Byrnes telephoned me that you wished me to come back to be Under Secretary. It all seems to me so mysterious, that I have been casting around for something to explain what brought me to your attention between my call in January 1945 and your appointing me in August. It hardly seems likely to have been Jimmie since he gave you my resignation and gave me your acceptance.

Don't disturb yourself about this but if any dim recollection stirs I should love to know of it.

Most affectionate Christmas greetings to Bess & yourself from Alice and me.

As ever,
Dean

January 23, 1967

Dear Dean:

I have searched my memory and try as I would, I cannot pinpoint the precise moment at which the decision crystallized in my mind that I wanted you in the Administration.

I had been aware of you long before I went to the White House and I am sure that my interest in you had to originate with me.

Sincerely yours,
Harry Truman

April 17, 1967

Dear Dean:

It has come to my attention that you had a birthday recently.

I hope it was a happy one, as I am sure it was, and that you will have many more like it.

Sincerely yours,

Harry Truman

April 21, 1967

Dear Boss,

The report about that birthday of mine was true and you were very kind to take note of it. My seventy-fifth year opened without noticeable pain. I am now getting accustomed to the idea, though it does run counter to an idea of myself which still hovers in my mind—that I am a promising lad and may get somewhere if I work hard and stay sober.

Poor old Adenauer is gone. Like Churchill he rather outlived his reputation and, as the British say, rather blotted his copy book in the last few years by the vindictive way he treated his less gifted successor. Both he and Churchill simply could not let go of power. Your predecessor had the same weakness but more reason for it. You were wise and right in stepping down as you did. As I look back, I know that I was tired out when we all left office. We might have saved Europe from much that has gone wrong since, if we had stayed on, perhaps two years, or even one year more. But I could not have lasted through another four.

I see John Snyder who keeps me posted on you and seems well and cheerful himself, and occasionally Harry Vaughan and Clark Clifford. The latter I think is a wise and helpful advisor to LBJ. He is better than I am at surmounting the difficulties in personal relations which make helping LBJ so difficult and disagreeable. I have about stopped the effort and dodge whenever I can. The phrase, "he is his own worst enemy", was never as true of anyone as it is of him.

How very appropriate it was of the Greeks to give you that old helmet last month. I was struck with the changes in head sizes over two and a half millennia. After my experience in 1964 with that old fool Papandreou over Cyprus, I began to wonder whether the Greeks were worth saving after all. The Turks certainly were.

You yourself will have a birthday coming up soon and Alice and I will soon have been married for half a century. Here's good luck to all of us, and to you and the boss much love from Alice and me.

Ever yours,

Dean

May 7, 1968

PRESIDENT HARRY S TRUMAN
WITH MUCH LOVE AND BEST WISHES FOR MANY HAPPY OCCA-
SIONS LIKE THE PRESENT FROM
DEAN AND ALICE ACHESON

February 28, 1969

Dear Boss,

The press gave us a bad turn about your going off to the hospital in an ambulance, but has now reassured us that you came back in your old style with your policeman-chauffeur at the wheel. So all seems well. Alice and I spent five weeks in the West Indies (and went to visit the Anthony Edens—now Avons). When we got back here the combination of the cold and the Republicans are driving us off to Florida for another two weeks.

My son-in-law who is staying on until the middle of March to let Bill Rogers find a replacement for him (as no-one will come to work for these people) says that the State Department has never been so bewildered and leaderless as it is now. A poor time and preparation for Mr. Nixon's journey to Europe. If he thinks his personality can affect negotiations with General de Gaulle, some one should tell him that better men have tried it and failed.

Affectionate greetings to Bess and to you from both of us.

Yours ever,

Dean

March 10, 1969

Dear Dean:

I was highly pleased to have your letter of February 28th, and took note of your comments with satisfaction. It was so nice to hear from you and I agree with what you had to say.

I am glad to report I am home and picking up where I left off—take a walk every morning when the weather is nice and am looking forward to the spring mornings.

Mrs. Truman joins me in sending you and Mrs. Acheson our very warmest regards.

Sincerely yours,

Harry Truman

Present at the Creation was Acheson's definitive memoir of his service in the State Department in four successive jobs. Acheson enclosed with this letter an advance copy of an article based on the final chapter of Present at the Creation, *in which he described the contributions to the Truman administration's foreign policy made by President Truman himself and by the Department of State. He titled this article, "The Greatness of Harry S. Truman." Acheson gave the article a kind of subtitle, running right below the title and above the author's name: "At night, knowing he was in the White House, even he slept better."*

August 12, 1969

Dear Mr. President:

Here is an article *Esquire* magazine is printing in its September issue. It is taken from my book, *Present at the Creation,* and I thought you might like to have it. The book will deal with the years 1941–1953, two-thirds of it or more being devoted to the years of great privilege when I was your Under Secretary and Secretary of State. I shall send you a copy of the book as soon as one is off the press—sometime in August, I hope. In writing about those years I came close to reliving them again with you and hope I have captured some of our spirit and purpose that made them such a wonderfully satisfying adventure and writing about them a fine way to spend another two years.

Alice joins me in most affectionate regards to you and Bess.

As ever,

Dean

August 27, 1969

Dear Dean:

I was happy to have a copy of the article *Esquire* is publishing in its September issue. I read it with interest and satisfaction and you were as kind as could be.

I am looking forward to your forthcoming book and, as you well know, I have a special interest in everything you have to say.

Bess joins me in sending warm regards to you and Alice.

Sincerely yours,

Harry S. Truman

September 3, 1969

Dear Boss,

One of the first copies of my book off the press has just been put in the mail to you. Without even asking your permission, I dedicated the book to you. You inspired and supported almost everything described in it. I hope you will find it a worthy account of what we tried to do together.

Alice sends her love to Bess and to you, as do I.

Faithfully,

Dean

September 15, 1969

Dear Dean:

I began to read your book as soon as it reached me, for I am always greatly interested in everything you have to say or write.

I deeply appreciate your dedicating the book to me as I recall with pleasure and satisfaction the years we have spent together shaping the American foreign policy.

With warm regards to Alice and you, in which Bess joins me.

Sincerely and gratefully yours,

Harry S. Truman

Truman and Acheson met for the last time at Truman's home on April 12, 1970. The occasion was a ceremonial gathering of members of Truman's administration on the twenty-fifth anniversary of Truman's succession to the presidency.

May 6, 1971

Dear Boss,

Our most affectionate greetings go to you with this birthday note. May you stay well and have many more of them. As the years pass your stature grows more and more imposing, not merely as the comparisons furnished are smaller and smaller, but also because what you did stands out more and more.

All of us who had the honor of serving under you will never forget the satisfaction of that experience.

Devotedly and respectfully,

Dean

May 14, 1971

Dear Dean:

I was greatly pleased by your kind and generous letter on my eighty-seventh birthday. Coming from you, this carries deeper meaning for me.

My thanks to you and Alice, in which Mrs. Truman is happy to join.

Sincerely yours,

Harry S. Truman

On October 12, 1971, Acheson suffered a heart attack. He died that same day. In his last letter to Truman, written a few months before, he expressed his abiding gratitude to his former chief.

Through his office in Independence, the President issued a final tribute:

America and the whole world have lost a great friend, diplomat and statesman. Dean Acheson was a friend of all mankind and served his country with honor and distinction. No one had a greater knowledge of world affairs and how to deal with them than he, while he was Secretary of State. Mrs. Truman and I have suffered a great personal loss in his passing.

A little over a year later, on December 26, 1972, Harry Truman died at his home. He was eighty-eight. The two friends' deaths brought to an end one of the most remarkable series of letters in the history of American politics and government. Although the long friendship was over, its effects on American politics and policy have continued to this day.

Dean Acheson and Harry Truman visit Yale University, where Truman lectured and met with students and faculty in April 1958.

Acknowledgments

The publisher acknowledges with thanks the permission generously given by Clifton Truman Daniel, Thomas W. Daniel, and Harrison Gates Daniel, President Truman's grandsons, and by the Honorable David C. Acheson, Dean Acheson's son, to publish letters to which they hold copyright.

Clifton Truman Daniel, Thomas W. Daniel, and Harrison Gates Daniel would like to thank Dr. Raymond Gesselbracht, Special Assistant to the Director of the Harry S. Truman Library, for his work in providing the President's letters used in this book and providing some of the explanatory headnotes, and Kacie Perna, assistant to Dr. Gesselbracht, for typing and formatting parts of the manuscript.

The Library would like to thank the Honorable David C. Acheson for also providing explanatory headnotes, and for furnishing answers to a myriad of factual questions regarding the events portrayed in this book.

The Library, the Daniels, and the Honorable David Acheson would like to acknowledge the book's editor at Knopf, Patricia Hass, for her enthusiasm for this project, her persistence in seeing it through, and her steady editorial hand.

Finally, all parties wish to thank David McCullough for his introduction and support.

List of Letters

Abbreviations

A: Dean Acheson

AF: Among Friends: Personal Letters of Dean Acheson, edited by David S. McLellan and David C. Acheson (New York: Dodd, Mead and Company, 1980)

DA: Papers of Dean Acheson, Acheson-Truman Correspondence File, Harry S. Truman Library

OTR: Off the Record: The Private Papers of Harry S. Truman, edited by Robert H. Ferrell (New York: Harper and Row, 1980)

PPP: Post Presidential Papers of Harry S. Truman, Harry S. Truman Library

T: Harry S. Truman

February 7, 1953: T to A (typed copy, 1 p., re luncheon thanks), PPP: Name File; also DA (typed, 1 p.).

February 7, 1953: T to A (typed, 1 p.), DA; also PPP: Name File (typed copy, 1 p.).

February 10, 1953: A to T (handwritten, 2 pp.), PPP: Name File; also *AF.*

February 18, 1953: T to A (handwritten, 4 pp.), DA.

February 21, 1953: A to T (handwritten, 2 pp.), PPP: Name File.

March 2, 1953: A to T (handwritten, 6 pp.), PPP: Name File.

March 6, 1953: T to A (typed copy, 1 p.), PPP: Name File; also DA (typed, 1 p.).

April 6, 1953: A to T (handwritten, 2 pp.), PPP: Name File; also DA (typed copy, 1 p.).

April 11, 1953: T to A (telegram, 1 p.), PPP: Name File; also DA (telegram, 1 p.).

April 14, 1953: A to T (typed, 2 pp.), w. enclosures, Drew Pearson, "Reasons Behind Dulles' Reversal," *Washington Post,* April 14, 1953; and John O'Donnell, n.d.; PPP: Name File; also DA (typed copy, 2 pp., and handwritten, 4 pp.); also *AF.*

April 18, 1953: T to A (handwritten, 4 pp.), DA.

April 24, 1953: T to A (typed copy, 1 p.), PPP: Name File; also DA (typed, 1 p.).

May 2, 1953: A to T (handwritten, 6 pp.), PPP: Name File.

May 25, 1953: T to A (typed copy, 1 p.), PPP: Name File, also DA (handwritten, 4 pp.); also *AF.*

May 28, 1953: A to T (handwritten, 6 pp.), PPP: Name File; also DA (typed copy, 2 pp.).

June 8, 1953: T to A (typed, 1 p.), DA.

June 23, 1953: A, Memorandum of Conversation (typed, 2 pp.), PPP: Name File.

June 23, 1953: A, Speech (excerpts), "Remarks of the Honorable Dean Acheson at Dinner Given in Honor of Former President and Mrs. Truman, June 23, 1953, Mayflower Hotel, Washington," PPP: Name File.

July 21, 1953: A to T (typed, 4 pp.), w. enclosure, Eddy Gilmore, "Writer Finds Mighty Russia Starting to Burst at Seams," *Washington Post,* July 19, 1953, PPP: Name File; also DA (typed copy, 4 pp.); also *AF.*

August 18, 1953: T to A (typed copy, 1 p.), w. enclosure, Samuel S. Freedman to T, August 10, 1953, PPP: Name File; also DA (typed, 1 p.).

September 2, 1953: T to A (typed copy, 1 p.), PPP: Name File; also DA (typed, 1 p.).

September 24, 1953: A to T (typed, 2 pp.), PPP: Speech File; also DA (typed copy, 2 pp.).

October 2, 1953: T to A (typed copy, 2 pp.), PPP: Name File; also DA (typed, 2 pp.); also *OTR*.

October 8, 1953: A to T (typed, 5 pp.), w. enclosure, "Post-War Foreign Policy, Second Phase," address by A at the Woodrow Wilson Foundation Dinner, New York, October 1, 1953, PPP: Name File; also DA (typed copy, 5 pp.).

October 21, 1953: T to A (typed copy, 1 p.), PPP: Name File; also DA (typed, 1 p.).

October 21, 1953: A to T (typed, 3 pp.), PPP: Name File.

November 5, 1953: T to A (handwritten, 4 pp.), DA.

December 3, 1953: A to T (handwritten, 2 pp.), PPP: Name File; also DA (typed copy, 1 p.).

December 26, 1953: T to A (handwritten, 4 pp.), DA.

January 28, 1954: T to A (handwritten, 3 pp.), DA.

February 5, 1954: A to T (handwritten, 6 pp.), PPP: Name File; also DA (typed copy, 3 pp.); also *AF.*

March 17, 1954 (Saint Patrick's Day): T to A (handwritten, 4 pp.), DA.

March 26, 1954: A to T (handwritten, 2 pp.), w. enclosure, " 'Instant Retaliation': The Debate Continues," *New York Times,* March 28, 1954, PPP: Name File; also DA (typed copy, 1 p.).

May 28, 1954: T to A (handwritten, 6 pp.), DA.

June 16, 1954: A to T (handwritten, 6 pages), PPP: Name File; also DA (typed copy, 2 pp.).

June 21, 1954: A to T (handwritten, 3 pages), PPP: Name File; also DA (typed copy, 1 p.).

June 27, 1954 (postmark): Bess Truman to A (handwritten, 1 p.), DA.

June 30, 1954: A to Bess Truman (typed copy, 1 p.), DA.

September 21, 1954: A to T (typed, 2 pp.), PPP: Name File.

October 14, 1954: T to A (handwritten, 5 pp.), DA.

October 19, 1954: A to T (handwritten, 7 pp.), probably w. enclosure, "The Responsibility for Decision in Foreign Policy," Autumn 1954. PPP: Name File.

January 11, 1955: T to A (handwritten, 2 pp.), DA.

January 20, 1955: A to T (handwritten, 6 pp.), PPP: Name File (AF); also DA (typed copy, 1 p.).

January 25, 1955: T to A (handwritten, 1 p.), DA.

January 31, 1955: A to T (handwritten, 2 pp.), PPP: Name File.

February 4, 1955: A to T (typed, 1 p.), PPP: Name File.

February 5, 1955: T to A (handwritten, 1 p.), DA.

February 9, 1955: T to A (telegram, 1 p.), PPP: Name File.

February 19, 1955: A and Mrs. A to T (telegram, 1 p.), PPP: Name File; also DA (telegram, 1 p.).

February 21, 1955: A to Bess Truman (typed copy, 1 p.), DA.

March 7, 1955: T to A (handwritten, 1 p.), PPP: Name File.

March 12, 1955: A to T (telegram, 1 p.), PPP: Name File.

March 29, 1955: T to A (typed, 1 p.), DA.

March 31, 1955: A to T (handwritten, 1 p.), PPP: Name File; also DA (typed copy, 1 p.).

April 20, 1955: T to A (handwritten, 2 pp.), DA.

April 29, 1955: A to T (handwritten, 6 pp.), PPP: Name File; also DA (handwritten draft, 4 pp., and typed copy, 1 p.).

June 7, 1955: T to A (typed copy, 1 p.; also typed draft, 1 p.), PPP: Name File.

June 21, 1955: A to T (typed, 10 pp.), PPP: Name File.

June 24, 1955: A to T (typed, 3 pp.), PPP; Memoirs File.

June 27, 1955: A to T (typed, 3 pp.), PPP: Memoirs File.

June 30, 1955: T to A (typed copy, 1 p.), PPP: Name File.

July 6, 1955: T to A (typed copy, 1 p.), PPP: Name File.

July 9, 1955: T to A (handwritten, 4 pp.), DA.

July 11, 1955: A to T (typed, 3 pp.), PPP: Name File; also DA (typed copy, 2 pp.).

July 18, 1955: A to T (typed, 12 pp.), PPP: Name File.

July 19, 1955: T to A (typed copy, 1 p.), PPP: Name File.

July 25, 1955: A to T (telegram, 1 p.), PPP: Name File.

July 25, 1955: A to T (typed, 14 pp.), PPP: Name File; also *AF.*

August 12, 1955: T to A (handwritten, 2 pp.), DA.

August 21, 1955: A to T (handwritten, 2 pp.), PPP: Name File.

October 14, 1955: A to T (typed, 2 pp.), PPP: Name File.

October 17, 1955: T to A (typed, 1 p.), DA; also PPP: Name File (typed copy, 1 p.).

October 18, 1955: T to A (typed copy, 1 p.), PPP: Name File.

November 9, 1955: A to T (typed, 1 p.), PPP: Name File.

November 10, 1955: T to A (handwritten, 4 pp.), DA.

November 21, 1955: T to A (typed, 1 p.), DA; also PPP: Name File (typed copy, 1 p.).

November 23, 1955: A to T (typed, 3 pp.), PPP: Name File, also *AF.*

December 8, 1955: A to T (handwritten, 4 pp.), PPP: Name File; also DA (typed copy, 1 p.).

December 9, 1955: T to A (typed, 2 pp.), DA; also PPP: Name File (typed copy, 2 pp.).

December 10, 1955: T to A (handwritten, 1 p.), DA.

December 14, 1955: A to T (typed, 2 pp.), w. enclosure, list, "Potsdam Papers Presumed to be in Mr. Truman's Custody, Copies of Which (Preferably Photocopies) are Desired by the Department of State," PPP: Name File; also DA (typed copy, 2 pp., without enclosure).

December 20, 1955: T to A (typed, 1 p.), DA; also PPP: Name File (typed copy, 1 p.).

December 27, 1955: T to A (typed, 1 p.), DA; also PPP: Name File (typed copy, 1 p.).

December 29, 1955: T to A (handwritten, 5 pp.), DA.

January 3, 1956: A to T (handwritten, 4 pp.), PPP: Name File.

January 19, 1956: T to A (handwritten, 2 pp.), DA.

February 9, 1956: A to T (typed, 1 p.), w. enclosures, letter, Eugene Rabinowitch to A, February 1, 1956 (typed, 1 p.); A to Eugene Rabinowitch, February 8, 1956 (typed copy, 2 pp.), re release of Acheson-Lilienthal Report, PPP: Name File.

February 21, 1956: T to A (handwritten, 3 pp.), DA.

February 23, 1956: A to T (handwritten, 4 pp.), PPP: Name File; also DA (typed copy, 1 p.).

March 26, 1956: T to A (handwritten, 2 pp.), DA.

March 27, 1956: A to T (handwritten, 6 pp.), PPP: Name File, also *AF.*

May 3, 1956: A to T (handwritten, 3 pp.), PPP: Name File.

May 9, 1956: A to T (handwritten, 2 pp.), PPP: Name File, w. enclosures, two notes re gift of books, *The Horse Soldiers* and *A Victorian Boyhood*; also DA (typed, 1 p.).

July 15, 1956: A to T (handwritten, 5 pp.), PPP: Name File.

July 20, 1956: T to A (handwritten, 4 pp.), DA.

August 21, 1956: A to T (handwritten, 4 pp.), PPP: Name File; also DA (typed copy, 1 p.).

August 29, 1956: T to A (handwritten, 2 pp.), DA.

September 1, 1956: A to T (handwritten, 2 pp.), PPP: Name File.

November 30, 1956: T to A (typed, 1 p.), DA; also PPP: Name File (typed copy, 1 p.).

November 30, 1956: T to A (handwritten, 2 pp.), DA.

December 4, 1956: A to T (handwritten, 4 pp.), PPP: Desk File; also DA (typed copy, 1 p.).

December 7, 1956: T to A (handwritten, 2 pp.), DA.

January 14, 1957: T to A (handwritten, 2 pp.), DA.

January 15, 1957: A to T (typed, 2 pp.), PPP: Name File; also DA (typed, 2 pp.); also *AF.*

January 26, 1957: A to T (handwritten, 2 pp.), PPP: Name File.

January 28, 1957: T to A (handwritten, 2 pp.), PPP: Name File.

February 12, 1957: A to T (handwritten, 1 p.), PPP: Name File.

March 15, 1957: T to A (not sent) (handwritten, 4 pp.), PPP: Name File, also *OTR.*

April 5, 1957: A to T (handwritten, 2 pp.), w. enclosure, Max Freedman, "Lessons in How to Master a Crisis," *Manchester Guardian,* n.d., PPP: Name File; also DA (typed copy, 1 p.).

April 8, 1957: T to A (handwritten, 8 pp.), PPP: Name File.

April 11, 1957: T to A (telegram, 1 p.), DA; also PPP: Name File (copy of telegram, 1 p.).

April 12, 1957: T to A (typed, 1 p.), DA; also PPP: Name File (typed copy, 1 p.).

April 17, 1957: A to T (typed, 1 p.), DA; also PPP: Name File (typed copy, 1 p.).

April 23, 1957: T to A (typed, 1 p.), DA; also PPP: Name File (typed copy, 1 p.).

May 7, 1957: A to T (handwritten, 2 pp.), PPP: Name File; also DA (typed copy, 1 p.).

May 27, 1957: T to A (telegram, 1 p.), DA: also PPP: Name File (copy of telegram, 1 p.).

June 1, 1957: T to A (handwritten, 4 pp.), DA.

June 5, 1957: A to T (handwritten, 7 pp.), PPP: Desk File, also DA (typed copy, 2 pp.); also *AF.*

July 10, 1957: T to A (handwritten, 2 pp.), DA.

July 10, 1957: A to T (handwritten, 2 pp.), w. enclosures, note from Barbara Evans, n.d.; note from Dean Acheson, n.d.; review of *Year of Decisions,* in *The Economist,* December 17, 1955, PPP: Desk File.

July 16, 1957: T to A (handwritten, 3 pp.), DA; also PPP: Name File (typed copy, 1 p.).

August 5, 1957: T to A (typed copy, 1 p.), w. enclosures, T to William Hillman, August 5, 1957, and teletype, "Is NATO a Lost Cause? Kill NATO and Doom Europe, Ex-Secretary Acheson Says," from *Western World,* w. note by William Hillman, "Mr. President, You sure need a cane and dictionary to wade through this one. Bill H.," PPP: Name File.

August 6, 1957: A to T (typed copy, 1 p.), DA.

August 14, 1957: A to T (typed, 2 pp.), w. enclosure, A to Lyndon B. Johnson, August 13, 1957, re civil-rights bill, PPP: Name File; also DA (typed copy, 2 pp.); also *AF.*

August 21, 1957: T to A (typed, 1 p.), DA; also PPP: Name File (typed copy, 1 p.).

August 28, 1957: A to T (typed copy, 2 pp.), DA.

August 31, 1957: T to A (typed, 1 p.), DA.

October 7, 1957: T to A (handwritten, 4 pp.), DA.

October 8, 1957: A to T (handwritten, 4 pp.), PPP: Name File; also DA (typed copy, 1 p.); also *AF.*

October 21, 1957: A to T (typed, 2 pp.), PPP: Trip File; also DA (typed copy, 2 pp.).

October 29, 1957: T to A (typed, 1 p.), PPP: Name File.

November 1, 1957: A to T (handwritten, 10 pp.), PPP: Name File.

December 5, 1957: T to A (typed copy, 1 p.), PPP: Name File.

December 18, 1957: T to A (typed, 1 p), DA; also PPP: Name File (typed copy, 1 p.).

December 20, 1957: A to T (typed, 3 pp.), w. enclosures, Elizabeth Finley, Memorandum for Mr. Acheson, December 11, 1957 (typed, 1 p.); Helen Lally, Memorandum to Mr. Justice Frankfurter, December 19, 1957 (typed, 2 pp.), PPP: Desk File; also *AF.*

January 24, 1958: T to A (handwritten, 2 pp.), DA.

March 25, 1958: A to T (typed, 2 pp.), PPP: Trip File; also DA (typed copy, 2 pp.).

March 28, 1958: T to A (typed, 1 p.), DA; also PPP: Name File (typed copy, 1 p.).

April 16, 1958: T to A (typed, 1 p.), DA; also PPP: Name File (typed copy, 1 p.).

April 18, 1958: A to T (typed, 1 p.), PPP: Name File; also DA (typed copy, 1 p.).

April 30, 1958: T to A (typed, 1 p.), DA; also PPP: Name File (typed copy, 1 p.), w. enclosure, T to Mr. Yalman (typed copy, 1 p.), April 29, 1958.

May 15, 1958: T to A (typed, 1 p.), DA.

July 15, 1958: T and A, transcript of telephone conversation (typed, 3 pp.), PPP: Name File.

July 29, 1958: T to A (handwritten, 1 pp.), w. enclosure, clipping, "Mrs. Acheson, Bishop's Widow," PPP: Name File, also *OTR.*

August 2, 1958: A to T (handwritten, 2 pp.), PPP: Desk File.

August 7, 1958: T to A (typed, 1 p), DA; also PPP: Name File (typed copy, 1 p.).

August 14, 1958: A to T (typed, 1 p.), PPP: Desk File; also DA (typed copy, 1 p.).

August 19, 1958: T to A (handwritten, 2 pp.), DA.

September 16, 1958: A to T (handwritten, 2 pp.), w. enclosure, clipping, "Washington Puts Peking to the Test," by Max Freedman, n.d., PPP: Desk File.

September 17, 1958: A to T (typed copy, 2 pp.), PPP: Desk File.

October 14, 1958: T to A (typed, 2 pp.), DA; also PPP: Desk File (typed copy, 2 pp., and typed draft with handwritten annotations, 2 pp.); also PPP: Name File (typed copy, 2 pp.); also *OTR.*

October 24, 1958: A to T (typed copy, 2 pp.), PPP: Desk File; also DA (typed copy, 2 pp.).

October 31, 1958: T to A (handwritten, 3 pp.), DA.

January 7, 1959: T to A (handwritten, 1 p.), DA.

January 22, 1959: T to A (handwritten, 2 pp.), DA.

January 27, 1959: A to T (handwritten, 4 pp.), PPP: Desk File; also DA (typed copy, 1 p.).

February 12, 1959: A to T (typed, 1 p.), w. enclosure, "What About Berlin?" by Dean Acheson (typed, 14 pp.), PPP: Desk File; also DA (typed copy, 1 p.).

February 19, 1959: T to A (handwritten, 3 pp.), DA.

April 10, 1959: T to A (typed, 1 p.), DA; also PPP: Name File (typed, 1 p., w. enclosure, A to Philip C. Brooks, April 1, 1959).

April 16, 1959: A to T (typed, 1 p.), PPP: Name File; also DA (typed copy, 1 p.).

April 22, 1959: T to A (typed, 1 p.), DA; also PPP: Name File (typed copy, 1 p.).

April 24, 1959: A to T (typed, 1 p.), PPP: Desk File; also DA (typed copy, 1 p.).

May 14, 1959: T to A (handwritten, 1 p.), DA.

May 20, 1959: A to T (handwritten, 2 pp.), PPP: Desk File; also *AF.*

May 26, 1959: A to T (typed copy, 3 pp.), DA.

May 29, 1959: A to T (handwritten, 2 pp.), PPP: Desk File; also DA (typed copy, 1 p.); also *AF* (misdated May 27).

June 2, 1959: T to A (handwritten, 1 p.), DA.

June 25, 1959: A to T (handwritten, 4 pp.), PPP: Desk File; also DA (typed copy, 1 p.).

July 12, 1959: T to A (handwritten, 2 pp.), DA.

August 22, 1959: T to A (handwritten, 4 pp.), DA; also PPP: Desk File (handwritten, 5 pp., a slightly different draft from the letter in DA); also *OTR.*

August 31, 1959: A to T (handwritten, 7 pp.), PPP: Desk File; also DA (typed copy, 3 pp.); also *AF.*

November 24, 1959: T to A (handwritten, 1 p.), DA.

November 30, 1959: A to T (handwritten, 2 pp.), PPP: Desk File; also DA (typed copy, 1 p.).

December 15, 1959: A to T (typed, 1 p.), PPP: Name File.

December 22, 1959: T to A (typed 2 pp.), DA; also PPP: Name File (typed copy, 2 pp.).

February 5, 1960: T to A (handwritten, 1 p.), DA.

April 10, 1960: T to A (handwritten, 2 pp.), DA.

April 14, 1960: A to T (handwritten, 4 pp.), PPP: Desk File; also DA (typed, 1 p.); also *AF.*

April 20, 1960: T to A (handwritten, 2 pp.), DA.

May 9, 1960: T to A (typed, 1 p.), DA; also PPP: Name File (typed copy, 1 p.).

May 23, 1960: A to T (typed, 2 pp.), w. enclosure, "The Persistence of Illusion: The Soviet Economic Drive and American National Interest," by Townsend Hoopes, *Yale Review,* Spring 1960, PPP: Name File; also DA (typed copy, 2 pp.); also *AF.*

May 27, 1960: T to A (handwritten, 2 pp.), DA.

June 27, 1960: A to T (handwritten, 4 pp.), PPP: Desk File; also DA (handwritten draft, 4 pp., dated June 28 written over June 26, and typed draft, 3 pp., dated June 28 written over June 26); also *AF.*

July 9, 1960: T to A (handwritten, 2 pp.), DA.

July 17, 1960: A to T (handwritten, 6 pp.), PPP: Desk File; also DA (typed copy, 2 pp.); also *AF.*

August 6, 1960: T to A (handwritten, 2 pp.), DA.

August 12, 1960: A to T (handwritten, 5 pp.), PPP: Desk File; also DA (typed copy, 2 pp.); also *AF.*

August 23, 1960: A to T (handwritten, 2 pp.), PPP: Desk File; also DA (typed copy, 1 p.); also *AF.*

August 26, 1960: T to A (handwritten, 2 pp.), DA; also PPP: Desk File (draft, handwritten, 3 pp.); also *OTR* (draft version of letter).

September 14, 1960: A to T (handwritten, 2 pp.), w. enclosures, A to John F.

Kennedy, September 15, 1960 (typed copy, 2 pp.), and "The President and the Secretary of State," by DA, PPP: Desk File; also DA (typed copy, 1 p., dated September 15).

October 3, 1960: A to T (handwritten, 2 pp.), PPP: Name File; also DA (typed copy, 1 p.).

October 9, 1960: T to A (typed, 2 pp.), DA; also PPP: Name File (typed copy, 2 pp.).

November 21, 1960: T to A (handwritten, 2 pp.), DA.

November 22, 1960: A to T (handwritten, 3 pp.), PPP: Desk File; also DA (typed copy, 1 p.); also *AF.*

November 26, 1960: T to A (telegram, 1 p.), DA; also PPP: Name File (copy of telegram, 1 p.; and handwritten draft by Truman of telegram text, 1 p.).

February 6, 1961: T to A (handwritten, 1 p.), DA.

March 23, 1961: A to T (typed, 2 pp.), w. enclosure, G. Bernard Noble to A, PPP: Name File; also DA (typed copy, 2 pp.).

March 28, 1961: T to A (typed, 1 p.), DA; also PPP: Name File (typed copy, 1 p.), w. enclosure, T to G. Bernard Noble, March 28, 1961.

May 3, 1961: A to T (handwritten, 2 pp.), PPP: Desk File; also DA (typed copy, 1 p.); also *AF.*

May 13, 1961: T to A (handwritten, 2 pp.), DA.

June 6, 1961: A to T (typed, 1 p.), PPP: Desk File; also DA (typed copy, 1 p.).

June 11, 1961: T to A (handwritten, 2 pp.).

June 24, 1961: A to T (handwritten, 5 pp.), PPP: Desk File; also DA (typed copy, 1 p.).

July 7, 1961: T to A (handwritten, 3 pp.), DA; also PPP: Desk File (handwritten, 3 pp., a slightly different version from the one in DA); also *OTR.*

July 14, 1961: A to T (handwritten, 2 pp.), PPP: Desk File; also DA (handwritten draft, 2 pp.); also *AF.*

July 18, 1961: T to A (handwritten, 4 pp.), DA.

August 4, 1961: A to T (handwritten, 6 pp.), PPP: Name File; also DA (typed copy, 2 pp.).

September 21, 1961: A to T (handwritten, 4 pp.), PPP: Name File; also DA (typed copy, 1 p.).

September 24, 1961: T to A (handwritten, 1 p.), DA; also PPP: Name File (handwritten copy, 1 p.).

September 25, 1961: T to A (handwritten, 1 p.), DA; also PPP: Name File (typed copy of handwritten letter, 1 p.): also *OTR.*

October 26, 1961: T to A (typed, 1 p.), DA; also PPP: Name File (typed copy, 1 p.).

November 28, 1961: A to T (handwritten, 3 pp.), PPP: Desk File; also DA (typed copy, 1 p.).

March 27, 1962: T, speech (handwritten, 2 pp.), DA; also PPP: Speech File (handwritten, 2 pp., original reading copy).

April 9, 1962: A to T (typed copy, 1 p.), DA.

April 20, 1962: T to A (typed copy, 1 p.), PPP: Name File.

May 3, 1962: A to T (handwritten, 4 pp.), PPP: Desk File; also DA (typed copy, 1 p.); also *AF.*

July 6, 1962: T to A (handwritten, 2 pp.), DA; also PPP: Name File (handwritten copy, 2 pp.).

August 6, 1962: A to T (handwritten, 4 pp.), PPP: Name File; also DA (typed copy, 1 p.).

August 8, 1962: A to T (typed, 2 pp.), PPP: Name File; also DA (typed copy, 2 pp.).

October 8, 1962: A to T (handwritten, 2 pp.), PPP: Desk File; also DA (typed copy, 1 p.).

October 12, 1962: T to A (handwritten, 3 pp.), DA.

December 14, 1962: A to T (typed, 1 p.), PPP: Name File.

December 18, 1962: T to A (handwritten, 2 pp.), DA.

December 20, 1962: T to A (handwritten, 2 pp.), DA.

January 19, 1963: A to T (typed copy, 2 pp.), DA.

February 15, 1963: T to A (typed, 1 p.), DA; also PPP: Name File (typed copy, 1 p.).

March 9, 1963: T to A (handwritten, 2 pp.), DA.

March 18, 1963: T to A (handwritten, 3 pp.), DA.

March 20, 1963: A to T (typed copy, 1 p.), DA.

March 29, 1963: T to A (typed copy, 1 p.), w. enclosure, T to W. P. Kennard, March 29, 1963 (typed copy, 1 p.), re history's judgment of Acheson; W. P. Kennard to T, March 11, 1963 (typed, 1 p.), PPP: Name File.

May 6, 1963: A to T (typed copy, 2 pp.), DA.

May 14, 1963: T to A (typed, 1 p.), DA; also PPP: Name File (typed copy, 1 p.); also *OTR.*

May 26, 1963: T to A (handwritten, 4 pp.), DA.

October 16, 1964: A to T (handwritten, 2 pp.), PPP: Name File.

January 12, 1965: T to A (typed, 1 p.), DA; also PPP: Name File (typed copy, 1 p.; also two typed drafts, one dated December 18, 1964, 1 p.).

July 10, 1965: A to T (handwritten, 4 pp.; also typed copy, 1 p.), PPP: Name File; also DA (typed copy, 1 p.).

August 4, 1965: T to A (typed, 1 p.), DA; also PPP: Name File (typed copy, 1 p.).

November 16, 1965: T to A (typed copy, 1 p.), w. enclosure, "Acheson's Contributions Reflected in Autobiography," review of *Morning and Noon* by Dean Acheson, by William McChesney Martin, Jr., PPP: Name File.

December 1, 1965: A to T (typed, 1 p.), PPP: Name File; also DA (typed copy, 1 p.).

December 10, 1965: T to A (typed, 1 p.), DA; also PPP: Name File (typed copy, 1 p.; also a second typed copy of the body of the letter only, 1 p.).

June 8, 1966: T to A (typed copy, 1 p.), w. enclosures, letters, Frank F. Jestrab to A, May 12, 1966, A to Rose Conway, May 16, 1966, and A to Frank E. Jestrab, May 16, 1966, PPP: Name File.

June 28, 1966: A to T (typed, 2 pp.), w. enclosure, draft letter (by A) from T to Senator Jackson, n.d. (typed, 3 pp.), PPP: Name File.

July 26, 1966: T to A (typed copy, 1 p.), w. enclosures, T to Henry M. Jackson, July 26, 1966 (typed copy, 1 p.), re need for continued support for NATO, PPP: Name File.

September 30, 1966: T to A (telegram, 1 p.), w. enclosure, obituary for Edward C. Acheson, PPP: Name File.

October 3, 1966: A to T (handwritten, 6 pp.), PPP: Name File; also *AF.*

October 19, 1966: T to A (typed copy, 1 p.), PPP: Name File.

November 16, 1966: A to T (handwritten, 4 pp.), w. enclosures, "Matter of Fact: 'Never Again Panmunjom,' " by Joseph Alsop, PPP: Name File.

November 21, 1966: T to A (typed copy, 1 p.), w. enclosures, memorandum, David Noyes to T, November 21, 1966, re search of documents re standstill order in Korea; Noyes enclosing letters, T to Joseph Alsop, March 19, 1965, and Joseph Alsop to T, March 12, 1965, PPP: Name File.

December 5, 1966: A to T (handwritten, 3 pp.), w. enclosure, M. B. Ridgway to A, November 21, 1966 (typed copy, 2 pp.), PPP: Name File.

December 17, 1966: A to T (handwritten, 4 pp.), PPP: Name File.

January 23, 1967: T to A (typed, 1 p.), DA; also PPP: Name File (typed copy, 1 p.).

April 17, 1967: T to A (typed, 1 p.), DA; also PPP: Name File (typed copy, 1 p.).

April 21, 1967: A to T (handwritten, 4 pp.; also typed copy, 1 p.), PPP: Name File; also *AF.*

May 7, 1968: A and Alice Acheson to T (telegram, 1 p.), PPP: Name File.

February 28, 1969: A to T (handwritten, 2 pp.), w. enclosure, "His Boss Was Tops," by Franz Daniel, *Springfield News Leader,* October 29, 1971, PPP: Name File.

March 10, 1969: T to A (typed, 1 p.), DA; also PPP: Name File (typed copy, 1 p.).

August 12, 1969: A to T (typed, 1 p.), PPP: Name File; also DA (typed copy, 1 p.).

August 27, 1969: T to A (typed copy, 1 p.), PPP: Name File.

September 3, 1969: A to T (handwritten, 1 p.), PPP: Name File.

September 15, 1969: T to A (typed copy, 1 p.; also typed draft, 1 p.), PPP: Name File.

May 6, 1971: A to T (handwritten, 2 pp.), PPP: Name File.

May 14, 1971: T to A (typed, 1 p.), DA; also PPP: Name File (typed copy, 1 p.).

October 13, 1971: T (press release, 1 p.), PPP: Name File.

Index

Page numbers in *italics* refer to illustrations.

Harry Truman shakes hands with Dean Acheson on January 21, 1949, as Mrs. Acheson looks on. The Achesons were leaving for the Big Three meeting on Western European unity in Paris.

A NOTE ON THE TYPE

This book was set in a typeface called Primer, designed by Rudolph Ruzicka (1883–1978) and first made available in 1954. The design of the face is totally lacking in manner and frills of any kind, but brilliantly corrects its characterless quality.

In the designs for Primer, Mr. Ruzicka exemplified the truth of a statement made about him by W. A. Dwiggins (1880–1956): "His outstanding quality . . . is *sanity*. Complete esthetic equipment, all managed by good, sound judgment about ways and means, aims and purposes, utilities and 'function'—and all this level-headed balance-mechanism added to [a] lively mental state. . . . Fortunate equipment in a disordered world."

Composed by North Market Street Graphics,
Lancaster, Pennsylvania
Printed and bound by Berryville Graphics,
Berryville, Virginia
Designed by Peter A. Andersen